Teaching Teenagers and Living to Tell about It

Gifted Treasury Series
Jerry D. Flack, Series Editor

Inventing, Inventions, and Inventors: A Teaching Resource Book. By Jerry D. Flack.

Mystery and Detection: Thinking and Problem Solving with the Sleuths. By Jerry D. Flack.

Teaching Teenagers and Living to Tell about It: Gifted Students and Other Creatures in the Regular Classroom. By Pamela Everly.

Teaching Teenagers and Living to Tell about It

Gifted Students and Other Creatures in the Regular Classroom

PAMELA EVERLY

1992
TEACHER IDEAS PRESS
A Division of
Libraries Unlimited, Inc.
Englewood, Colorado

TEACHER IDEAS PRESS
A Division of
Libraries Unlimited, Inc.
P.O. Box 6633
Englewood, CO 80155-6633

Library of Congress Cataloging-in-Publication Data

Everly, Pamela.
    Teaching teenagers and living to tell about it : gifted students
and other creatures in the regular classroom / Pamela Everly.
    xiv, 209 p. 22x28 cm. -- (Gifted treasury series)
    Includes bibliographical references and index.
    ISBN 0-87287-894-5
    1. Gifted children--Education--United States.   2. Curriculum
planning--United States.   3. Independent study.   I. Title.
II. Series.
LC3993.9.E94   1992
371.95--dc20
                                                        91-39553
                                                          CIP

To my friend and partner, Debbie Robbins,
> Who taught me to make my ideas practical,

To my friend and mentor, Jerry Flack,
> Who gave me the opportunity to write them down,

To my friend and husband, Keith,
> Who helped me get them down on paper,

And to my son, Macklin,
> Who took his naps and made it all possible!

Contents

Part 1
THE INFRASTRUCTURE

Part 2
APPLICATIONS

Acknowledgments

Several elements of this book were contributed by other writers and artists. The sections on group performance courses and the music segment of the interdisciplinary units on composition were written by Jean Simons of the Brigham Young University Departments of Music Education and Choral Music. The recordsheet graphs and room map were done by Anthony Staley, a junior at Air Academy High School at the United States Air Force Academy, and the planning grids and music evaluation sheets were drawn by my husband, Keith Everly. All of the cartoons and several of the line drawings were executed by Matthew Ableman, a sixth-grader at Timberview Middle School in Colorado Springs, Colorado, and the drawing of the student file folder was contributed by Sallyanne Hayden, a fourth-grader at High Plains Elementary School, also in Colorado Springs. My thanks to all of them for helping me bring my plans and ideas to life and for contributing their time, efforts, and expertise.

Preface

Who can say how many gifted students are in a given classroom? For that matter, who can say how many nongifted students are in a given classroom? Until our abilities to define and identify giftedness improve, there will always be some unidentified gifted students who will fall through the cracks and end up in regular classrooms full time. Until our abilities to provide adequate programming for gifted students improve, there will always be some identified gifted students in the regular classroom either full or part time. Until then, regular classroom teachers will be responsible for meeting the needs of these students while they are also struggling to meet the needs of all of the other students in their charge. It is a Herculean task at best. The model described in this book is an effort to meet the needs of those teachers, and through them, the needs of all of their students.

This model, called Rewrite, was constructed by regular classroom teachers who were frustrated by the difficulty of meeting individual needs in a traditional classroom setting. Our classes were overcrowded and underfunded, but fortunately we had a supportive principal who encouraged us to do our best within our means. As long as we spent no extra money, requisitioned no new supplies or materials, changed no class or room assignments, and covered the material required by the district, we could do anything we wanted that was productive. In short, as long as we stayed out of trouble and didn't mess up our students' education, we were safe. This sounds terribly harsh and restrictive, but in fact it forced us to be as pragmatic as possible in developing the model. As a result, we came up with a workable and transferable product.

Rewrite is based on several premises. It assumes that different people have different needs, interests, and abilities. It assumes that students must learn to become independent and responsible for their own learning and behavior if they are to become successful adults and that it is the responsibility of teachers to help students become that way. Finally, it assumes that because the students are the ones taking the class, the teacher shouldn't be doing the work for them. This amounts to a revision of the hidden curriculum of dependence taught in traditional classrooms in which students are forced by roles and situations to be almost completely dependent upon the teacher. It is a rewriting of that curriculum, hence its name, Rewrite.

The planning, teaching, and management strategies and processes used in the Rewrite model can help restructure classrooms in practical ways to increase opportunities for teaching and learning. Although the suggestions and recommendations presented in this book are teacher-tested, they are not cast in stone. Not only is every student unique, but every teacher is, too. So is every class, for that matter. Very few teachers will find themselves able to adopt everything in this book as presented. Most will instead find ways to adapt the elements of Rewrite to their own styles and teaching situations, but this is as it should be. Rewrite was constructed by two very different teachers working together to create a system they could both use. I have only found two teachers who have quit using it altogether—one because she was comfortable with her old ways of doing things and one because she felt guilty having so much extra time on her hands.

When I started this book, I was excited about the prospect of finally working in a format that would allow me to explain the Rewrite model completely. I was naive. Rewrite is too flexible and adaptable for me to cover in a single work all of the adaptations and variations developed by the teachers who have employed it. Instead, I have tried to provide a guidebook for restructuring the traditional classroom so that teachers will be able to reorder their classrooms to meet the special needs of their students, their curricula, and their teaching positions.

Part 1 of this book provides a rationale for incorporating Rewrite into the regular classroom. It also contains guidelines for planning curriculum, assembling instructional materials, and establishing management procedures to improve learning, build student independence, and increase teacher availability and productivity. Part 2 is the applications section of the volume and deals with four specific concerns voiced by teachers when first presented with Rewrite. The first concern is how to switch over from a traditional model to Rewrite without undue pandemonium. The second addresses the questions of teachers of different kinds of subject areas. This is particularly important because so many of the examples in part 1 come from the language arts area, for which Rewrite was originally developed. But because subject areas tend to fall into categories defined by activity types instead of actual academic relationships, three additional categories beyond the reading and writing type of subjects are covered. These include classes that require a great deal of hands-on activity, those that require group participation such as drama or choir, and those that instruct and employ student aides. Interdisciplinary instruction is the third area of concern covered in the applications section, and the fourth is final exams that test both subject area knowledge and student independence.

Teachers using this book will find many ways to improve the learning experiences of all of their students, gifted or not. In fact, many teachers might say that the ideas presented here are appropriate for every student, not just the gifted ones. Very true. But because so many of our gifted students are unidentified and most or all of the identified ones are present in regular classrooms, we need to provide ways for all students—not just the learning disabled or the underachieving or the regular students—to work up to their potential. And as they do, we can find out what their special talents and problems are. Rewrite gives them a change to show us who they are so we can nurture them.

– 1 –
Where Are the Gifted?
A Rationale for the Regular Classroom

Are Neanderthals Really Extinct?
A True Story

Slack-jawed and gangly, they slumped in their seats. Who among them had remembered to bring a book, let alone homework? They had just set a new world record—100 percent failure on a spelling test. And not just any spelling test. This had been a spelling test with all the answers written on the blackboard.

"How come you told the other classes about our test grades?" one thin voice mewled. It took effort to actually move the jaw and lips when speaking. This was a class deep in the throes of that dreaded disease—hormone haze.

"Because I was so impressed with your achievement. Never in my nine years of teaching have I ever had an entire class flunk a test. I wanted to share that with everyone so they could all appreciate your accomplishment."

Acid burns did not seem to affect them too much. Caustic words only made some of them shift in their seats and others scowl. The scowls were an improvement over the earlier, mindless expressions, and the shifting showed that they were indeed alive and had not come here under remote control.

"Well, are you going to let us take it again?" Wheedle, wheedle. A faint glimmer of hopefulness crept into the vacuous eyes.

"What for? Would you study for it the second time any more than you did the first?"

At least they'd learned to be honest. No one tried to tell me they'd study. They knew they wouldn't. That was one sign of their maturity—they had come to recognize their weaknesses and live down to them.

"So why should I go through another set of F's?"

"Some of us might do better," one girl suggested.

"Have I ever given you a second chance on a test?"

"No."

"Well, since you knew that and still didn't study, I see no reason to give you a second chance. Now please get out the worksheets that are due today."

"I lost mine."

"I threw mine away."

"I never got one." This from the one who is, unfortunately, *never* absent. Not physically anyway.

"Are you going to tell us how we did on our tests?"

Long pause. Twenty-five pairs of eyes slide over to the boy dragging his head up off his desk. Even the low-density people are astounded at the existence of a total vacuum in their midst. Two or three kids swear at him in a counterpoint to the giggles and groans of the others. A descant chimes out over the chorus.

"Are we still your favorite class, Mrs. E?"

ODD MAN OUT

Despite the apparent profusion of tomato varieties available in seed catalogs and garden centers, there are really only two main types of tomatoes—determinate and indeterminate. Determinate tomatoes grow to a certain height and then just branch out and produce fruit without ever expanding outside a certain envelope of space. Indeterminate types have no height limit and continue to increase in size as long as they receive the elements necessary for growth. Unless the plants are mature, the only way the gardener can tell determinate from indeterminate types is to know which seeds are which. Tomato seeds all look pretty much alike, however, and unless they come out of labeled packets, the only way to distinguish them is to plant them, let them grow, and see what happens. This is not usually a problem unless the gardener plants indeterminate types in an area with restricted space, because these types must have unlimited space in which to grow or they will never produce their full capacity of fruit. The best way to make sure that all the seeds will have enough room is to provide each plant with the maximum space possible.

It may seem unlikely, but the eighth-grade class in "Are Neanderthals Really Extinct?" had a large proportion of indeterminate types, otherwise known in educational circles as *gifted and talented*, *TAG*, and *G/T*. Many of them were underachieving and/or unidentified gifted, but gifted nevertheless. There were as many reasons for their underachievement as there are factors influencing the ultimate growth of indeterminate plants, whether in the internal makeup of the plant or the growth environment. These gifted students, both those formally identified and those who had not been identified, had been placed in a class with the more classic types of low-achieving students. Consequently, their growth toward their potential capacities had reached a point of almost absolute inertia. The course itself, though, was not an offering of the school's Special Education program. It was a regular course that, through a quirk in the school's scheduling and programming policies, had evolved into a set of classes that typically had no large, middle group of regular students. Instead, it was a sort of inverse bell curve of enabled and disabled students. This sort of situation doesn't occur very often, but it does serve to throw into strong relief a common predicament of gifted students in regular classrooms. Gifted students are, for at least part of their school day, almost without exception placed into mainstreamed classes that fail to consistently and effectively meet their needs, often resulting in a stunting of their growth.

PROBLEMS, PROBLEMS!

It is rarely, if ever, the intention of educators to inhibit or make dysfunctional the gifted students in their care. Problems in identification and assessment as well as in availability and management of programming resources often interfere with the schools' abilities to serve members of this special population whether these students are in or out of special gifted/talented programs. It is difficult to assess the magnitude of these problems because no comprehensive national figures are available on the actual number of gifted students in the total population. Neither are comprehensive statistics available on the total number of gifted programs in place or on their effectiveness. There are, however, some figures available that indicate just how severe the problem of underserved gifted really is.

Depending on how the gifted/talented student is defined and what standards for identification are used, there are anywhere from 2.5 million to 5 million gifted students in the U.S. school population today.[1] Of these, only about 1 million are receiving any programming at all. Of that million, according to Dr. Mary Frasier, the 1987 president of the National Association for Gifted Children, "as high as 90 percent are in programs that are not adequate to meet their needs."[2] Figures are not available on the projected 40 to 50 percent of the gifted population who have not even been identified, but it is clear that present efforts to meet the needs of gifted students fall far short of the mark.[3]

Identification and assessment of giftedness is a definite handicap to the schools' efforts to serve gifted students. In order to identify and assess something, one must know what it is. But giftedness per se is not an easy quality to define. One need only look at the abysmal identification rate of 50 to 60 percent and the reported inadequate programming rate of up to 90 percent to realize that the usual methods of identification and assessment are somewhat ineffective. There have been many attempts to codify a definition of giftedness, ranging from specific scores on IQ and achievement tests to surveys of teachers, family members, and peers of a given individual to find out whether they think that person is gifted. Both ends of the continuum help in identifying gifted students, but because giftedness often takes quite some time or special conditions to manifest itself, it can be many years before a gifted individual's special needs can be recognized and met. About all that can be stated conclusively regarding a definition of giftedness is that it involves a greater potential for growth, learning, and intelligence than is normally present in the general population. John Feldhusen, director of the Gifted Education Resource Institute at Purdue University, describes this view concisely: "The gifted are not *unique* individuals; they are simply *qualitatively* different from some other people by virtue of superior potential for development of their talents or abilities."[4] Using potential as a criterion makes it possible to describe giftedness without being too restrictive. Every human being has potential, and that potential is unique to every human being. What distinguishes the gifted student from the crowd is a potential to go further, faster, and sometimes with greater drive than most other people. That potential may exist in one area or in many areas. It varies from one gifted individual to another.

The only problem with using potential as an identifying criterion is that it can't be measured. Potential is not *here and now*, it is *there and then*, and *there and then* is a place into which no one can see clearly since it is in the future. Because it is unlikely that ESP or crystal balls will be used as standard identification and assessment instruments by the educational establishment, one is left with two options—to do one's best with present tests and techniques to predict student potential or to set up programming that enhances every student's chances of developing talents and abilities to full potential so that gifted students, even the unidentified, have the opportunity to stretch beyond the usual goals and objectives set for regular students.

In an extensive attempt to find out how gifted students are identified and served in the nation's schools, the Sid W. Richardson Foundation of Texas canvassed four thousand schools and school districts in 1985. Of the 1,572 responses they received, they discovered that 91 percent of the programs used teacher nominations as a condition of enrollment, 90 percent achievement test scores, 82 percent IQ tests, and 50 percent grades.[5] It hardly needs to be pointed out that there are many accusations and controversies in educational and psychological circles about the reliability and validity of tests that measure human intelligence and potential for future achievement. In fact, a large part of the controversies revolve around the very nature of human intelligence. Without agreement on what exactly is being measured, it is more than a little difficult to construct measurement instruments of any real accuracy. About the only conclusion that all but the most hard-nosed of psychometrists can agree on is that these tests are only indicators of ability and potential, not absolute, infallible measures. Add to this the finding that only 20 percent of all inservice G/T teachers and an even smaller percentage of regular classroom teachers are trained in Gifted Education, and teacher nomination as a criterion becomes a doubtful standard for placement, too.[6]

As things stand now, accurate identification and assessment of human intelligence and potential are simply not possible given today's technologies. So much so that even the 50 percent figure of unidentified students is only a rough estimate based on statistical projections. Still, with that 50 percent figure, one can assume that at least that percentage of gifted/talented students are receiving no services for their special needs and are spending their school career exclusively in the regular classroom.

But that is not the end of the problem. For many gifted students, resources are just not available to provide appropriate programming. In 1981, as part of a consolidation plan, gifted and talented education program resources at the national level were combined with twenty-nine other special types of educational resources under Chapter 2 of the Educational Consolidation and Improvement Act. As of 1986, five years after the consolidation, only 13 percent of all school districts receiving Chapter 2 funds had set aside any of that funding for gifted programming. Of those that did, the average allotment made was $1,000.[7] Although it is true that new legislation has been passed to support development of G/T programs since that time, the fact remains that budget, personnel, and resource considerations limit the amount and type of programming schools can provide. Cutoff lines must often be set for enrollment, based on the resources available rather than on the actual size and needs of the gifted population in a given district. As a result, many students who would ordinarily qualify for gifted programs are excluded from the very programming set up to meet their needs. Even for those students who do get in, the programs are generally only part-time accommodations for full-time needs.

Sometimes Even Identification Doesn't Help the Gifted!

A friend of mine is a teacher in one of the largest school districts in the country. The district is a wealthy one and has a larger than usual gifted population. Even so, this district found itself in the position of having to cut back its gifted programming. In order to accommodate the new budget constraints, the district calculated what percentage of the services they would have to cut and simply cut that percentage of gifted students from the program rolls. The number of gifted students in the district didn't change, only the number of eligible students. In fairness to the district, they did not pretend that the students were suddenly nonexistent. Instead, they informed the regular classroom teachers that it would now be their responsibility to individualize for the gifted students in their classrooms. It filled the square for the district, but left the regular classroom teachers squarely facing a new problem — serving the needs of the gifted in the regular classroom. The funny thing was that the problem had always been there, but now the teachers had to admit it.

In light of these limitations, it would appear that the only place where all the gifted can be found is in the regular classroom. The unidentified gifted are obviously there, and for the most part the identified must spend at least a portion of their time there. The regular classroom teacher, therefore, is the only person who has the best opportunity to meet their needs on a full-time basis. Unfortunately, many regular classroom teachers believe that, for one reason or another, meeting the special needs of gifted students should not be their responsibility and often resent the perceived added burden to do so. They seem to feel that the gifted students are bright enough and capable enough to get along on their own and therefore have no real claim on the teacher's overscheduled and valuable time. The facts, meager though they are, would indicate otherwise.

In his testimony before the Senate Subcommittee on Education, Arts, and Humanities, Senator Bill Bradley reported that an estimated 50 percent of gifted students are underachieving.[8] Nancy Lukenbill, president of the Council of State Directors for Programming of the Gifted, reported that in a study undertaken by Dr. Ken Seeley for the Clayton Foundation in Colorado, 16 percent of the adjudicated youths in his sample were found to be gifted.[9] Using the more conservative estimate of 3 to 5 percent of the total population as gifted, this is more than three times the usual proportion of gifted to the rest of the population. In the executive summary of his report to the foundation, Dr. Seeley pointed out that a literature review of previous research showed that as many as 15 to 30 percent of gifted students drop out of school.[10] Clearly, these figures, though restricted to a few studies, indicate that the idea that gifted students will make it on their own is not true for a large segment of that population. Sue Hovey, a G/T teacher and a member of the NEA Executive Committee put it this way:

> There is a danger in believing that because these young people are gifted, they are guaranteed success in life. Precisely because they are gifted, they are in some senses at risk. Many students have both the talent and drive to challenge their energies in productive ways, but many others need to be challenged over and over again to keep that spark alive.[11]

LOOKING FOR SOLUTIONS

There are many factors that influence the fruitful development of gifted students, but the importance of contact and interaction with teachers who nurture and challenge is extremely important if the "spark" referred to by Ms. Hovey is to be fanned into full flame. Figure 1.1 offers questions teachers may ask themselves for determining their impact on students.

◇ *Could You Be a Significant Teacher?*

1. Do you encourage your students to strike out on their own?

2. Do you encourage your students to explore their own interests even if it's not in the curriculum guide?

3. Do you provide for differences in individual style and ability?

4. Do you encourage your students to go at their own paces even if they're faster than average?

5. Do you encourage your students to become independent learners?

6. Do you encourage them to set their own goals and purposes?

7. Do you use a problem-solving approach in presenting new knowledge?

8. Do you model the processes you want your students to use?

9. Do you encourage students to use higher levels of thinking?

10. Do you make sure that your students have a thorough grounding in the basics with the view that they will use that knowledge in more creative processes?

11. Do you provide opportunities for your students to recombine and transform their basic knowledge into original products?

12. Do you provide an environment that allows and encourages students to work at their maximum capacities?

Fig. 1.1.

As John Feldhusen puts it, "Growth in the areas of one's talents and abilities may be slow or rapid depending upon the conditions of nurturance at home, in school, and in the community."[12] In an attempt to discover what some of these conditions of nurturance might be, the researchers conducting the Richardson study canvassed a sample of highly productive, gifted adults—the MacArthur Fellows. These are artists and scholars who have shown evidence of unusual creative potential in their professional lives by virtue of their achievements and who have been selected by the John D. and Catherine T. MacArthur Foundation to receive annual monetary awards ranging from $24,000 to $60,000 for five years. Two of the major findings to come out of the survey seem contradictory. The MacArthur Fellows report that certain teachers and certain types of teachers were instrumental in helping them become successful professionals. Curiously enough, the consensus is that school in its traditional format did just the opposite. Teachers and school go together like soybeans and cafeteria food, so how could one be a deeply positive influence and the other such a negative one?

> A true teacher defends his pupils against his own personal influence.
> —A. Bronson Alcott, *Orphic Sayings*

To begin with, the significant teachers allowed their gifted students the freedom to strike out on their own, to explore independently and to go ahead at their own paces. The traditional school format fostered conformity and made independence and individualization difficult, if not impossible, by encouraging teacher-centered classrooms in which teachers decide all goals and set the pace for all students. The significant teachers taught through problem-solving approaches that encouraged the use of higher-level thinking and modeled the processes used by professionals in the subject area. The traditional school format encouraged the teaching of facts, rules, and lower-level thinking. Finally, the significant teachers insisted that their gifted students have a thorough grounding in the basic knowledge of their subject areas, thus giving their students the necessary tools to strike out on new frontiers. The traditional school format set standards of minimum competency and did not make provision for those students capable of much more. In short, the significant teachers, like good gardeners, provided an environment which allowed for the maximum growth of all their students. They let the needs of their students, rather than the conventions of the traditional classroom, dictate how and what their students would learn. By providing student-centered settings for learning, they countered those aspects of the traditional classroom which tend to stunt rather than enhance the growth of indeterminate types of students. But with all of these characteristics, it is interesting to note that most of these significant teachers were not Gifted Education specialists. Rather, they were regular classroom teachers who responded to the special needs of their students without having seen the labels on the seed packets. They understood that regular classroom does not necessarily mean traditional classroom and took steps to provide adequate space for their indeterminate students' growth.

A SIGNIFICANT INFLUENCE

Today it is still impossible to infallibly identify and assess giftedness or to know each student's potential. Consequently, there is only one set of professionals who come in contact with all of the gifted students in a school population—the regular classroom teachers. They are the ones who have the greatest contact with identified and unidentified gifted students. They are the ones with the greatest opportunity to be instrumental in the nurture of great minds and talents. They are the ones who have the chance to become the significant teachers in the lives of these students, and through the contributions of those students, to extend their significance far beyond their classrooms.

Bibliography / 7

NOTES

1. Dr. Mary Frasier, U.S. Congress, Senate, Subcommittee on Education, Arts, and Humanities of the Senate Committee on Labor and Human Resources, *Hearings*, 100th Cong., 1st sess. on S. 303, 18 September 1987, S. Doc. No. Y 4.L 11/4:S.hrg. 100-379.

2. Ibid.

3. Ibid.

4. John Feldhusen, "An Introduction," in *Toward Excellence in Gifted Education*, ed. John Feldhusen (Denver, CO: Love Publishing, 1985) 13.

5. June Cox et al., *Educating Able Learners: Programs and Promising Practices* (Austin, TX: University of Texas Press, 1985) 33.

6. Bill Bradley, U.S. Congress, Senate, Subcommittee on Education, Arts, and Humanities of the Senate Committee on Labor and Human Resources, *Hearings*, 100th Cong., 1st sess. on S. 303, 18 September 1987, S Doc. No. Y 4.L 11/4:S.hrg. 100-379.

7. Ibid.

8. Ibid.

9. Nancy Lukenbill, U.S. Congress, Senate, Subcommittee on Education, Arts, and Humanities of the Senate Committee on Labor and Human Resources, *Hearings*, 100th Cong., 1st sess. on S. 303, 18 September 1987, S. Doc. No. Y 4.L 11/4:S.hrg. 100-379.

10. Kenneth Seeley, "High Ability Students at Risk: A Research Report," in *Gifted and Talented Education in Colorado*, eds. Elinor Katz and Aline Joseph (Denver, CO: Program for Educational Quality [Colorado Department of Education, 201 E. Colfax, Denver, CO 80203], 1985) 275.

11. Sue Hovey, U.S. Congress, Senate, Subcommittee on Education, Arts, and Humanities of the Senate Committee on Labor and Human Resources, *Hearings*, 100th Cong., 1st sess. on S. 303, 18 September 1987, S. Doc. No. Y 4.L 11/4:S.hrg. 100-379.

12. Feldhusen, 13.

BIBLIOGRAPHY

Alcott, A. Bronson, "Orphic Sayings." *Dictionary of Quotations*. Ed. Bergen Evans. New York: Avenale Press, 1968.

Cox, June, et al. *Educating Able Learners: Programs and Promising Practices*. Austin, TX: University of Texas Press, 1985.

Deci, Edward L., and Joseph Porac. "Cognitive Evaluation Theory and the Study of Human Motivation." In *The Hidden Costs of REward: New Perspectives of the Psychology of Human Motivation*. Eds. M. R. Lepper and D. Greene. Hilldale, NJ: Lawrence Erlbaum Associates, 1978.

Feldhusen, John. "An Introduction." In *Toward Excellence in Gifted Education*. Ed. John Feldhusen. Denver, CO: Love Publishing, 1985.

Seeley, Kenneth. "High Ability Students at Risk: A Research Report." In *Gifted and Talented Education in Colorado*. Eds. Elinor Katz and Aline Joseph. Denver, CO: Program for Educational Quality, Colorado Department of Education, 1985.

U.S. Congress. Senate. Subcommittee on Education, Arts, and Humanities of the Senate Committee on Labor and Human Resources. *Hearings*. 100th Cong., 1st sess., 18 September 1987. S. Doc. Y 4.L 11/4:S.hrg. 100-379.

— 2 —
At Home on the Range
Building Student Independence

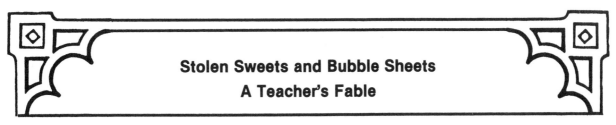

Stolen Sweets and Bubble Sheets
A Teacher's Fable

A few years ago, my teaching colleague Debbie and I stole half of a banana cream pie from the cheerleaders' fundraising booth at the Halloween dance and huddled in a remote office to bury our sorrows in meringue and custard. Neither one of us had the weight gain pattern for that sort of behavior. Neither of us cared, either. All we wanted was gratification—and that day the only kind left seemed to be oral.

What had driven these two compassionate, intelligent, and responsible teachers of America to such depths? Perhaps it was the fact that Halloween in a junior high school is a harrowing experience at best. Perhaps it was the false weather report that had us both sweltering in sweaters and gabardine in a building where the windows were riveted shut to keep the latches from breaking. Perhaps it was the kid with a six-foot kite string that he had been pulling back and forth through his pierced ear all afternoon.

Actually, it was none of these. These are, after all, simply normal fare in the life of a public school. It was the last day of the quarter, grades were due in by sundown, and a host of fallen souls had been descending upon the two of us all day with cries of anguished despair as the full implications of Judgment Day were made clear to the poor sinners. Really, what was left for us but a stolen pie consumed in secret fulfillment of buried gustatory lust?

What was left? Olympic-class whining and complaining, of course. We had worked ourselves into stupors over the past nine weeks. The kids wouldn't turn stuff in. If they did, it was full of silly mistakes. We had been spending hours grading papers every night and scrambling to make special accommodations for individual needs as prescribed by the Special Education department. For nine whole weeks, we had had to direct all class activity and take responsibility for all successes and failures in the class. We had had between 180 and 200 kids a day to keep track of, and half of their parents had called in the last few days to bully or beg us to take late work. And now ... now the kids were going home to Halloween festivities, and we were stuck with piles of smudged student papers, a pair of electronic calculators we'd gotten as book club teacher bonuses, and a stack of bubble sheets. We had the dreaded records secretary waiting in the office with a box of number 2 lead pencils should any of the marks on the bubble sheets not be suitably dark or shiny. We were paying in sleep, sweat, and writer's cramp for our students' inability to accept responsibility for themselves or their work.

What it all came down to, we decided, was this: If the kids were the pupils, why were we doing all the work?

Moral: The *kid* is the one taking the class!

THE TRADITIONAL HIDDEN CURRICULUM

It's a good question. Why *do* the teachers end up doing all the work of managing everyone's learning, behavior, evaluation, and error correction if the kids are the ones taking the class? Shouldn't students be responsible for their own learning? Shouldn't they also be learning to manage their own behavior, set their own goals, evaluate their own work, and correct their own mistakes? Certainly they should. After all, there will be no constant guidance available to them once they graduate from school. They should begin learning to do these things when they begin school and get better and better at them until they go out on their own as autonomous adults. Unfortunately, too many students remain dependent and irresponsible throughout their school years and then find the expectations of the real world to be a rather rude surprise. Why does this happen? It happens because the traditional school classroom arrangement teaches a hidden curriculum and teaches it effectively:

1. Depend on the teacher for everything.

2. Do nothing on your own initiative.

3. Keep up (or back) with the rest of the class.

It is a version of this hidden curriculum that the Richardson Foundation found to be one of the most universally reported inhibitors to the MacArthur Fellows' development into productive professionals. They found that, in contrast to the positive influences of significant teachers, "our school system, public and private, most often rewards patterns of behavior inappropriate for an independent thinker, researcher, or artist."[1]

If students do somehow emerge from the traditional classroom with the skills and attitudes of an independent adult, it is not because of its teacher-centered, rule-oriented atmosphere of conformity. It is often because of mitigating factors such as the significant teachers so highly praised by the MacArthur Fellows. As one of the Fellows, biologist Michael Ghiselin, commented in his survey response, "there is no important connection between what is demanded of a student and what is needed by a scholar."[2] Another Fellow, molecular biologist John Cairns, shared the observation that "we reward students for conformity, whereas nonconformity is required for success in the academic sciences."[3] These are serious problems in the education of the gifted if they are to be the future discoverers and creators of new knowledge, art, and technologies in our society. These are the people who will be the most likely to stretch our frontiers and in so doing, be the most likely to find themselves almost completely alone on those frontiers. As any individual must do sooner or later, these gifted students will have to be able to function autonomously, without the constant guidance and direction of a teacher and may have already reached that point. They will have to be able to discipline themselves to strive for goals and evaluate for themselves how well they have achieved those goals. They will have to be at home out on the range. To force them to forego the opportunities to learn these things as children and adolescents is to deprive them of the tools they must have to function at full capacity as adults.

But gifted students are not the only ones who need to become independent. Teaching these things in the regular classroom benefits all class members. All students need to attain autonomy. Sooner or later, all of them will find themselves in situations where they will need to learn something new or solve a problem or evaluate their own performances without the direction and supervision of a teacher. Whether they reach this point at the edge of a new frontier or on settled ground, at age twelve or forty-two, they too will need to have the tools to function independently.

A CURRICULUM FOR INDEPENDENCE

Gifted or not, students are handicapped in their efforts to acquire these tools whenever they are denied the opportunity to learn what the tools are and how to use them. Giving them the opportunity to learn is vital. It is not natural for students to avoid academic and personal autonomy. On the contrary, research done in the relatively new field of cognitive science supports just the opposite view. In their article on human motivation, Deci and Porac summarize the findings of this research:

> [Humans are] in constant interaction with the environment, operating on the environment and adapting to it. By nature, they strive to be competent and self-determining in these interactions, because competence and self-determination have important survival value. People need to feel effective, to feel like they can bring about desired outcomes. This need for competence and self-determination is the psychological basis for intrinsic motivation.[4]

The interaction Deci and Porac refer to is the basis of the learning process. By interacting with their environment, people are able to make observations and draw conclusions about the environment and how they relate to it, whether it be a concrete or abstract relationship. These conclusions or generalizations, called schemata, are either hooked onto existing schemata of knowledge possessed by the learner or used to modify them. The more complete and consistent the structure and the more accurately they reflect the real world, the more competent the individual is to operate within that world. The more competent an individual is, the better able he or she is to exercise positive self-determination.

Teachers can inadvertently rob students of competence by overemphasizing the value of isolated, lower-level knowledge and skills in class and by forcing them to engage in activities that seem to have little or no relevance. Students do not become truly engaged cognitively and affectively in such tasks because they do not care about them or see the value in them. Indeed, why should they, since they have little or nothing to say about what, how, or when something is learned and do not have the experience to see the value of the skills and knowledge in the greater scheme of things. In their eyes, they are powerless to act on their own. The teacher decides what will be learned, when it will be learned, and how it will be learned. This is doubly counterproductive. Not only are the students *not* learning the material presented, but through the natural process of drawing generalizations from their interactions with the environment, they are learning that school consists largely of meaningless activities, that they are not moving toward greater competence, that they do not possess any great measure of self-determination, and that learning as a formal activity is useless. As a result, their instrinsic motivation shrivels and teachers are forced to resort to such motivational strategies as extrinsic reward and competition. When these are the types of lessons learned in school, it is little wonder that gifted students, who have notoriously voracious appetites for learning, become so discouraged that they fall into underachieving patterns of behavior and fail to live up to their potentials.

PROVIDING STRUCTURE
FOR INDEPENDENCE

Many teachers will argue that these decisions must be made for students, and that students are incapable of making informed decisions about what subject matter should be studied. To some extent, they are correct in this. If students knew enough about the subject area to make these kinds of choices, they wouldn't need to take the class. The point to be made here is that teachers need to make decisions on what, how, and when something should be taught, but once those decisions are made, they need to structure learning activities in such a way as to foster interaction (with the emphasis on *action*) between students and the subject matter. This will enable them to take advantage of students' natural drives to achieve competence and self-determination. In so doing, they will become students who are intrinsically motivated to achieve—independent learners. See figure 2.1 for suggestions on assignments that foster autonomy.

◇ *Assignments That Foster Autonomy*

Teachers can foster student autonomy through instructional tasks that provide choices of approach and product. By developing instructional tasks that require students to make choices about focus, format, and complexity, teachers can help students learn to make appropriate choices and gain confidence in their abilities to make choices on their own. Compare and contrast the examples of traditional assignments and assignments designed to promote independent thought and action.

Instead of ...
Write a five-paragraph theme entitled, "How I Spent My Vacation."

Substitute ...
Pretend you have unlimited resources for a two-week vacation. Put together a travel portfolio which includes an itinerary, estimated expenses, maps, information on accommodations, meals, and attractions, and any other materials you would find helpful.

Instead of ...
Assemble a collection of 25 species of butterflies properly labeled and mounted on a display board.

Substitute ...
Choose a particular type of insect and put together a presentation to teach others about its different species.

Instead of ...
Describe the lifestyle of an ancient Egyptian peasant family.

Substitute ...
You are an archaeologist working in Egypt. Your workers unearthed the remains of an ancient peasant village and you spent most of the season working there. Now your sponsors back home want to see what you've been doing. Put together a report, presentation, or exhibit to show them what you discovered.

Instead of ...
Build a gingerbread house using the directions on pages 54-58. You will be graded on how well your house matches the example in the book.

Substitute ...
Your cousin was the witch Hansel and Gretel pushed into the oven and you have inherited her gingerbread house. The only problem is that you don't have quite the same Rococo tastes as your cousin. Design and build your own gingerbread house using gingerbread, royal icing, and any other edible materials you need. Recipes and construction procedures are in the book on pages 54-58.

Fig. 2.1.

What this means in real terms is that instructional units should engage the student in active manipulation of the subject matter in meaningful situations. Drill and practice of a skill or rehearsal of facts and rules isolated from their natural contexts do not allow students to learn to use these skills, facts, and rules in productive ways. Walter Doyle of the Research and Development Center of Teacher Education at the University of Texas at Austin sums it up this way:

> Students learn whatever curriculum they have an opportunity to follow. If, for example, students spend time calculating answers to multiplication problems, they will learn *how* to multiply. If, in addition, they solve problems in which they choose from several operations the ones appropriate to a particular problem, they will learn *when* to multiply. From this perspective, the quality of schooling is affected by the character of the academic work students do and the relation of this work to the expected outcomes of schooling.[5]

This is not to say, however, that there is no place for instruction in lower levels of knowledge and skills for the gifted. On the contrary, one of the findings of the Richardson study was that many of the MacArthur Fellows attached great importance to accumulating and building a solid knowledge base within a field of competence. To summarize this conclusion, the remarks of Renaissance scholar Paul Oskar Kristeller were cited:

> Danger lies in the current cult of creativity and self-expression, which serves as a pretext for not teaching solid knowledge even to gifted students. Behind this is the false assumption that gifted persons produce everything out of nothing or out of themselves, without having learned anything. The fact is that a gifted person needs even more knowledge than others before he or she can hope to make a significant contribution to his or her field.[6]

Support knowledge and skills should not be excluded from the curriculum simply because they involve lower levels of thinking. There is nothing wrong with lower-level thinking as long as students realize that it is not an end in itself and is used in the performance of more complex tasks. Otherwise students come out of school thinking that mathematics is about long division, reading is about phonics, and science is about memorizing the proper names of things. By placing instruction of skills and lower-level knowledge within their methodological contexts, that is, in the types of real situations in which they are used, students learn how and when to apply those skills and knowledge to further their competence and self-determination. See figures 2.2a and 2.2b, page 14, for an example of putting things in context.

For instance, in putting together an instructional unit on narrative writing, the teacher should structure the primary task to model the writing processes used by writers in creating narrative works. Because it is the main focus of the unit, most of the instructional time should be allotted to it, thus communicating its importance to the students. That time should be spent observing and practicing strategies and tactics such as invention, data-gathering, and organization; drafting of the actual document; editing and revising the piece; and final proofreading and preparation for publication— or in a classroom situation, for submission to the teacher for credit. Within the context of the learning experience, applicable skills such as recognizing cause and effect relationships, organizing by chronological order, or the elements of plot structure can be taught. (The actual management mechanism for doing this in the regular classroom, a primary element of the Rewrite system, will be discussed in a later chapter.) In this way, students learn not only how to organize events in chronological order or how to structure a plot, but they learn to apply these skills by using them to synthesize a narration of their own choosing. Figure 2.3, page 15, shows a process for narrative writings.

Putting Things in Their Natural Context

Take a good look at the object pictured. Have you ever seen one of these before? Chances are if you have never lived in Michigan's Upper Peninsula, you won't recognize it. Guess what it is, what it's used for, and what it's made of.

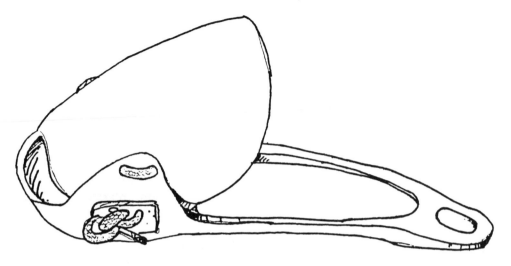

Fig. 2.2a.

 Here's the same object in its natural context. Now do you know what it is? It's a snowshoe binding invented by a man named Bob Maki who lives in upper Michigan. He makes them out of neoprene taken from old inner tubes. The boot heel goes in the round hole and the tension from the stretched rubber keeps the toe of the boot firmly in the binding. Do you see how important context can be?

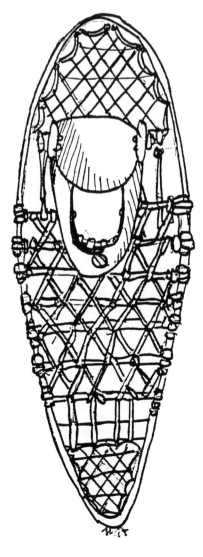

Fig. 2.2b.

◇ *A Process for Narrative Writing*

Phase I: Prewriting

Invention: Read aloud the story of *Alexander and the Terrible, Horrible, No Good, Very Bad Day* by Judith Viorst to the class.

Have students brainstorm lists of their best and worst days.

Have students choose one to three items as possible foci.

Have students do clusters on each day to see which would be the most productive to write about.

Data Gathering: Have students do free-writing exercises on their chosen topic to help them remember every possible detail.

Organization: Have students organize their material into chronological and cause and effect relationships.

Phase II: Drafting

Give students time in class to get started on their first drafts so they will have something to work on at home.

Phase III: Editing/Revising

Have students share their first drafts with peers in small editing groups using grading rubrics to help in editing and revising.

Repeat the drafting phase for another draft and then repeat the editing step.

Have students prepare final copies and then have them turn in all of their phase I, II, and III work so they will learn that all of the process is valuable and not just the finished product.

Fig. 2.3.

PROVIDING OPPORTUNITIES FOR LEARNING

Another advantage of teaching skills and lower-level knowledge in this context is the increased opportunity for elaboration on the basic presentation for learners. This is important because retention of material is enhanced by successive processing of incoming information. When students take the input provided by the teacher through explanation and modeling and manipulate it to synthesize products of their own, they are gradually transforming the input from something foreign and external into something uniquely personal that is tied in to their own cognitive schemata. This series of transformations is called *elaborative processing* and is thought by cognitive scientists to be one of the primary processes of learning and human memory.

This type of processing cannot take place if students are not attending to the input or making an effort to transform and transfer the information from short- to long-term memory. To capture and hold their attention, both the content and presentation of the input must have some value apparent to the prospective learner.

> The thing I like about Rewrite is that I don't have to jump start my classes everyday anymore. The students know what to do without my telling them, they like what they're doing, and they do more than I would have had them do under the old system.
> —Utah junior high school teacher

Ideally, the value placed on the new material should appeal to and stimulate students' intrinsic motivation by explicitly helping them to move toward competence and self-determination. Setting up instructional tasks that appeal to their interests and provide appropriate challenge are most effective in getting and holding student attention. Since a wide range of abilities and interests typically exist in a mainstreamed classroom, the teacher should provide a set of tasks from which students can choose to fulfill the requirements of the instructional unit. These tasks should provide opportunities for students of varying interests and learning styles. They should also be designed in graduated degrees of complexity from highly structured tasks for students of low ability and/or motivation to open-ended tasks for those of high ability and/or motivation. See figure 2.4 for task examples.

◆ *Tasks That Provide a Range of Challenges*

Here is an example of a unit assignment that provides many ways for students of varying learning styles, talents, and abilities to show that they understand the basics of narrative expression.

Choose either one of the best or worst days of your life and then pick one of the ways below to tell about it:

1. Write a short story.
2. Write a children's book.
3. Do a photojournalism spread.
4. Make a cartoon strip.
5. Write a ballad or an epic poem.
6. Write a letter to your best friend.
7. Write a half-hour television script.
8. Present any other ideas for narration to the teacher for approval.

Fig. 2.4.

At first, it may be that able students of low motivation will choose tasks that are too easy for them, but as they experience success and make gains in self-determination and competence, their intrinsic motivation will increase. Deci and Porac describe this process of motivational and cognitive growth in this way:

Intrinsic motivation underlies an ongoing cyclical pattern in which people seek out and conquer challenges that are optimal for their capacities. When people encounter challenges, they turn their attention to conquering the challenges. If there are not challenges appropriate for them, they seek challenges. These challenges must, however, be ones for which they are equipped. If the challenge is too difficult, they will avoid it until they have the capacity for dealing with it; if the challenge is too easy, they will seek more difficult ones.[7]

Gifted individuals are often characterized by a greater capacity for task involvement than normal people. However, the task must be something that captures their interest before they will commit to it. If no such challenges are given in the regular classroom, gifted students will sometimes seek out activities, often disruptive or counterproductive, to challenge themselves (see figure 2.5). Conversely, if the challenges presented in the classroom are beyond students' capabilities, they will seek out activities that are better suited to their abilities.

◇ *Twenty Ways to Beat Boredom*

Contributed by Mrs. Palmer's tenth-grade TAG English class, Liberty High School, Colorado Springs, Colorado.

1. Distract the teacher.
2. Talk loud in the back of class. Then, when the teacher asks you a question, he or she gets mad if you know the answer.
3. Administrators always leave the smart people in charge of classes. Make the best of this awesome opportunity.
4. Bother other people.
5. Do homework for other classes.
6. Write stories.
7. Bring candy and food to class and see how long you can get away with it.
8. Play paper football and basketball in class.
9. Work very slowly by writing each letter perfectly.
10. Read novels, newspapers, and magazines.
11. Invent codes and puzzles.
12. Write in your journal about time, space, existence, life.
13. Sit in class and just let your brain take a little nap.
14. Break your pencil so you can get out of your seat to sharpen it. Walk slowly to the sharpener, stopping to read posters and papers on the wall, and return to your desk slowly.
15. Write down ideas for future stories and then follow with details about individual characters.
16. Try to see the hand move on the clock so you can make a wish.
17. Ask ridiculous questions and act like you don't understand so the teacher will go over and over it.
18. Imagine the teacher living your life.
19. Sing to yourself and tune other people out.
20. Read the wrong story on purpose.

Fig. 2.5.

By providing constructive instructional outlets for gifted students' energies, teachers can help these students develop and focus their abilities in productive ways that will benefit them for life. Students will not only experience increased motivation to conquer challenges, but as they gain repertoires of knowledge and skills along with methodological, communicative, and metacognitive strategies, they will be enabled to seek out and conquer greater challenges without any external guidance or prodding beyond encouragement and expressions of interest. Then they can truly function as independent learners who are both intrinsically motivated and academically equipped to go as fast and as far as they can.

A PLAN FOR DEVELOPING INDEPENDENT LEARNERS

Using the regular, mainstreamed classroom as the primary setting, Rewrite develops these independent learners through two principal means: academic instruction and motivational improvement. Of these two, the dominant focus is academic instruction. Every aspect of classroom time, resources, behavior, and management is focused on supporting the academic progress of the students. All activities are consciously structured by the teacher to maximize academic learning and develop student responsibility. At the same time, they are structured to minimize the amount of time teachers need to spend in such activities as lecturing, evaluating, and managing the daily routines of a class. This promotes learning and independence by providing opportunities for active student involvement in learning activities and for finding and meeting challenges. It is the students, instead of the teacher, who spend the bulk of the class time and energy manipulating and processing the subject matter, which is as it should be. After all, the *kid* is the one taking the class!

NOTES

1. June Cox et al., *Educating Able Learners: Programs and Promising Practices* (Austin, TX: University of Texas Press, 1985) 27.

2. Ibid.

3. Ibid.

4. Edward L. Deci and Joseph Porac, "Cognitive Evaluation Theory and the Study of Human Motivation," in *The Hidden Costs of Reward: New Perspectives of the Psychology of Human Motivation*. eds. M. R. Lepper and D. Greene (Hillsdale, NJ: Lawrence Erlbaum Associates, 1978) 151.

5. Walter Doyler, U.S. Department of Education, "Effective Secondary Classroom Practices," in *Reaching for Excellence: An Effective Schools Sourcebook*, ed. Regina M. J. Kyle (Washington, DC: E. H. White, 1985) 57.

6. Cox et al., 26.

7. Deci and Porac, 151.

BIBLIOGRAPHY

Cox, June, et al. *Educating Able Learners: Programs and Promising Practices*. Austin, TX: University of Texas Press, 1985.

Deci, Edward L., and Joseph Porac. "Cognitive Evaluation Theory and the Study of Human Motivation." Eds. M. R. Lepper and D. Greene. In *The Hidden Costs of Reward: New Perspectives of the Psychology of Human Motivation*. Hillsdale, NJ: Lawrence Erlbaum Associates, 1978.

Doyle, Walter. U.S. Department of Education. "Effective Secondary Classroom Practices." In *Reaching for Excellence: An Effective Schools Sourcebook*. Ed. Regina M. J. Kyle. Washington, DC: E. H. White, 1985.

– 3 –
The Academic Environment
Curriculum Planning for Independence

What Do They Really Need to Know?
A Fable for Teachers

One of my first teaching jobs included a ninth-grade honors speech and drama class, a course the other English teachers at that junior high would have killed for, but one that I dreaded. I had taken the one public speaking class I had needed to get my teaching certificate and I had had *no* instruction in drama whatsoever. I hated skits. I hated reading plays aloud in class with everyone taking a part for a portion of the period, and I was firmly convinced that my head would fall off if I got up on stage and pretended to be somebody else. I hid my opinions, however, and decided to concentrate on speech first while I got my courage up for the drama segment. To avoid getting too theatrical too soon, I decided to work on problem-solution speeches, a fairly cut-and-dried format and a good chance to teach research skills, which was something I knew I could do.

I put together a wonderful lesson on using the *Readers' Guide to Periodical Literature*. It had great visual aids, an attention-getting step, opportunities for the students to practice using the *Readers' Guide* in a nonthreatening atmosphere, and practical application to their immediate need which was getting enough material to write a good speech and get a good grade. The next day I planned for us all to go to the library to do actual research on actual speech topics with actual periodicals.

My explanations were flawless. The students were attentive. I had all the right questions. They had all the right answers. When I was sure they had the idea, I asked, "Now, does anybody have any questions?" I knew they wouldn't. The lesson had been perfect.

"Yeah," said one of the students. "What's this for?"

There's always one. I went through an abbreviated version of my explanation, outlining the elements of the entries. "Okay?" I asked.

"No. I still don't see how to use this," she persisted. Several others in the class grunted in agreement.

I went through it once again, more than a little disgruntled at my students' obtuseness in the face of such masterful teaching. "Now do you get it?"

"No." The students were starting to get upset by *my* obtuseness. "We still don't know how to use this!"

"What do you mean, you don't know how to use it?" My voice was more than a bit shrill. Didn't they realize what a great lesson plan this was? "It's for finding magazines in the library!"

"But we *know* where the magazines are! They're on the magazine racks!"

"Not those! The old magazines! The ones that aren't on the rack anymore!"

"There aren't any old magazines in the library. Mrs. S. takes them off when the new ones come in and tosses them!" they insisted.

"No, she doesn't. She keeps them in the back room! You tell her what issue you want to look at and she gets it for you!"

Their eyes lit up with discovery. "You mean we can look at the old magazines if we tell her which ones we want?"

"Yes!"

"And all we have to do is use the *Readers' Guide* to find the ones we want?"

"Yes!"

"Wow! What a cool idea!"

Moral: Teach the kids what they need to know.

WHAT INDEPENDENT STUDENTS NEED TO KNOW

In the last chapters the importance of a thorough grounding in content knowledge and skills and training in content area methodologies was discussed. These two areas are the primary curriculum planning. They fit one inside the other like nested bowls (see figure 3.1), the methodological processes providing the context and structure for the presentation of knowledge and skills.

Fig. 3.1. Nested bowls.

Methodological instruction includes the processes used by professionals in investigation, problem solving, communication, synthesis of original products, and evaluation. Content skills are used within these processes to manipulate and shape the raw material of the content area—knowledge. In order for students to produce a product on their own, they must understand the nature of the product and the methodology used to produce it, and be able to use content area skills to transform the knowledge into the finished product. With these relationships in mind, it is a relatively simple matter to plan a curriculum that helps students become self-sufficient in the subject area. In planning such a curriculum, teachers need to answer two questions:

1. *What* do the students need to learn?

2. *How* can they learn it best?

By considering these questions at each level—methodologies, skills, and knowledge—it is possible to put together a curriculum plan in short order. Since methodologies provide the context for the other elements, it is most productive to start planning at that level and use it to choose the components of the other elements.

To decide what methodologies should be taught, it is often helpful for teachers to examine the community expectations for students at that grade level. These expectations are usually codified in the form of a scope and sequence chart. Even though gifted students are capable of performing at higher levels than most students, they are still expected to achieve competence in the forms mandated by the community. They can still participate in and gain from instruction that is methodologically based, employing the same processes to produce a more complex product. For example, at the beginning of junior high or middle school, English students are expected to learn about personal and school communication so that they will be able to function within a secondary school setting. The personal and school communications of gifted students will of course be of a greater complexity than the minimum standards set by the school, but they will still be of the same basic types as those of the rest of the class. These types of communication often include such things as letter writing, oral and written explanation, description of observations and thoughts, narration of a series of events, and production of written and oral reports. This is what must be taught in the course, although there are, of course, many skills and knowledge areas that must be mastered to perform well in the communication areas. But since these must be sequenced within their broad, methodological contexts, the first curriculum planning decisions to be made concern these broad areas. Sometimes school districts sequence these communication areas for teachers; sometimes teachers have a great deal of latitude in deciding on an order of presentation. By setting up the broad areas of instruction first, it is possible to sketch out a coherent plan for an entire quarter of instruction in a relatively short time.

> I really like Rewrite planning. When I use it, I know my kids are getting a coherent curriculum because I can make sure that the units really build upon one another.
> —classroom teacher, Monument, Colorado

The concern then becomes how the students should learn the methodologies, skills, and knowledge of the content area. How can the students best learn the methodologies? How can they best learn the skills? How can they best learn the content knowledge? The answers to these questions hinge on three basic principles:

1. Students learn best when they are allowed to construct their own schemata and when they can involve themselves in experiential exploration of the material.

2. Students remember best when elaborative processing is maximized.

3. Students learn and remember best when they are motivated to learn and remember, when they care about what they are learning.

With these principles in mind, teachers can select categories of activities for inclusion in their classes that will prove the most productive for student learning. These categories provide the structure of the course by setting up consistent expectations for types and durations of activities. The planning grid shown in figure 3.2 allows for a course with five basic categories of activities, but any reasonable number can be used.

UNIT TASK #1	SKILL #1a	VOCAB #1a	READING-WK #1	TERM PROJECT SUBTASK #1
	SKILL #1b	VOCAB #1b	READING-WK #2	TERM PROJECT SUBTASK #2
UNIT TASK #2	SKILL #2a	VOCAB #2a	READING-WK #3	TERM PROJECT SUBTASK #3
	SKILL #2b	VOCAB #2b	READING-WK #4	TERM PROJECT SUBTASK #4
UNIT TASK #3	SKILL #3a	VOCAB #3a	READING-WK #5	TERM PROJECT SUBTASK #5
	SKILL #3b	VOCAB #3b	READING-WK #6	TERM PROJECT SUBTASK #6
UNIT TASK #4	SKILL #4a	VOCAB #4a	READING-WK #7	TERM PROJECT SUBTASK #7
	SKILL #4b	VOCAB #4b	READING-WK #8	TERM PROJECT SUBTASK #8

Fig. 3.2. Blank curriculum planning grid.

Unit Tasks

In order to actively explore methodological processes, students need opportunities to use those processes to produce a product. By observing the students' use of methodology and the quality of the resulting products, teachers can tell how well students have mastered the course material on all levels. Since this type of work involves the elaboration and manipulation of the course content in highly complex ways, it is probably an even better indication of a student's grasp of the material than a formal test. These methodological tasks also build autonomy and can increase motivation to learn if they are structured so as to appeal to varied interests and abilities. This type of instructional activity, due to its complexity and importance relative to skills and knowledge, should engage students for the duration of an entire unit. It constitutes a category called *unit tasks*. Because unit tasks provide the context for the other activities of the course, the first column of the grid is labeled "Unit Tasks."

Units should be two to three weeks in length so that students have enough time to achieve success in the unit task, yet are able to move through the material quickly enough to see their success. In an average nine-week quarter, this would mean planning for three three-week or four two-week unit tasks. The planning grid shown allows for four two-week tasks. This only accounts for eight of the nine weeks in a standard quarter, but it is often wise to build in a one-week safety margin to allow for unexpected events such as assemblies, snow days, and illness. Any extra days can be taken up by term project work, which will be explained in more detail in chapter 6.

The first step in filling the grid is to return to the scope and sequence of broad curriculum areas. In the case of the previously mentioned junior high English class, the teacher might choose to begin with process descriptions as shown in figure 3.3. In process writing, support skills could include recognition of cause and effect relationships, use of chronological order, and two grammatical devices for avoiding the use of second person pronouns, passive voice and imperative mood. Since there are more than two skill areas, the process segment of the course is expanded to two unit tasks. In this case, the teacher chooses writing instructions on how to make something or how to play a game for the first unit task and writing an owner's manual for a device invented by the student for the second task. Notice that in both of these tasks, the assignment is both clearly defined and open-ended. Students may choose how simple or complex they wish to make their final product and in the process demonstrate their understanding and mastery of the content of the unit. There is also room for individual interests and creativity, allowing for maximum personal involvement in the tasks.

◇					
UNIT TASK #1 **PROCESS #1 WRITING DIRECTIONS**	SKILL #1a	VOCAB #1a	READING-WK #1	TERM PROJECT SUBTASK #1
	SKILL #1b	VOCAB #1b	READING-WK #2	TERM PROJECT SUBTASK #2
UNIT TASK #2 **PROCESS #2 OWNER'S MANUAL**	SKILL #2a	VOCAB #2a	READING-WK #3	TERM PROJECT SUBTASK #3
	SKILL #2b	VOCAB #2b	READING-WK #4	TERM PROJECT SUBTASK #4
UNIT TASK #3	SKILL #3a	VOCAB #3a	READING-WK #5	TERM PROJECT SUBTASK #5
	SKILL #3b	VOCAB #3b	READING-WK #6	TERM PROJECT SUBTASK #6
UNIT TASK #4	SKILL #4a	VOCAB #4a	READING-WK #7	TERM PROJECT SUBTASK #7
	SKILL #4b	VOCAB #4b	READING-WK #8	TERM PROJECT SUBTASK #8

Fig. 3.3. Planning grid with unit tasks.

Skills

Skill activities are different from unit tasks in that they involve less complex modes of thinking and are subsumed within the context of the unit task. If the skills do not have immediate and obvious application to the unit tasks, they are not appropriate for inclusion in that particular unit. Skill modules are sequenced to match the demands of the unit task as shown in figure 3.4. Since understanding cause and effect and chronological order are more basic and necessary in describing processes, they are put first. Passive voice and imperative mood are more abstract skills and apply more to the stylistics of the writing rather than its intrinsic meaning, so they are placed within the context of task 2, after the students are already familiar with process description.

UNIT TASK #1 **PROCESS #1 WRITING DIRECTIONS**	SKILL #1a CAUSE AND EFFECT RELATIONSHIPS	VOCAB #1a	READING-WK #1	TERM PROJECT SUBTASK #1
	SKILL #1b CHRONOLOGICAL RELATIONSHIPS	VOCAB #1b	READING-WK #2	TERM PROJECT SUBTASK #2
UNIT TASK #2 **PROCESS #2 OWNER'S MANUAL**	SKILL #2a PASSIVE VOICE	VOCAB #2a	READING-WK #3	TERM PROJECT SUBTASK #3
	SKILL #2b IMPERATIVE MOOD	VOCAB #2b	READING-WK #4	TERM PROJECT SUBTASK #4
UNIT TASK #3	SKILL #3a	VOCAB #3a	READING-WK #5	TERM PROJECT SUBTASK #5
	SKILL #3b	VOCAB #3b	READING-WK #6	TERM PROJECT SUBTASK #6
UNIT TASK #4	SKILL #4a	VOCAB #4a	READING-WK #7	TERM PROJECT SUBTASK #7
	SKILL #4b	VOCAB #4b	READING-WK #8	TERM PROJECT SUBTASK #8

Fig. 3.4. Planning grid with unit tasks and skills.

YABBUT ...

Yabbut if I've sequenced my unit tasks and a skill in the second unit needs to be learned before the first unit task can be accomplished, what do I do?

Response: One of two things can be done. Either flip-flop the unit tasks or insert another unit task before task 1 that provides a better preparation for it than the last task of the previous quarter.

Skill modules are usually allocated at a rate of one per week. This allows students to focus clearly on the mastery of a particular skill area and also contributes to a consistent schedule of expectations which helps students learn to manage their time independently.

Knowledge

Knowledge of facts and rules, the raw material that is transformed by the application of skills within methodological processes into a product, is the next category of activity (see figure 3.5). The raw material of language arts is words, so "Vocabulary" would serve as a basic category for this class. In other subject areas, however, an equivalent category might be "Facts and Rules" or "Content Knowledge." It would include drill and practice in this area so that students would be able to use the appropriate content knowledge in the completion of their unit tasks.

UNIT TASK #1 **PROCESS #1 WRITING DIRECTIONS**	SKILL #1a CAUSE AND EFFECT RELATIONSHIPS	VOCAB #1a VOCAB. CHAP. 1	READING-WK #1	TERM PROJECT SUBTASK #1
	SKILL #1b CHRONOLOGICAL RELATIONSHIPS	VOCAB #1b VOCAB. CHAP. 2	READING-WK #2	TERM PROJECT SUBTASK #2
UNIT TASK #2 **PROCESS #2 OWNER'S MANUAL**	SKILL #2a PASSIVE VOICE	VOCAB #2a VOCAB. CHAP. 3	READING-WK #3	TERM PROJECT SUBTASK #3
	SKILL #2b IMPERATIVE MOOD	VOCAB #2b VOCAB. CHAP. 4	READING-WK #4	TERM PROJECT SUBTASK #4
UNIT TASK #3	SKILL #3a	VOCAB #3a	READING-WK #5	TERM PROJECT SUBTASK #5
	SKILL #3b	VOCAB #3b	READING-WK #6	TERM PROJECT SUBTASK #6
UNIT TASK #4	SKILL #4a	VOCAB #4a	READING-WK #7	TERM PROJECT SUBTASK #7
	SKILL #4b	VOCAB #4b	READING-WK #8	TERM PROJECT SUBTASK #8

Fig. 3.5. Grid with tasks, skills, and vocabulary.

Reading

In our culture, much of our knowledge is communicated through print media. Most subject areas have a body of literature with which students must become acquainted if they are to be considered educated in that area. Gifted students need to become familiar with this body of literature so that they can use it as a starting point for discovery. Also, like other students, they need to become comfortable in the forms, vocabulary, and content of the literature so that they can educate themselves when it becomes necessary. Therefore, another category might be reading, as shown in figure 3.6. Reading in the example English class is regarded in two ways: reading for information and reading for pleasure. The teacher can decide how many pages, readings, or books the students should read in the course of the quarter and account for them in whatever units are desired. Accounting by number of pages read, for example, provides a flexible base which can include both required readings and any recreational reading a student completes.

◇	UNIT TASK #1 PROCESS #1 WRITING DIRECTIONS	SKILL #1a CAUSE AND EFFECT RELATIONSHIPS	VOCAB #1a VOCAB. CHAP. 1	READING-WK #1 1-50 pp.	TERM PROJECT SUBTASK #1
		SKILL #1b CHRONOLOGICAL RELATIONSHIPS	VOCAB #1b VOCAB. CHAP. 2	READING-WK #2 51-100 pp.	TERM PROJECT SUBTASK #2
	UNIT TASK #2 PROCESS #2 OWNER'S MANUAL	SKILL #2a PASSIVE VOICE	VOCAB #2a VOCAB. CHAP. 3	READING-WK #3 101-150 pp.	TERM PROJECT SUBTASK #3
		SKILL #2b IMPERATIVE MOOD	VOCAB #2b VOCAB. CHAP. 4	READING-WK #4 151-200 pp.	TERM PROJECT SUBTASK #4
	UNIT TASK #3	SKILL #3a	VOCAB #3a	READING-WK #5 201-250 pp.	TERM PROJECT SUBTASK #5
		SKILL #3b	VOCAB #3b	READING-WK #6 251-300 pp.	TERM PROJECT SUBTASK #6
	UNIT TASK #4	SKILL #4a	VOCAB #4a	READING-WK #7 301-350 pp.	TERM PROJECT SUBTASK #7
		SKILL #4b	VOCAB #4b	READING-WK #8 351-400 pp.	TERM PROJECT SUBTASK #8

Fig. 3.6. Grid with tasks, skills, vocabulary, and reading.

Term Projects

This leaves one more type of activity—investigation. It encompasses all of the previous categories and increases motivation by encouraging students to set goals for in-depth exploration of their own interests within the subject area. In this activity, students choose a particular topic or project that is of personal interest to them within the subject area and take the entire quarter to investigate it. They use the methodologies, skills, and knowledge gained from the other segments of the course. Because the process should take the entire quarter, it is called the *term project*. To make this long-term activity more achievable and to teach investigative processes and time management, the teacher breaks down the term project into eight subtasks. Each subtask roughly corresponds to one week in the quarter, although students may vary in the amount of time they take to accomplish each subtask.

Since developing positive attitudes toward using language for one's own purposes is an important goal in any English class, term projects in the example class are extremely varied. Students may research and write reports; create original works of their own such as novels, plays, or class newspapers; make field notes on a series of experiments or experiences; or write articles and submit them to magazines for publication. (See chapter 6 for suggestions on term projects.)

Because the term projects are often so varied, the requirements for completing them must also be varied. (When all students are working on similar projects, the requirements can become more specific.) The requirements are actually subtasks that must be completed to produce a project of high quality. In this class, the teacher decides to mimic the process used by writers or other creative professionals when they undertake a project for a particular sponsor. First the writer must prepare a proposal for the project and then get it approved. Then informational sources must be located and compiled into a working bibliography. Once this is accomplished, the writer must take notes from the sources and organize the data and ideas obtained into a presentational format. The writer then composes a rough draft of the project, takes it to an editing group of other students who are also involved in term projects, and then revises the draft on the bases of personal judgment and peer criticism. The final subtask is to publish the project in some way so as to make it available to the entire class and a larger audience if possible.

A Completed Structure

All of these course and category elements are filled in at the appropriate locations on the grid. The teacher now has a quarter plan that looks like the one shown in figure 3.7. The entire quarter is roughed out except for two more unit tasks and the corresponding skill modules. Since the students are also supposed to be learning about oral communication, the teacher decides to have each student do a demonstration of how to do something they know how to do well. The students need to know how to make a speech outline and use note cards. These are all good support skill modules and fit easily onto the planning grid under the skills category.

UNIT TASK #1 PROCESS #1 WRITING DIRECTIONS	SKILL #1a CAUSE AND EFFECT RELATIONSHIPS	VOCAB #1a VOCAB. CHAP. 1	READING-WK #1 1-50 pp.	TERM PROJECT SUBTASK #1 PROPOSAL
	SKILL #1b CHRONOLOGICAL RELATIONSHIPS	VOCAB #1b VOCAB. CHAP. 2	READING-WK #2 51-100 pp.	TERM PROJECT SUBTASK #2 TEACHER APPROVAL
UNIT TASK #2 PROCESS #2 OWNER'S MANUAL	SKILL #2a PASSIVE VOICE	VOCAB #2a VOCAB. CHAP. 3	READING-WK #3 101-150 pp.	TERM PROJECT SUBTASK #3 WORKING BIBLIO.
	SKILL #2b IMPERATIVE MOOD	VOCAB #2b VOCAB. CHAP. 4	READING-WK #4 151-200 pp.	TERM PROJECT SUBTASK #4 NOTES & ORGANIZING
UNIT TASK #3	SKILL #3a	VOCAB #3a	READING-WK #5 201-250 pp.	TERM PROJECT SUBTASK #5 ROUGH DRAFT
	SKILL #3b	VOCAB #3b	READING-WK #6 251-300 pp.	TERM PROJECT SUBTASK #6 EDITING GROUP
UNIT TASK #4	SKILL #4a	VOCAB #4a	READING-WK #7 301-350 pp.	TERM PROJECT SUBTASK #7 FINAL DRAFT
	SKILL #4b	VOCAB #4b	READING-WK #8 351-400 pp.	TERM PROJECT SUBTASK #8 PRESENTATION

Fig. 3.7. Grid with tasks, skills, vocabulary, reading, and projects.

At this point, the teacher decides that the students will have fulfilled the course requirements for process writing and moves on to another area. Narration is dependent on cause and effect and chronological order and follows process nicely. The teacher decides that students will need to learn about direct and indirect quotations and sets each of those as skill areas. The planning grid shown in figure 3.8 is now full.

UNIT TASK #1 PROCESS #1 WRITING DIRECTIONS	SKILL #1a CAUSE AND EFFECT RELATIONSHIPS	VOCAB #1a VOCAB. CHAP. 1	READING-WK #1 1-50 pp.	TERM PROJECT SUBTASK #1 PROPOSAL
	SKILL #1b CHRONOLOGICAL RELATIONSHIPS	VOCAB #1b VOCAB. CHAP. 2	READING-WK #2 51-100 pp.	TERM PROJECT SUBTASK #2 TEACHER APPROVAL
UNIT TASK #2 PROCESS #2 OWNER'S MANUAL	SKILL #2a PASSIVE VOICE	VOCAB #2a VOCAB. CHAP. 3	READING-WK #3 101-150 pp.	TERM PROJECT SUBTASK #3 WORKING BIBLIO.
	SKILL #2b IMPERATIVE MOOD	VOCAB #2b VOCAB. CHAP. 4	READING-WK #4 151-200 pp.	TERM PROJECT SUBTASK #4 NOTES & ORGANIZING
UNIT TASK #3 PROCESS #3 "HOW TO SPEECH"	SKILL #3a OUTLINING	VOCAB #3a VOCAB. REVIEW CHAP.	READING-WK #5 201-250 pp.	TERM PROJECT SUBTASK #5 ROUGH DRAFT
	SKILL #3b NOTECARDS	VOCAB #3b VOCAB. CHAP. 5	READING-WK #6 251-300 pp.	TERM PROJECT SUBTASK #6 EDITING GROUP
UNIT TASK #4 NARRATION #1	SKILL #4a DIRECT QUOTATIONS	VOCAB #4a VOCAB. CHAP. 6	READING-WK #7 301-350 pp.	TERM PROJECT SUBTASK #7 FINAL DRAFT
	SKILL #4b INDIRECT QUOTATIONS	VOCAB #4b VOCAB. CHAP. 7	READING-WK #8 351-400 pp.	TERM PROJECT SUBTASK #8 PRESENTATION

Fig. 3.8. Completed planning grid.

PLANNING FOR EVALUATION

One of the goals of Rewrite is to free up teacher work time to allow for more interaction with students and more planning time. By setting up the evaluation criteria at the curriculum planning stage using the Rewrite record-keeping system, grading time can be cut down significantly. Most teachers who adopt this system of record keeping and evaluation cut the amount of time they spend calculating midterm and quarter grades by 90 percent or more even if they have been using a computer program to process their grades. In addition, the Rewrite record-keeping/evaluation system provides a graphic representation of the course content and structure for students. Students are then able to chart their success within the context of the entire course and see the extent of teacher expectations for the class. Feedback on their progress is constant and instant, and they come to realize that *they* are the ones who are responsible for their grades, not the teacher. This graphic representation shows them that their time use and behavior affect their success and provides them with a sense of autonomy and responsibility. Because they understand that they have control over their grades and success, their levels of intrinsic motivation are increased. Teachers and students become colleagues in the achievement of a common goal rather than adversaries in a power struggle. The entire ethos of the classroom is improved.

> These record sheets are great! I haven't had an argument with a student over grades in ages! There's nothing to argue about. It's all right there on the paper for the student to see.
> —high school teacher, Layton, Utah

To set up this record-keeping/evaluation system, the planning grid is transformed into a bar graph format with each category of activity represented by a bar on the graph. Since the example English class has five types of activities, there will be five bars on the graph. The activities follow:

1. Unit tasks

2. Skills

3. Vocabulary

4. Reading

5. Term projects

They are represented on the bar graph in figure 3.9.

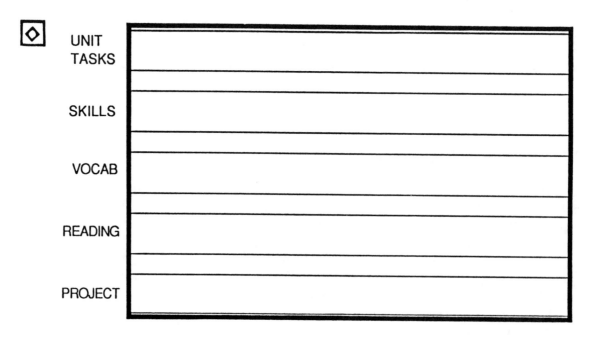

Fig. 3.9. Empty bar graph to be developed into record sheet.

The teacher fills in each bar with the number of credit units required to account for each activity area. To do this, it is only necessary to decide on the grading method for each category and then count the total number of units for each activity on the planning grid. As students successfully earn credit, they color in the appropriate number of squares on the record sheet. Because each category is separated from the others, each can be graded differently. One category can be given grade points, others mastery credit, and still others credit for satisfactory completion as in the term project sub-tasks. It is important to be able to do this, since the categories involve such different types of thinking and content. Following is a description of how the teacher of the example English class would analyze the categories for grading method.

Unit Task

The unit task is variable in the areas of topic and complexity, but there are definite concepts that must be mastered to complete it successfully. These are the concepts that form the basis for evaluation and include such things as how well the methodology was used to incorporate the strategies, tactics, and content knowledge of the unit into a finished product, how well the demands of the unit task activities were met, and how well the student succeeded in producing an original product of high quality. Obviously, regardless of what topic or level of complexity was chosen by each student, there is a great range of variability in the potential quality of the finished task. To provide a continuum for grading this variable product, unit tasks are best graded on a letter grade scale from A to F and figured with a 4.0 grade-point system in which A corresponds to 4.0, B to 3.0, C to 2.0, and D to 1.0.

On the record sheet in figure 3.10, since there are four unit tasks, the teacher has put 16 points as the total possible points to be earned in this category (4.0 × 4 tasks = 16). If the student earned an A (4.0) on task 1, he or she would fill in four squares. Then, if he or she earned a B (3.0), a C (2.0), and another A (4.0) on the next three tasks, the student would fill in three squares, two squares, and four squares, respectively. The total number of grade points or credit units would be 13.

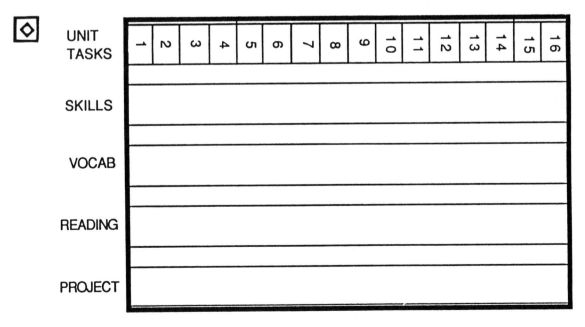

Fig. 3.10. Record sheet with unit tasks.

Skills and Knowledge

In general, these activities involve primarily empirical matter that is easily measured through external behavioral objectives. They also lend themselves well to mastery learning and evaluation techniques. A certain percentage of correct answers on a packet of exercises or a quiz can be set for each module and students can work on the modules until they receive a passing grade.

YABBUT ...

Yabbut what if a kid takes six weeks to finish one module? He or she will be hopelessly behind by the end of the quarter!

Response: Meeting deadlines is an important life skill and Rewrite places strong emphasis on teaching students to meet completion deadlines. Students are expected to attempt every assignment, seek help for what they realize they don't understand, and turn in their best effort by a certain deadline. In the case of skill and knowledge modules, this is usually at the end of the week they were assigned. If a student does not achieve mastery of the topic in that time, the paper is returned with a "Revise" grade and no credit is given. The student then has two days from the return date to revise the assignment and turn it in again. If the student fails the module once again, the teacher immediately knows that the student is having real difficulty with the concepts since the previous "Revise" grade is already recorded both in the gradebook and on the paper itself. The teacher can then meet with that student and any others who are having difficulty and clear up misunderstandings. If the student still does not pass the module on the third try, the teacher can choose to either extend the number of chances or to close out the assignment for that student and deny credit, depending on the circumstances. The advantages of this process are that the teacher only needs to work with those students having trouble with the concepts rather than making the entire class sit through the remediation, and students can learn to see mistakes as opportunities to learn, so that risk-taking is not as daunting as under the traditional hidden curriculum.

Since mastery of the module is what counts, the teacher needs to provide only one square for each module instead of percentage point values as shown in figure 3.11. As the student passes skill and knowledge modules, he or she fills in one square for each earned credit, regardless of the order of assignment and completion.

UNIT TASKS	1	2	3	4	5	6	7	8	9	10	11	12	13	14	15	16
SKILLS	1		2		3		4		5		6		7		8	
VOCAB	1		2		3		4		5		6		7		8	
READING																
PROJECT																

Fig. 3.11. Record sheet with mastery modules.

Reading

Reading, unless it is structured in extremely well-defined assignments, also can be accounted for by recording the successful completion of a number of units, such as pages, articles, or books. To represent these units on the graph, the teacher can mark off intervals similar to those on a thermometer or barometer. When the students have received confirmation that their reading credits have been recorded in the teacher's gradebook, they can fill in the appropriate amount on the bar graph. Figure 3.12 shows a record sheet with reading units.

UNIT TASKS	1	2	3	4	5	6	7	8	9	10	11	12	13	14	15	16
SKILLS	1		2		3		4		5		6		7		8	
VOCAB	1		2		3		4		5		6		7		8	
READING	1-50 pp.		51-100 pp.		101-150pp.		151-200pp.		201-250pp.		251-300pp.		301-350pp.		351-400pp.	
PROJECT																

Fig. 3.12. Record sheet with reading units.

Term Project

Oddly enough, although term projects are highly complex and extremely varied, they also lend themselves to a pass/fail system of grading similar to that in the skill and knowledge categories. The teacher allots one square to each subtask as shown in figure 3.13. Particularly in this area, as well as in reading, it is possible to individualize by ability. If a gifted student turns in a project proposal for a project that is obviously too simple in light of the student's abilities, the teacher can have the student revise the proposal until it is more in line with the student's potential. Likewise, if a student with learning problems turns in a proposal for a project that is too difficult or complicated and therefore likely to result in failure to complete it, the teacher can help revise the proposal to match it more appropriately to the student's capabilities.

On the surface, it may appear that the criteria for grading the term project are different for each student, but actually they are the same: How well is each student working to capacity and achieving his or her potential? Since each student in the class is doing a different project, it is impossible for students to compare grades to see if everybody is being graded the same. As each subtask is handed in for assessment, the teacher can decide whether or not that particular student is working to capacity. If not, the subtask is returned for further work. If the work is satisfactory, the student can record credit for that square and proceed to the next subtask in the project.

UNIT TASKS	1	2	3	4	5	6	7	8	9	10	11	12	13	14	15	16
SKILLS	1		2		3		4		5		6		7		8	
VOCAB	1		2		3		4		5		6		7		8	
READING	1-50 pp.		51-100 pp.		101-150pp.		151-200pp.		201-250pp.		251-300pp.		301-350pp.		351-400pp.	
PROJECT	PROP. SBMISSN		TEACHER APPROVAL		WORKING BIBLIO.		NOTETAKE & ORGANIZE		ROUGH DRAFT		EDITING GROUP		FINAL DRAFT		PRESENT PBLCATN	

Fig. 3.13. Record sheet with project subtasks.

Common Denominators

Because there are different credit systems for each area and all of the areas must be combined into one grade for report cards (usually a letter grade), a method for reconciling these differences is needed. This is done by figuring out the quarter grade cutoffs for each bar and arranging the credit points accordingly. Figure 3.14 shows an example of a zoned record sheet, and figure 3.15 provides suggestions for making them.

UNIT TASKS	1	2	3	4	5	6	7	8	9	10	11	12	13	14	15	16
SKILLS	1		2		3		4		5		6		7		8	
VOCAB	1		2		3		4		5		6		7		8	
READING	1-50 pp.		51-100 pp.		101-150pp.		151-200pp.		201-250pp.		251-300pp.		301-350pp.		351-400pp.	
PROJECT	PROP. SBMISSN		TEACHER APPROVAL		WORKING BIBLIO.		NOTETAKE & ORGANIZE		ROUGH DRAFT		EDITING GROUP		FINAL DRAFT		PRESENT PBLCATN	
	F		D		C				B						A	

Fig. 3.14. Zoned record sheet.

Tips on Making Record Sheets

1. Decide how you will grade each category. What sort of credit units will be used? (Pass/fail? Letter grades? Number of pages?)

2. Count up the number of credit units needed for each category. Use the planning sheet to make sure everything is accounted for.

3. Make a bar graph with one bar for each category.

4. Draw grade zones horizontally across the bar graph.

5. Calculate the cutoff points for each bar. If there is a fraction, round down to give the student the benefit for completing an assignment.

6. Divide each grade zone of each bar into the maximum number of credit units necessary to earn that grade.

7. Number the squares to help students keep track of credit.

8. Number the squares consecutively and do not worry about labeling each square with a particular assignment title. The graph is intended to show how much has been earned, not which assignments have been passed.

9. Try to keep an odd number of bars on the graph. When there is an even number and the student has a 50-50 split between two grades, say an A and a B, there is no way to justify choosing one grade over the other.

10. If an even number of bars cannot be avoided, try to include some sort of tiebreaker such as a book report or extra credit tally. This will provide valid justification for choosing one grade over another in a 50-50 split.

Fig. 3.15.

As the student progresses and receives credit for successfully completed work, he or she fills in a square in the corresponding category. At the end of the quarter, the filled in squares on each bar will reach into a grade zone. Usually, students are consistent enough in their work to have most of the bars end in the same or adjacent zones. When this is the case, it is possible to tell at a glance what letter grade the student has earned for the quarter. On this record sheet (see figure 3.16), the student has three bars in the B zone, one in the A zone, and one in the C zone. The A and the C average out to a B. Along with the three B grades, this gives the student a B for the quarter.

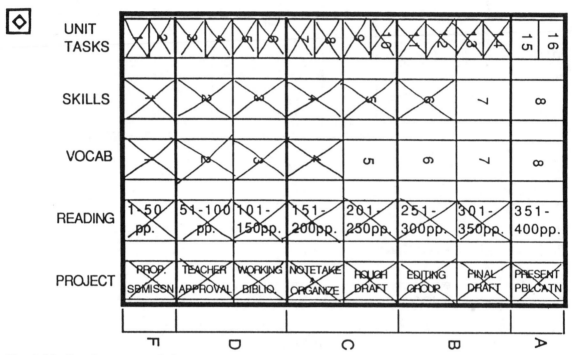

Fig. 3.16. Consistent record sheet.

There are some students, however, who have widely varying grades among the categories because of poor self-management or learning disability. When this occurs, it is necessary to average the grades from each bar to arrive at a quarter grade. Even this process is made easier than most traditional grading systems, since the number values to be averaged are quite small. First, the teacher assigns a grade point value to each bar on the graph. On the graph shown in figure 3.17, the student has earned A's in unit task and term project and receives a 4.0 value for each of those categories. In skills, the student has earned a D and in vocabulary a C, or a 1.0 and a 2.0, respectively. The student has earned a B in reading, or a 3.0. The grades to be averaged are small in number and value and an average can be quickly calculated. This student's raw score is 14. Fourteen is divided by the number of categories, resulting in a 2.8 grade-point average for the quarter.

Another advantage of the record sheet is that the number values used to figure inconsistent grades are always whole and small. Every student's raw score is averaged by the same number of categories, so the teacher can draw up a cutoff chart for quick reference if desired. The chart shown in figure 3.17 is based on a five-category class. Notice that the largest raw score that can be accumulated is 20.0 (5 × 4.0), which gives a very manageable number of possible scores.

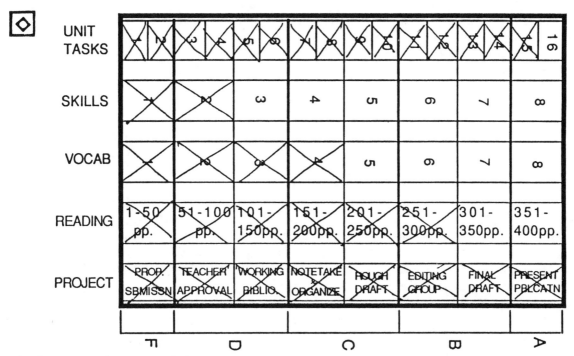

Fig. 3.17. Inconsistent record sheet.

> With the record sheets, students can see that grades are not judgments, only records of performance. They can finally see *they* are responsible for the grade they get — not me!
> —junior high school teacher, Layton, Utah

> I like these sheets. I don't have to ask the teacher to tell me what grade I'm getting. I already know.
> —junior high school student, Layton, Utah

Using Record Sheets and Gradebooks

The record sheet has two functions: to provide ongoing feedback of student performance and to speed up the calculation of student grades. The gradebook serves only one real purpose: to provide a master record of student grades. (Specific guidelines for setting up a Rewrite gradebook are included later in the text.) The record sheet spends most of the quarter in the hands of the students and is used by the teacher only for calculating grades or conferencing with students, parents, and other educators.

Most teachers find it convenient to staple the record sheets inside a manila folder for each student that serves as a work file for that student. The work file is labeled with the student's name and stays in the classroom, usually in a file box. It contains graded work and any work in process the student wishes to keep there. The only time the folder leaves the room is at the request of a parent or administrator. It is signed out by the student upon presentation of a written request and must be returned the next day so that it will always be available to provide feedback during class meetings. If the file is lost while it is signed out, the gradebook record can be used to reconstruct the recordsheet.

Some teachers find that their students simply cannot handle the responsibility of keeping their record sheets. In those cases, they hand out the sheets at intervals during the quarter and have the students update them. At the end of the quarter, the teacher collects the record sheets, uses them to quickly calculate grades, and then keeps them on file should there be any questions regarding a particular student's work.

SETTING UP THE
GRADEBOOK RECORD

Nobody is perfect, and no student is perfectly responsible, even after several quarters of Rewrite. Students lose their record sheets or fill them in incorrectly or don't fill them in in a timely manner. Then when it comes time to figure their grades, their record sheets are unusable. For this reason, the teacher must have a master record of student performance—the gradebook. Traditionally, the gradebook has been an object of veneration for students and a virtual badge of office for classroom teachers. In the Rewrite classroom, "The Gradebook" becomes the "gradebook," a simple record of what each student has accomplished during the year. Because students have ongoing information about their grades in the form of record sheets, the cloak of awe and mystery surrounding "The Gradebook" evaporates. Students come to see their record sheets as the primary records of their grades, and the teacher's gradebook becomes what it really always was, a record, an account of student achievement. Only now the students see it that way, too.

Within the Rewrite framework, the gradebook serves one function—that of a master record of data already recorded on student record sheets. It organizes the data in a more compact format than do the record sheets, and because of this, it is somewhat more difficult to read and use to calculate. But if there are ever any questions about the accuracy of a student record sheet, the gradebook always holds the final word.

Traditional gradebooks are organized to reflect calendar relationships. Each column represents a class meeting, and sets of columns are often divided into weeks. This sometimes makes it difficult to make accurate, readable records when more than one score is earned on the same day. By the end of the quarter, most of these gradebooks resemble hieroglyphic tablets excavated from ancient ruins.

A Rewrite gradebook is organized on a different principle than the calendar. It is organized by activity category, just as the planning grid and record sheet are. Sets of columns that are usually reserved for specific calendar weeks in a traditional gradebook are reserved for different categories of activities instead. Each column represents a particular assignment, and the teacher fills in the appropriate score as each student successfully completes an assignment, much like the record sheet. But the gradebook has the capability of charting student performance much more accurately than the record sheet and maintaining compact records on many students at once.

Regular gradebooks can be adapted to Rewrite record keeping, but ordinary ledger paper is even more adaptable. The sets of columns and rows are already numbered and the paper itself comes in many different formats. Some have only eight or ten sets of columns per page and others have up to fifteen or twenty, so it is possible to choose a format that best fits a particular course. In addition, the paper comes in tablets that are punched so pages can be inserted into a loose-leaf notebook. The teacher of the example English class has chosen only five activity categories, so eight-column ledger paper, one of the smaller formats, serves nicely for the gradebook (see figure 3.18). The planning grid once again serves as a guide, using sets of columns for types of activities and individual columns for specific assignments. The first step in formatting the page is to label the sets of columns. The mythical English teacher chooses set 1 for student names, set 2 for unit tasks, set 3 for skills, set 4 for vocabulary, set 5 for reading, and set 6 for term projects. This leaves two unused sets. To allow for student bonuses and any extra work or activities that might occur during the quarter, set 7 is labeled "Extra Credit." Even though it has this label, it can be used for anything from recording attendance at assemblies to compensation for student aide work. This leaves set 8 free for recording midterm and quarter academic grades along with citizenship or semester grades or any other type of cumulative grade. Figure 3.19 shows a labeled gradebook page.

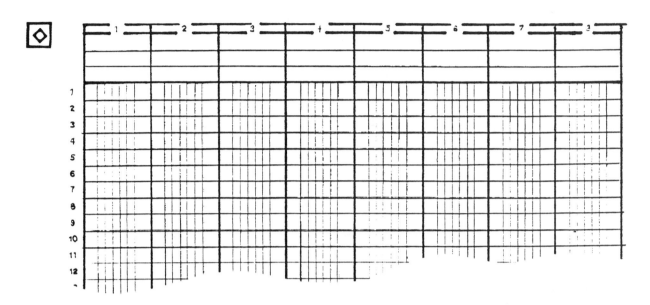

Fig. 3.18. Blank ledger paper.

Fig. 3.19. Labeled gradebook page.

The second step in setting up the gradebook is to allow columns for specific assignments. The assignments do not need titles at this point, only numbers to identify prospective assignments. In figure 3.20, page 40, the teacher has numbered four columns to represent the four unit tasks.

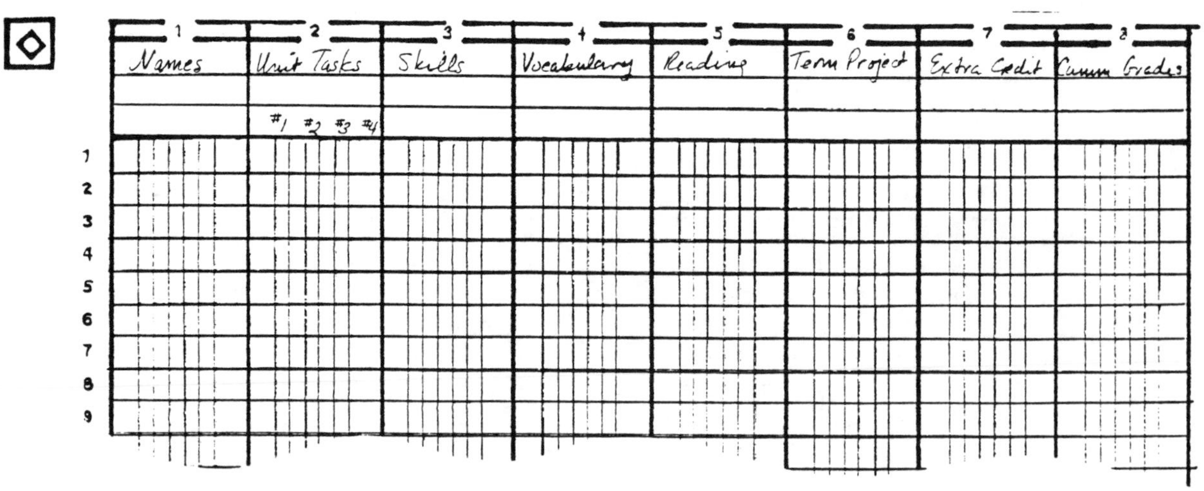

Fig. 3.20. Unit task columns.

The astute reader will have noticed by now that each columnar set has seven columns, one for each day of the week, since accountants work with calendar relationships and the paper is printed for their use. However, all of the other activity categories have eight modules. The solution to this problem is simple. Reserve two rows for each student record and record four modules on the top row and four on the bottom. This, too, leaves plenty of room for any extra notations the teacher may wish to make during the course of the quarter (see figure 3.21).

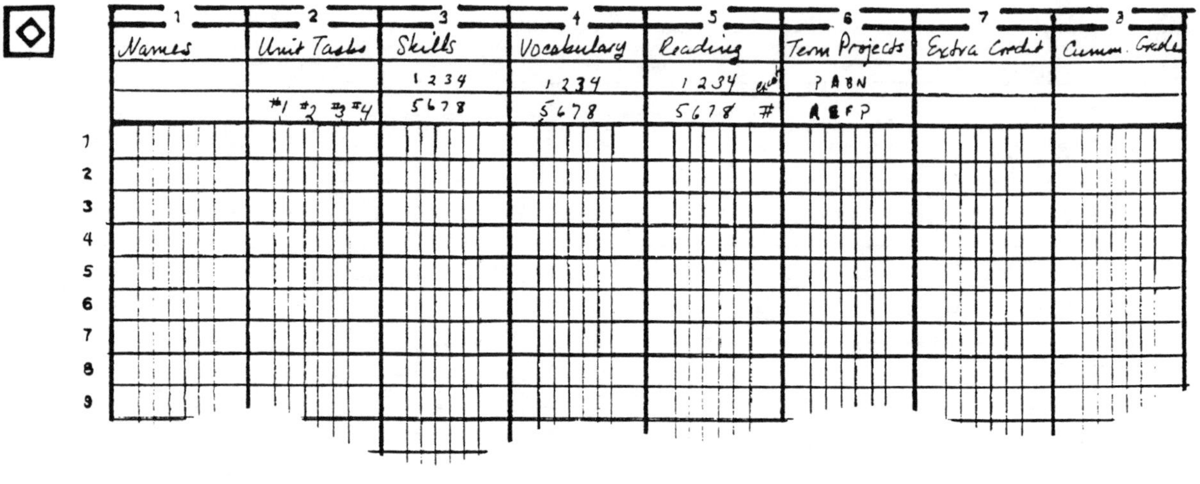

Fig. 3.21. Blank student entry.

Using the Gradebook Record

The gradebook is now ready for class information to be entered. Using the enrollment lists, student names are registered in the name column, every other row (figure 3.22). As students earn credit in unit tasks, their letter grades are filled in in the appropriate squares as shown in figure 3.23.

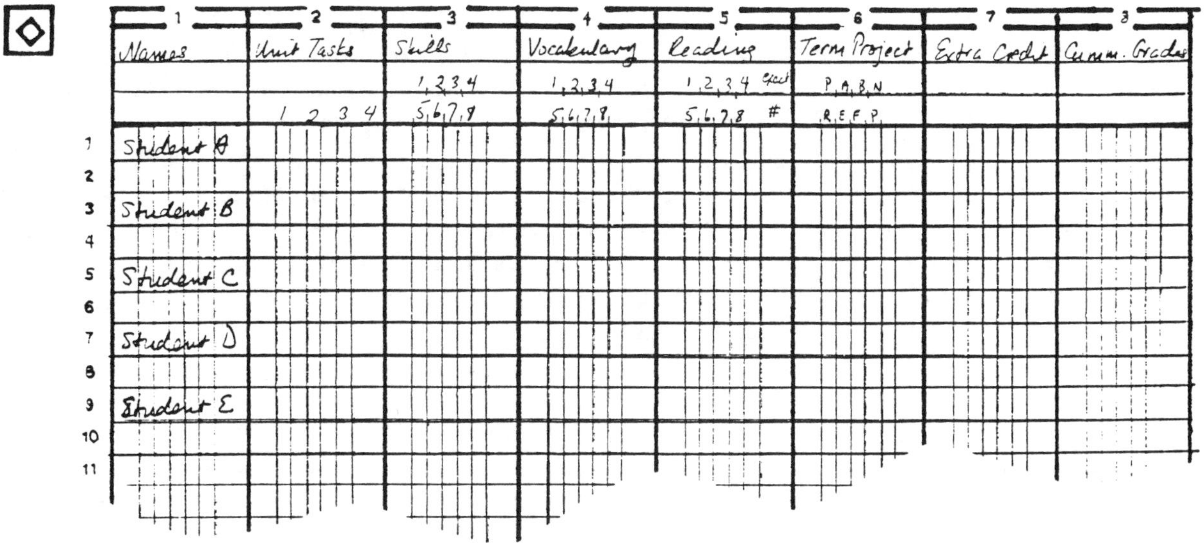

Fig. 3.22. Names filled in.

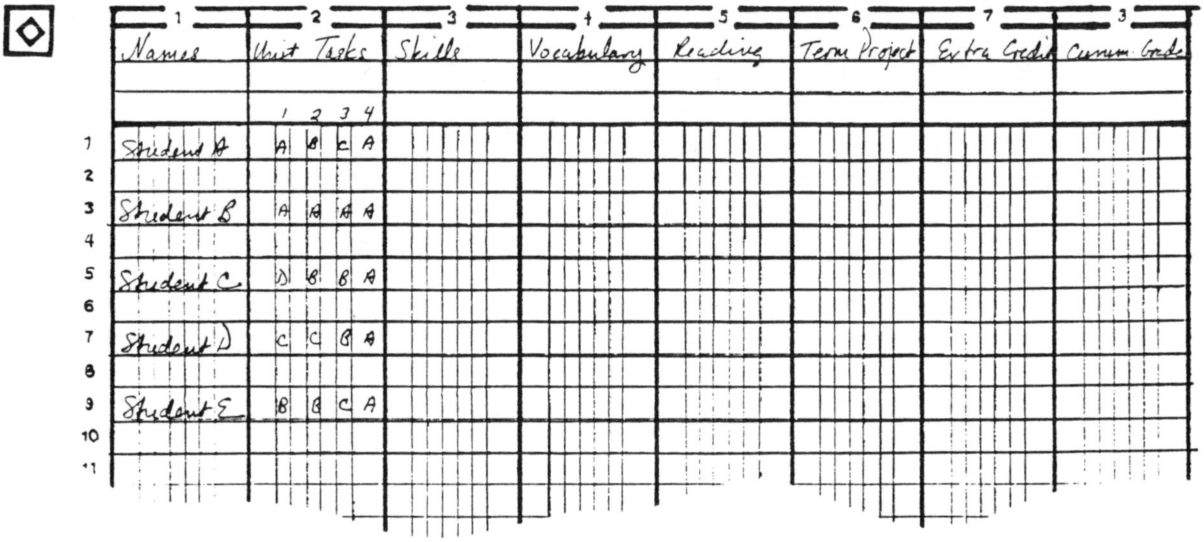

Fig. 3.23. Names and unit task grades.

Skill, vocabulary, and term project subtasks are all graded on a pass/fail/revise system, so letter grades are not used in recording student credit in these areas. Instead a P is recorded in the appropriate square if the student passed the work, an R if the student needs to try again on the assignment, and an F if the final deadline passed and the student chose either not to attempt or not to revise the work.

Even though students will usually only see a P or an R on their returned papers, the advantages of having the P/R/F options for the gradebook record are several. First, it enables the teacher to see whether an assignment has been attempted (a P or an R), ignored altogether (a blank space), or attempted and received (R), or not revised (F). Second, it enables the teacher to see which students are having trouble with a particular area so that a remediation group can be formed to work with those students. In this way, only those students who need extra help need meet with the teacher. The others can go on with the regular program. This practice places no stigma on remediated students, since sooner or later everyone will need help with something, and there are so many other activities going on simultaneously that an extra group off to the side is hardly noticed.

Reading credit can be recorded in several ways. The teacher may designate each square to represent a certain number of pages or assignments or simply write in numerical values in squares labeled "Midterm" and "Quarter." If summaries or book reports or some other means of checking on student reading is preferred, the teacher can either designate squares to represent each unit of measurement or keep a running tally in one of the larger squares in the column set. Figure 3.24 shows an example of a filled-in gradebook page.

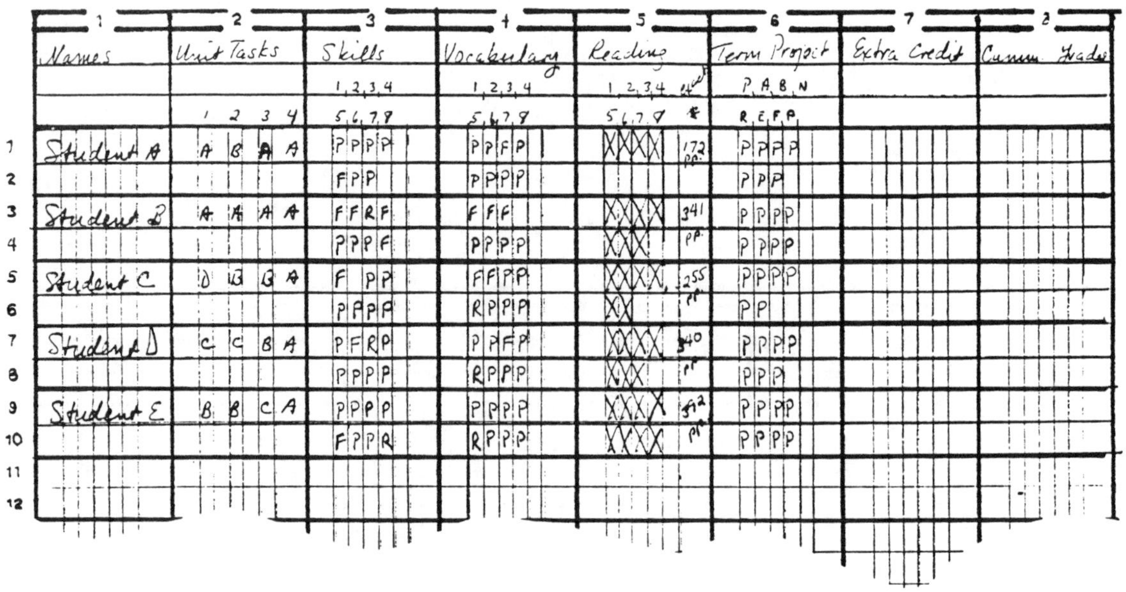

Fig. 3.24. Filled-in gradebook page.

Judgment Day

When the gradebook is all filled in with student performance records, its effect is that of a record sheet that has been dismantled and has had the bars laid end-to-end horizontally. Although this record could be used to figure grades, it is not nearly as easy to do so as with the student record sheets. Rather than use the gradebook for this purpose, the teacher collects the student record sheets twice per quarter to calculate midterm and quarter grades. To make sure that the student record sheets are accurate, the Judgment Day procedure is used.

Twice each quarter the teacher announces dates for Drop Dead Day and Judgment Day, the two national holidays of Rewrite. Drop Dead Day is the last day that work is accepted before computing grades. If any students try to turn in work after Drop Dead Day, the other students and the teacher are entitled to say, "Drop dead!" in unison and the discussion is over. Judgment Day follows Drop Dead Day by one to three days, depending on how long the teacher needs to complete grading student work for that grading period. On Judgment Day, the Book is opened and Accounts are settled.

What this means in practical terms is that one class day is set aside for quiet, individual work while the teacher reads aloud the recorded credit units for each student from the gradebook. While the teacher reads the record, the corresponding student checks to make sure that his or her record sheet accurately reflects the gradebook record. At this time, students can let the teacher know where they want to have their bonus squares counted. (Bonus squares can be earned in several ways and will be discussed in later chapters.) Also, if there are any discrepancies regarding work that the student claims was turned in and graded but of which the teacher has no record, the student can produce the graded paper from his or her work file so that the gradebook can be corrected. (No evidence, no gradebook change!) A student aide can check the records of absent students and the teacher places bonus squares in the most advantageous spots on the record sheets so that the students receive the maximum possible benefit from their bonus work.

The entire process takes about thirty to forty minutes for a class of forty pupils. For most teachers, the remaining ten to fifteen minutes of the class is time enough to calculate grades from the record sheets for the entire class. No class time is really wasted in this procedure, because each student has to spend only about one minute engaged in the Judgment Day festivities. The rest of the class period is available to the students to work on projects, unit work, or reading. The only real limitation is that no group work can be done, as the noise and attention levels required for group work would interfere with record checks.

CONCLUSION

After looking over Rewrite materials and results, a teacher once remarked to the author, "Golly, this is great! I'd love to use it, but I don't have time." The author's reply was, "If you'd use it, you'd *have* the time." The three processes described in this chapter—filling in the planning grid, constructing student record sheets, and setting up the gradebook—may seem time-consuming. In fact, they save time—hours and hours of it—before, during, and after the grading period.

Most planning grids can be roughed out in a half hour or less. If it takes longer than that, the teacher is trying to be too specific and using the grid to plan the precise details of each unit. That is not the purpose of the grid. This grid is intended to serve two major functions. It provides a basis for setting up record sheets and gradebooks by enabling the teacher to establish the number and types of learning activities that will be included in the quarter's curriculum. It also serves as a shopping list when it comes time to plan individual units. When teachers know what kind of materials are needed, they can focus their unit planning and material preparation much more quickly and effectively than when they are simply getting along from one week or day to the next. As one of the first teachers to adopt this system commented, "Ever since I started using this program, I've been able to go shopping on weeknights like normal people!" And, with a planning grid, the record sheet and gradebook can be set up even before the teacher knows the specifics of each unit.

Unless the teacher using Rewrite curriculum planning is particularly clumsy with rulers and graph paper, even the record sheet and gradebook are quick to set up. The minimal time invested in these two activities yields an enormous return on time usually spent calculating grades, arguing with students over calculating grades, answering questions like, "Can you tell me what my grade is so far?," entering records into a digital computer program, waiting for the program to print out grade slips for each student, waiting for a turn to use the computer if it's necessary to share, hunting through cramped gradebook entries to see if a student is making progress, explaining the principles of responsibility and accountability to students and sometimes to parents, and/or calculating grades with a calculator. Another of the teachers at the junior high where Rewrite was first developed was enthusiastic over the positive payoffs resulting from implementing Rewrite planning and record keeping. Her observation was, "I love it! I can actually use planning days to plan instead of to fill out bubble sheets!"

With Rewrite curriculum planning, the stage is set for learning and teaching. Both teachers and students can know from the first what the expectations for the quarter are. Students can receive constant feedback on their performance and the teacher can tell at a glance how each student is doing. Because the goals are clear, both teachers and students can see where they are headed. For students, this heightens intrinsic motivation and autonomy because they no longer have to depend on the teacher to find out what will be required of them from moment to moment. For teachers, the sense of motivation and autonomy are increased because they no longer need to be at the mercy of a textbook and a schedule. Instead, they can use the time and energy gained to do what they really want to do—teach.

— 4 —
The Classroom Environment
Management Planning for Independence

Class of the Living Dead
A Teacher's Horror Story

Zombies, that's what they were. They sat there looking at me through the entire set of instructions, eyes open, upright in their seats, even moving about a bit as one would expect living beings to do. They nodded in the right places, smiled in the right places, even opened their books to the right page, but they weren't really living, breathing souls. They were academic zombies, and as soon as I finished my spiel and turned them loose to work on their own, they would start coming.

Most of them waited until I sat down at my desk. Then they began to rise from their seats in ones and twos and stiffly made their way up the aisles to my desk, frowning at a blank work-sheet or fixing a fishlike stare on me as they approached. The first one said, "I don't get it," and dropped the paper on my desk as though I were not aware of its contents.

"What don't you get?" I asked.

"I just don't get it."

Vague questions had become a pet peeve of mine ever since the Great *Readers' Guide* Debacle with the speech class. "If you can't ask a specific question, I can't give you an answer."

This was calculated to force the student to actually read the assignment so one of two things would happen. Either the student would realize that he or she really did understand the instructions or formulate a question I could answer. This particular student asked a question. I answered as efficiently as I could, since the air was growing thick with the stench of corn nuts and taco chips, the primary nourishment of the students who were crowding in around my desk. The student listened to my answer, nodded, and then pushed back through the crowd to his desk.

The next zombie stepped up, a total distance of about two inches. "I don't get it."

"What don't you get?" It began to occur to me that I had been through this before. After listening to my specific question retort, the student frowned, read the directions, and asked exactly the question the first student had. It occurred to me that I had been through this before, too, and likely would be again. Clearly it was a well-designed strategy to draw me into the zombie corpus. Even if I did not succumb, I knew that my sweaters would be permanently saturated with corn nut and taco chip fumes. Something had to be done.

My first strategy consisted of writing out the answers to the most common questions I received on large cards, numbering them, and posting them on the walls. Among others, these included, "Yes," "No," "Put it in the in basket," "Look in the out basket," and "On the top shelf of the bookcase under the front window." Then I put one more sign up. It read, "If the answer is on the wall, don't ask the question!" From then on, when the zombies asked their repetitive questions, I could just say, "One," or "Eighteen," instead of going through the whole thing ad infinitum. The problem with this was that it just made them read the answer off a card. I decided to try something else.

I wrote, "The answer lady will return in fifteen minutes. Try it yourself first," on the blackboard. Then I took a chair out into the hall and waited. Maybe if there were no teacher to cling to, they would discover their own resources, i.e., their brains and volition. Unfortunately, this was less than successful, too. Not only did it seem strange, if not actually irresponsible, to my principal for me to be sitting in the hall when there were obviously a large number of students who needed some serious teaching pronto, but the students merely went into neutral and idled for fifteen minutes until I came back in. Then the onslaught began again, the zombies slowly, deliberately moving up the aisles, intoning, "I don't get it. I don't get it."

At first I tried to fend them off, but I soon saw that there was no way to survive without escaping. I tried one last survival trick from my college classroom management courses—I screamed at them to get back to their seats and rushed into my glass-walled office, slamming and locking the door behind me. The students stared after me for several seconds, their mouths hanging loosely from their ears and then slowly, deliberately, plodded back to their desks, chanting, "I still don't get it. I still don't get it." I watched from the sanctuary of my office. Yes, I was safe in here and class would be over soon, but could I manage to get out before the bell rang and the next horde came in? I might be trapped in here until lunchtime, when the bell would turn them into a battalion of shrieking berserkers as they converged to wreak havoc in the cafeteria. I waited and watched, biding my time and praying that somehow I would be able to escape.

Moral: Always leave some room for the living!

A MANAGEMENT POWWOW

In a way, it was a relief to discover that Debbie was experiencing the same plague in her classroom and that I wasn't the only target. We decided that it was us or them. We would have to build mechanisms into our program that would not just shift responsibility onto a generation of academic gumdrops who were ill-prepared for assuming it, but we would have to make the shift as easy for them as possible, especially at the beginning. It seemed best to streamline the ways in which students could obtain explicit instructions, additional explanations and materials, and ongoing feedback without disrupting the laboratory atmosphere we were seeking to maintain and without adding to our workload, which would make us less available to students.

We set to work designing a total environment that would communicate Rewrite's hidden curriculum to our students and prepare them for life in the "real" world:

Rewrite Hidden Curriculum

1.   Try to do as much for yourself as you can.

2.   Take initiative and responsibility in positive ways.

3.   Go at your own pace and do your best.

We knew that the procedures we established would have to be sensible and simple so that our students would be able to pick them up quickly. We also had been told by our principal that we would have no access to additional supplies, money, or personnel in implementing these procedures, since our school was on a tight budget. In addition, we could in no way change our schedules or class assignments. In short, we had to work with what we already had and stay within the greater context of our traditional school.

It wasn't as much of a problem as one might expect. As we examined the parameters of the problem, we realized that the solution mainly involved using the elements of the traditional classroom in different ways. By modifying these elements—teacher/student roles, information, time, and space—we could achieve our goals and stay within the limits our principal had defined. We decided to try to employ two basic principles in our modifications. First, we would try to shift as much responsibility for learning and personal management as possible to the students, and second, we would try to create structures that were static and therefore constantly accessible to all students regardless of ability or style.

TEACHER/STUDENT ROLES

The traditional teacher/student paradigm portrays the teacher as the Source of All Knowledge, Information, and Decisions. It also presents the teacher as the Bearer of All Responsibility, a role guaranteed to produce an eventual core meltdown. The traditional teacher has only so much time and energy to give to instruction, explanations, and feedback and consequently tends to do this in a whole-class situation, leading the students in unison activities.

Problems with this situation arise when some students don't grasp the concept under study as quickly as the bulk of the class and others grasp it more quickly. In the former case, the students will rarely, if ever, be able to get the full amount of assistance and practice they need to master the material and will gradually feel as though they have lost control over their learning situation. In the latter case, the students will be faced with the prospect of sitting idly by, waiting for the rest of the class and trying to make the boredom bearable, becoming aware that they, too, have lost control over their learning situation. This promotes a relationship of "us and them" rather than a more collegial one of teacher and learners working together toward a common goal. However, by changing the traditional definitions of teacher and student, many of the problems associated with the traditional paradigm can be solved.

The first change is in the definition of roles. Teachers in a Rewrite classroom become resources instead of sources. They become guides and colleagues in a process of active discovery instead of merely dispensers of knowledge. Once this change is made, other members of the class can become teachers, too. Students who have mastered a concept or skill can help others who are having trouble with it. Students who have understood instructions easily can help those who have not done so. And students who are engaged in similar learning processes can give feedback and encouragement to one another. Instead of one teacher in a classroom with many students as in the traditional classroom, there are many teachers and students in the Rewrite classroom. There can be cooperative learning groups, editing/peer response groups, research teams, and formal and informal peer tutoring, all in addition to the more expert and specialized guidance of the teacher.

Along with the increased opportunities to receive help, there are other advantages that result from this change in teacher/student roles. Students who master material more quickly can benefit from teaching other students. As they organize and communicate their knowledge, they process it more thoroughly, thus internalizing it better and receiving extra practice in communication and leadership skills. This is particularly important for gifted students because they must develop the ability to communicate and collaborate with less able colleagues if they are to be successful as adults. But it is important to keep in mind that this experience will not be limited to gifted students. Everyone, even gifted students, has trouble grasping some new idea or skill at some time or another. Sooner or later, every student in the class will be called upon to share his or her expertise with another student. This allows every student, gifted or not, to assume a leadership role in the class.

Finally, the Rewrite teacher/student paradigm is more representative of the way the "real" world works. Adults often work cooperatively on projects and are expected to seek help and feedback from one another on their own. When students experience similar work settings and requirements in the classroom, they gain work and social skills which will stand them in good stead as they enter the work world.

INFORMATION

An element of the regular classroom that is tied closely to the definition of roles is information. When teachers are sources rather than resources, they are the repositories of all information. Some of that information is shared freely by the teacher and some of it is traditionally held back and obtained by students only at appointed times or when students manage to pry it out.

Quarterly grading expectations and students' progress are part of the information that is traditionally held close by the teacher. Just as traditionally, students try to elicit this information by asking questions like, "What am I getting so far?" or, "How many more of these will we have to do?" Keeping this information from students is comparable to the Internal Revenue Service's refusing to tell adults how much tax they can expect to have withheld from their paychecks each week. Students have a right to know where they stand and what is expected of them. To deny them this information is to rob them of both self-determination and responsibility. By directing students' attention to the record sheets presented in chapter 3, these questions can be readily and privately answered without taking up any valuable teacher time.

Other elements of information traditionally withheld by the teacher include unit plans, activity instructions before the activity is scheduled, class schedules, and ongoing feedback on students' performance. Certainly the teacher must still make the bulk of decisions about these things, but these decisions can be communicated in ways that do not take up teacher or class time, ways that are static in their availability, and that do not demean students by forcing them to come begging. Instead, they can be disseminated in ways that teach them to take the initiative in finding the necessary information, such as unit overviews, calendars, and evaluation rubrics.

There are always some students who progress at a faster pace than the teacher estimates in a unit schedule. To communicate unit plan overviews and preclude the infamous cry of "What do I do next?" teachers can provide each student with a checklist of unit activities such as that shown in figure 4.1. These unit plans need not have specific dates for when each supporting activity will be performed, only the order and number of activities. Each item on the checklist should have a brief explanation so that students can refer to it to refresh their memories concerning teacher instructions and expectations. This method has the advantage of making the information constantly accessible to students. At first, students often forget to use the checklist and persist in asking the teacher what they should do next, but after a few reminders to look at it, they discover that they can indeed find answers on their own. This new-found ability often seems to add to the students' feelings of autonomy and self-esteem. At the same time, students are learning about planning techniques by seeing how they are used in the teacher's checklist format.

A second method of providing ongoing information about class schedules is a rather prosaic one—a calendar. Teachers can use calendars in several ways, depending on the constraint of their situations. For teachers with only a few different class preparations, one large calendar is usually enough for all the classes. The calendar should be posted in an easily accessible spot in the classroom so that students can consult it at their leisure without disturbing the rest of the class. All known due dates should be posted on the calendar and students' attention should be directed to it whenever they request information on due dates or scheduled events. Before long, they learn to take responsibility for finding out about schedules and to stop asking the teacher for this information. For some teachers, it may be necessary to have a different calendar for each class. In this case, one bulletin board or display area can be set aside exclusively for calendar information or a bulletin board/ display area for each class can include a calendar along with any other pertinent items.

◇ ***Rewrite English Program***
Language Task 1: Biographical Sketches
Unit Checklist

This task is intended to help you get to know your classmates, learn how to write a biographical sketch, and learn to be a good editor. You must complete *all* of the steps below to try for an A.

_______ 1. Make a list of interview questions that you think would tell you a lot about what somebody else is really like.

_______ 2. Interview another student in your class. Ask him or her the questions you made up. Add any other questions you think of while you're interviewing. *Take notes! You will have to turn them in with your paper!*

_______ 3. Choose the most important, interesting, and unique things about your partner and introduce him or her to the class. Be sure to tell the *most* interesting and unique things about that person.

_______ 4. Write a short biographical paragraph about your partner. It should be about the right length to fill up a large index card for a display of classmembers. Take it with you to your editing group.

_______ 5. In your editing group, read your paragraph aloud to the other students. Then let them read your paper while you read their papers silently. Make suggestions for improving their papers and tell them what they did well.

_______ 6. Using the comments of your group as a guide, revise your paragraph and take it to a second group meeting for checking and proofreading.

_______ 7. Fix any remaining errors and prepare your final draft to hand in. Your final draft must be on standard-sized notebook paper, in ink, with 1-inch margins on both sides. Your name, period, and the date must be in the upper right-hand corner of your paper. With your final draft, hand in all of your interview notes and rough drafts so you can get credit for everything you did.

Fig. 4.1.

Finally, information regarding the grading criteria and expectations for each unit task can be made constantly available to students by use of a rubric (see figure 4.2).

◇ *Biographical Sketches Rubric*

All papers will be graded according to the following guidelines:

An A paper has all or most of the following:
- Prewriting notes, two rough drafts, and final drafts
- A definite angle
- Logical organization
- Basic information and several interesting and unique things about the person
- Few or no errors in spelling, grammar, or format

A B paper has all or most of the following:
- Prewriting notes, one rough draft, and final drafts
- A definite angle
- Logical organization
- Basic information and only a few interesting or unique things about the person
- Some minor errors in spelling, grammar, or format that do not interfere with meaning

A C paper has all or most of the following:
- Prewriting notes or rough draft with a final draft
- An angle, but not clearly defined
- Errors in organization
- Missing some basic information about the person and has only one or two interesting or unique items
- Serious errors that interfere with meaning

A D paper has all or most of the following:
- Only a final draft
- No definite angle
- Poor organization
- Only basic information and no interesting, unique details
- Many serious errors that interfere with meaning

An F paper has all or most of the following:
- Only a final draft
- No definite angle or organizational plan
- Is difficult or impossible to understand
- Does not fulfill the requirements of the assignment

Fig. 4.2.

A rubric is a set of evaluation criteria drawn up ahead of time by the teacher. It should be given to the students at the beginning of the unit along with the checklist and any known due dates. The rubric clearly tells the students what they must do to earn a certain grade in much the same way that adults produce products to specifications. (For further discussion on preparing rubrics, see chapter 5, page 82.) This resource has several advantages. First, it provides ongoing information about teacher requirements and takes away much of the frustration of trying to second guess the teacher's expectations for student performance. Second, it serves as a way for students to receive clarification on this information independently, without running to the teacher to see "if this is okay."

> I like these rubrics. When I was in school, if I did a paper for a teacher and got a bad grade on it, all I knew was that, of all the possible ways I could have done the paper, I had picked the wrong way. That meant that my revision options were only infinity minus one instead of infinity. That doesn't happen to my students.
> —English teacher, Colorado Springs, Colorado

Third, it provides a valuable tool for use in peer response/editing groups, cooperative learning groups, and peer tutoring situations. Students can refer to the rubric when working together and use it as a guide to their activities. Fourth, it puts the primary responsibility for error correction on the students, since they know far ahead of time what the teacher expects from their work. Fifth, along with the checklist, it is a convenient way to show parents, administrators, and special education teachers what the objectives of the unit are. Finally, it streamlines the grading process for teachers and ensures more consistency in grades since grading with rubrics involves matching of characteristics with prespecified criteria rather than complex subjective judgments. This is because the major decisions about evaluation are made before the teacher sits down to grade papers. Rubrics can also be used as checklists to let students know what weaknesses and strengths were found in their work. Instructions for constructing rubrics will be presented in detail in chapter 5.

TIME

None of these modifications in teacher/student roles and the handling and dissemination of information can function productively in a traditional classroom where time is dribbled out in strict allowances for specific activities. If all students must use their time in identical amounts for identical activities, then it is impossible for students who *need* extra time to achieve mastery to *take* that time. It is likewise impossible for students who master material quickly to function as peer tutors or to go on to more challenging activities, since they must mark time until the teacher is ready to go on. It is impossible for students to seek out and find needed information or to adjust to the needs of their individual schema-building the amounts of time they spend in different activities.

A further time limitation of the traditional classroom is the idea that all students must spend their time in the same way at any given moment. Every student constructs schemata in highly individual ways, taking in information as needed, and not necessarily as it is formally presented. By insisting that all unit activities be done in a specific order, in a specific amount of time, and in unison, teachers can severely inhibit the construction of cognitive schemata. This is not to say that time management must be done away with altogether. On the contrary, students need to learn time management skills to function well both in and out of school. Deadlines and schedules are very real parts of our society.

In the adult world, one person may take all weekend to finish a set of basic household responsibilities. Another may rush around for half of Saturday, finish everything, and use the rest of the weekend for more pleasurable pursuits. Either way, they both finish in time to return to work on Monday. They have both met their deadlines and worked according to their own styles and preferences, although they have made very different choices about how they approached their tasks. Similarly, students can still accomplish their goals and meet their deadlines even if they do not do so in exactly the same way that the teacher would have.

When I took my first microcomputers course in the early 1980s, my instructor was a man named Jim. (His last name shall remain unknown to protect his identity.) Jim was a good teacher and was patient with all of us in the Microcomputers for Teachers class. He was good at explaining things and at reducing our apprehension at dealing with such a high-tech machine as a 28K microcomputer.

Several times during the course, however, it became clear to me that Jim and I had very different work styles. It was clear to Jim, too, but he put my "odd" behavior down to such things as daydreaming, laziness, and slowness. What was it that I used to do in his class that produced this clash, you ask? I didn't type data continuously into the computer the way he did.

What's wrong with that, you wonder? Nothing at all, really. It was my habit to think about what I should type into my program and get it straight in my head before I started typing. It was Jim's habit to plunge ahead, typing and retyping as he saw his work take shape on the screen. Whenever he saw me sitting motionless, staring at the screen, he would accuse me of "just sitting there" or "doing nothing" and would urge me to "get to work." Because he always had to be typing to be working, it did not occur to him that someone else could be working and not typing! Had he been a Behaviorist, I might have understood his perception of the situation, but the man was a dyed-in-the-wool Piagetian! I decided to attribute his behavior to the possibility that he hadn't quite reached the stage of formal operations yet.

How can time use be made more flexible in a regular classroom? The procedures are actually quite simple, particularly when unit activities are active and exploratory and based on the application of knowledge and skills to methodologies. When introducing a new unit and modeling the strategies and processes involved in producing a unit task, it is almost always necessary to do so in the traditional, teacher-led format, but once the unit activities are explained and the knowledge and skills presented, the students need opportunities to explore, practice, and elaborate. The teacher cannot do it for them, so any further regimentation is often unnecessary, if not actually counterproductive. The students can be turned loose to work on their assignments.

If unit tasks are given at the rate of one every two weeks and skills and knowledge modules one every week, it means that during any given week, students will have one unit task, one skill module, and one knowledge module to work on. If the teacher presents these early in the week and sets a due date for weekly assignments at the end of each week and for unit tasks at the end of every other week, students can have several days of relatively unstructured time in class. (It is *relatively* unstructured because there are still definite expectations for how this time should be used.) Those students who wish to can finish their mastery modules first and then devote themselves to their unit tasks. Figure 4.3 shows a sample unit calendar.

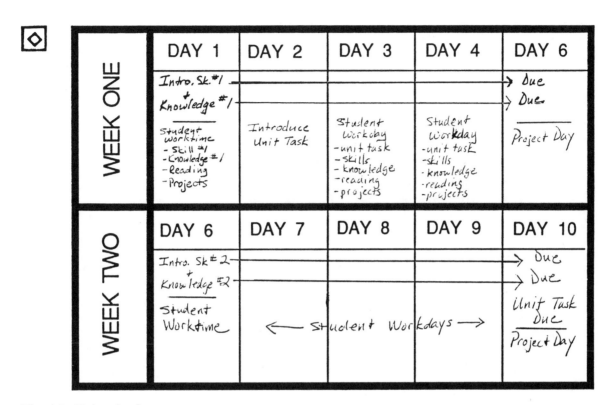

	DAY 1	DAY 2	DAY 3	DAY 4	DAY 6
WEEK ONE	*Intro. Sk.#1* → *Knowledge #1* → ___ *Student worktime* *- Skill #1* *- Knowledge #1* *- Reading* *- Projects*	*Introduce Unit Task*	*Student workday* *-unit task* *- skills* *- knowledge* *-reading* *- projects*	*Student Workday* *-unit task* *-skills* *- knowledge* *-reading* *-projects*	→ *Due* → *Due* ___ *Project Day*
	DAY 6	DAY 7	DAY 8	DAY 9	DAY 10
WEEK TWO	*Intro. Sk #2* → *Knowledge #2* → *Student Worktime*	← *Student*	*Workdays* →		→ *Due* → *Due* *Unit Task Due* ___ *Project Day*

Fig. 4.3. Unit calendar.

Other students may wish to switch back and forth between activities in a more simultaneous type of work style. Still others may choose to get as far ahead as possible on the assigned tasks and then spend the rest of their class time on such things as reading or term projects. Those with extra time can tutor other students, work at a classroom job (a topic covered later in this chapter), make up missed work, or revise returned assignments. On a well-run work day, there can be as many as six or seven different activities going on in a Rewrite classroom, but they are all focused on one goal— exploration and mastery of the subject matter.

CHANGING TIME ZONES

It is often difficult for students to adapt to these different concepts of time use after years of being told how to spend their time. There are several procedures that are helpful in assisting students learn to manage their own time. At the beginning of each period, the teacher can list the various "legal" activities for that day. The teacher can review these items—referred to as "today's menu" in figure 4.4—*briefly* with the class along with any impending due dates. At this point, the teacher can also ask whether there are any student work groups that need to meet. If there are, the teacher can then specify when and where those groups should meet in the classroom. Once this is done, the class can be given the rest of the period to do their work. The teacher can then spend that time working with students who need specialized help, developing curriculum materials, or taking care of clerical responsibilities. If any students try to request clearly posted information from the teacher, they should have their attention directed to the proper source. If a due date is requested, they should be referred to the calendar; if unit requirements are questioned, they should first be referred to the checklist and rubric. If students do not seem to know what they should be doing, their attention should be drawn to the daily menu. In these ways, menial demands on teacher time are minimized. This helps teachers to become more accessible to those students needing specialized help and students to learn to help themselves whenever possible.

Fig. 4.4.

SPACE

Shifts in time utilization require similar shifts in space utilization. In the traditional classroom, all the students do the same thing at the same time, excepting, of course, the souls who have been cast out into the back corners to engage in copying the dictionary or some other punitive activity. This is perfectly reasonable within the traditional context, since only one activity is usually going on at a time. But in a Rewrite classroom, many activities are occurring simultaneously, and room space must accommodate all of them without wreaking undue hardship on anyone else. This is not an unnatural situation. In a normal community, residents go about their various activities side by side without seriously disrupting the fabric of society. They observe certain courtesies and laws and their activities are relegated to specific places and circumstances. A similar system can be set up in a regular classroom.

The first step in customizing space utilization in a Rewrite classroom is to list the needs of the class. There will be various management functions that must be accommodated. There will be students working alone. There will be peer tutoring taking place. There will be small groups meeting. There may be a need to provide a class library or reference area and maintain it. There may be special use areas with special equipment for courses such as science or industrial arts or typing. All of these necessities must be taken into account.

Certain management functions are common to most, if not all, classrooms. Attendance must be taken and recorded, announcements shared, materials passed out, papers returned and collected, records of student grades kept, and students returning from absences briefed on what they missed. Traditionally, these functions are dealt with in a whole-class format, which often takes up large amounts of collective class time. But most of these functions can be carried out in ways which do not detract greatly from learning time.

ASSIGNED SEATING

Usually students have assigned seats that are placed in a static arrangement dictated by the teacher. This helps in taking attendance, since empty seats are easy to match to absent students. This system works well and can still be used in a Rewrite format, particularly since it makes counting heads quick and accurate. It is also extremely helpful for substitute teachers who need to identify students as easily as possible. However, once attendance is taken, any announcements made, and materials distributed, students need to be able to go to the place in the room where they can best carry out their work. Once the day's work is finished, students can return to their arranged seats to be dismissed by the teacher.

> I always tell my students on the first day of class that the seats they are sitting in do not belong to them, they belong to the class and that we will use the seats as the class needs to use them.
> —Debora Robbins

PAPER FLOW

Passing out and collecting papers can take staggering amounts of time away from class work. It is often done by the teacher or perhaps a student helper and is the sort of mindless task that does not require special certification from the state. Any person of reasonable reading ability and discretion can do it without unduly disrupting the classroom routine. It need not fall to the teacher, whose specialized training can be put to much more effective use.

Two simple procedures can accomplish this process quickly and unobtrusively. The first modification is to do away with returning and collecting homework as a formal activity. This is done by setting up "In" and "Out" baskets for each class. Since students will be working at their own paces, they will be turning in work at different times. Some will finish early and others on time. By providing "In" and "Out" baskets, teachers enable students to turn in work whenever they finish it. The teacher can grade it as it comes in and return it via the "Out" basket. This naturally staggers the turn-in times for student papers and cuts down on the periodic "mountains" of student papers needing grading. The baskets can be placed in an accessible, but unobtrusive space so that students using them will not disturb students who are working.

Sometimes, however, the "Out" basket can get quite full or the teacher may not wish students to be rummaging through it to find their papers. Student aides, called management aides, can be used to alleviate this problem. Management aides, one of several types of student aides employed in a Rewrite classroom, are responsible for helping the teacher with clerical and room management tasks. They apply for their jobs by filling out an application form furnished by the teacher (see figure 4.5) and are hired for one academic quarter. Their rate of payment is one free square anywhere on their record sheets at the end of the quarter, to be paid on Judgment Day. Management aides can, at the beginning of each period, pass out the graded papers in the "Out" basket.

◇ *Job Application*

Fill out all sections of the questionnaire below to apply for a job as a classroom aide. Remember that your term of employment will be for one quarter and that you will receive one free square on your record sheet in payment at the end of the quarter.

Name_____Period_____Quarter_____

Job you are applying for _____

1. Why do you want to be hired for this particular job?

2. What experience do you have that would help you do a good job in this position?

3. What other qualifications do you have?

4. What other work experience have you had?

5. What additional information would you like me to be aware of in considering you for this job?

Fig. 4.5.

If the "Out" basket happens to fill up again during the course of the class period, they can pass papers out again if they have finished their academic work for the day. Management aides can also help in taking and recording attendance, preparing class materials for distribution, and passing out activity materials. At the teacher's discretion, they can also assist in recording grades and in correcting mastery-type assignments. And they are wonderfully handy for taking messages or escorting petty criminals to the main office when necessary.

STUDENT FILES

Maintaining records of student progress and making records available to students also requires a static method of management. Individual student files are an excellent way to do both simultaneously. Another static solution to the necessity of maintaining student records that requires a space allotment is the use of student files. Each student is issued a file folder in which to keep a record sheet, any graded work, and any work in progress (see figure 4.6). These files are kept in the classroom so that they will always be available for teacher or student use. The files can be kept in separate file boxes for each class or all of the classes' folders can be kept in one large file box or drawer separated by dividers. Management aides pass out the files at the beginning of each hour while the students are seated in their assigned places. They can collect the files and put them away at the end of the hour when the students are once again back in their assigned seats. It is often helpful to color code each class' files by drawing a narrow stripe across the top of the label tab with a colored marker. It is then a simple matter for anyone to correctly put away a file which has been left out by matching the color code to the correct file box.

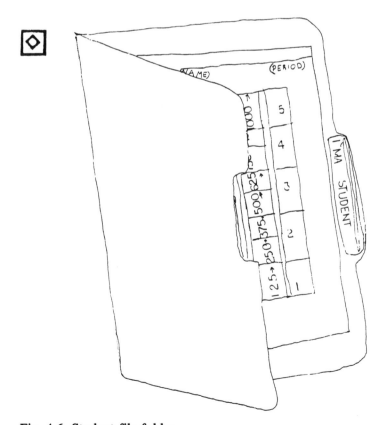

Fig. 4.6. Student file folder.

There are several other practical matters to consider in the management of student files, but they can be distilled into two laws:

1. Things get lost.

2. Things get heavy.

To address the first problem, students should not be allowed to remove their file folders from the room without the knowledge and permission of the teacher. The only reason files should be removed from the room is by request from a parent or the administrative or counseling staff. If students need to work on an assignment at home, they may take only those materials home; they must leave the file in the room. When the student brings in a written request (which serves as a record of the location and routing of the file until it is returned), the teacher staples the file shut through the middle so nothing will fall out or get lost and relinquishes the file to the student for a specified period of time, overnight or over a weekend or vacation. Another useful practice in keeping things from getting lost is to print record sheets on colored paper so they are easily distinguishable from other papers and then to staple them inside the file folder.

One of the functions of the student file is to keep all of a student's graded work on hand for revision work and to prove that work was actually completed in the event of a discrepancy between the gradebook record and the student record sheet. It doesn't take long for the files to get full. They get heavy and fall apart or the management aides drop them. To cope with this problem, a secondary Judgment Day ceremony is held at midterm. The teacher follows a routine similar to the Judgment Day procedure (see chapter 3) at the end of the quarter with only a few changes. No free squares are given out at this time, and the students retain their record sheets. Once teacher and student are satisfied that their records match for the first half of the quarter, all graded work can be removed from the file and taken home. This leaves only the record sheets and the student's current work in the file after midterm.

CURRENT HANDOUT FILE

To assist new or absent students who arrive in the middle of a unit, another set of files is maintained, a materials file. This file contains extra copies of all current handouts. Any students who need a new copy of the assignments can get them from this file without having to ask the teacher. When management aides finish passing out new materials, they can put the extra copies in the file. Some teachers like to use "absent eyes" aides in addition to the handout file. Management aides give the files of any absent students to these aides when they finish passing out files at the beginning of the hour. The absent eyes aides get copies of any new materials for each file and place them in the file along with a short note on class activities and the assignment for that day. If there are any questions when the absent student returns, the absent eyes aide who took care of the student's file can try to answer them first. If there are still questions, the returning students can ask the teacher specific questions about the materials.

For those teachers who would prefer to keep the files of absent students in the file box, class journals provide an alternative to personal notes from the absent eyes aides. Each day, an absent eyes aide is assigned as the class journalist. The aide takes charge of the class journal (any type of notebook will do) and records any announcements, activities, and assignments that were given in class that day. When absentees return, they can check the entries for the days they missed and get any missed handouts from the current handouts file.

NEW STUDENTS

Few situations are more disruptive and difficult to handle from a management standpoint than the arrival of a new student at midyear, mid-quarter, or mid-unit. It is next to impossible to orient a new student properly while continuing with planned activities in the traditional classroom. It is also extremely difficult for a new student to absorb new surroundings, people, and procedures for several classes simultaneously. It is made even more difficult for them because they are arriving at a time when the rest of the school is already functioning at a normal pace rather than the slower one followed the first couple of weeks of school. In a Rewrite classroom, the flexibility of time, space, and teacher/student roles along with the free flow of information make it easier for new students to orient themselves quickly to the new class. The situation can be approached in two different ways depending on the needs of the moment. Either the teacher can handle new student orientation exclusively or he or she can share the responsibility with the absent eyes aides.

In either case, it is a good idea to have some sort of static reference on class procedures for new students. A self-published booklet or learning kit works well. A bulletin board display works as well. Whichever orientation aid is chosen, it must be something the new students can refer to freely as often as necessary. New students have so much to absorb at once that it is easy for them to confuse the requirements and procedures of different classes. The orientation materials should contain samples of all types of classroom forms (record sheets, checklists, rubrics, etc.), a vocabulary list defining management and materials terms (unit task, student file, skill module, term project, rubric, etc.), a list of grade types for each activity category (four squares = A for unit tasks, one square = pass for skills, etc.), classroom rules and jobs, and a rough quarter schedule.

When the new student arrives, he or she sits down with the teacher or absent eyes aide, whoever has more time. The teacher or aide goes through all of the orientation materials with the student. Once this material is covered, the student is then taken on a tour of the room and shown the location of the "In" and "Out" baskets, classroom resources, the current handout file, student files, and various activity areas. While on the tour, the guide can point out students who are engaged in various types of activities as examples of the topics mentioned in the orientation materials. The new student is then given a file with a record sheet and assigned to one or two absent eyes aides who will help with settling in. When the new student feels ready, he or she is then given a quiz on all of the orientation material. The quiz should count for real credit on the record sheet, should not be looked on as something arduous, and should be as straightforward as possible. The point of the quiz is to find out whether the new student knows where to find out what he or she needs to know. It is not to find out how much the poor soul can memorize in a vacuum. For this reason, the quiz should be open book, with the new student encouraged to look up or ask someone else about answers that he or she is not sure of. The one-week orientation unit in part 2 provides model unit materials.

Another problem created by the arrival of new students during the course of a quarter has to do with record sheets. Since they have not been present for all of the activities, they cannot fill in an entire record sheet as it was planned in the part of the quarter remaining. Therefore, a small modification must be made in the record sheet to accommodate these students' special situations. To be fair, new students should not be expected to make up required class work from before their arrival. This class work should be stricken from their record sheets and at least one unit replaced with their orientation work. It will then be possible to treat the record sheet in the same way as the others at the end of the quarter when figuring grades.

ACCOMMODATING SIMULTANEOUS ACTIVITIES

Once students have received their files, announcements, and menu options in their assigned seats, they are encouraged to break up and go to that part of the room best suited for their activities. These locations are designated ahead of time by the teacher. There must be areas where students can work quietly and individually without the distraction of conversation. There must also be areas set aside where small groups can meet without disturbing those involved in individual work. These areas can be set aside on a flexible, daily basis or they can be permanently designated by the teacher. Figure 4.7 shows a map of a room divided into several areas. One area can be a "quiet zone" for individual work. Two or three areas can be set aside in the corners or back of the room for small group meetings. Another area can be set aside for peer tutoring, teacher/student conferencing, and makeup quizzes and tests. The functions of these areas should be as strictly enforced as public zoning laws are in the community and students should be clear on what types of behavior are appropriate in each area. But however the space is divided, whenever alternate uses are necessary, they must be approved by the teacher before they can take place. With this system, students learn that different things are expected of them in different places (a situation analogous to the adult world). This makes monitoring of student behavior simpler for the teacher since any activity taking place outside its designated area will be immediately obvious to all.

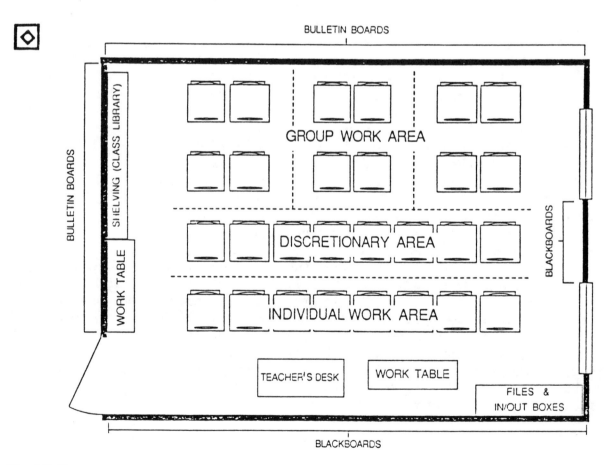

Fig. 4.7. Room map.

SPECIAL RESOURCE AREAS

Most subject areas use some type of special references or equipment and many classroom teachers like to include samples of these references and equipment in their classrooms. English and social studies teachers may have libraries of reference books, study aids, and reading selections. Classes with heavy orientations toward hands-on applications like industrial arts, home economics, art, and band may have sets of specialized supplies and equipment that must be accommodated and taken care of. Math classes may have calculators, computers, and gaming supplies; science classes may have combinations of all of these. Whatever the special resource area, however, there are some basic procedures which can be instituted to protect them while making them available to students.

Students should be made aware of all of the teacher's requirements for use and maintenance of the area. They should be acquainted with the contents of the areas and their proper uses. They should learn how to care for this special material and equipment and understand that such things are often expensive and difficult to replace. They should also understand that the availability and use of these things is a privilege and that irresponsible use will result in the loss of that privilege.

So far this sounds exactly like a traditional classroom. Well, there's nothing wrong with tradition when it accomplishes what is needed. However, the teacher work load for much of the running of these special areas can be delegated to specially trained classroom aides. These aides should be among the most trustworthy in the class and should be thoroughly trained and tested in their jobs before beginning them for it will be their responsibility to check materials and supplies in and out, to report any misuse or accidents within the special area, to make sure that everything is properly put away at the end of the hour, and to pass on any special instruction to the next class' special resource aides. These jobs are especially appropriate for gifted students because they are usually better at picking up the more complicated knowledge necessary for managing special resource areas and, if they fulfill their promise and strike out on their own at an early age, they will need to know how to run and care for a lab or studio, or special reference collection. The sooner they can learn these skills, the sooner they will be able to devote their primary attention to the less mundane aspects of their chosen fields. Furthermore, the experience gained in this class job may enable them to find part-time work in a real lab or studio or research area under the mentorship of professional scientists, artists, or other scholars.

The resource aides are not expected to supervise students working in the areas, only to facilitate the proper procedural flow. Particularly in science labs, home economics, and industrial arts classrooms, there are many potentially dangerous items. When students are using these items, they must be supervised by the teacher at the teacher's discretion. But because students will be working at different paces, it is likely that a sizable portion of the class will be engaged in less volatile activities in the other room areas. This can cut down on the number of students the teacher must supervise at one time. Also, since many students will be helping and teaching one another, the teacher can work more closely with those students using special resources if they need it. For a more detailed discussion of the adaptations necessary in laboratory-type classes, see the chapter on special problems in part 2.

CONCLUSION

The changes in this chapter are extensive and in some ways perhaps even radical, but they have all proven workable in many different classroom settings by many different kinds of classroom teachers. Many of them were collected by Debbie and me over the years through contact with other teachers and professionals from fields other than education. Many others we invented and developed on our own, refining them as we encountered problems. Even now, we still modify them according to the people and resources available to us. But they work. Students *do* become more responsible over time and they *do* become more motivated to learn and to take the initiative in achieving their goals. Two separate midyear incidents made this very clear to me.

Every teacher has nightmares. One of mine is that it is 1:45 P.M. and I suddenly realize it's a school day. I had thought it was a holiday and stayed home without calling a substitute. I panic, wracking my brains for some halfway decent excuse for forgetting to come to work, but I can't think of one. At this point I usually wake up in a cold sweat, delighted to see that it is 3:00 A.M. or Saturday. Somehow it never occurs to me that the office probably would have called me shortly after the start of first hour.

One day in the middle of winter, I succumbed to the flu that had been decimating our students and bringing our class size down close to national averages. When I called in for a substitute, my principal assured me all would be well, and I went back to bed, secure in the knowledge that my students knew what they should be doing and that the aides would help the sub sort things out.

The next school day, a Monday, I returned to work. Debbie greeted me with the news that our principal, Jim, had been unable to find subs for everyone since so many teachers were sick. She had, therefore, told Jim not to worry about my classes. They could get along on their own as long as she checked in with them from time to time. I was horrified. Debbie is, in my opinion, always taking crazy chances. (Of course, she has the same opinion of me!) I didn't want to go look at my room.

"It's okay," Debbie assured me. "They were fine. I had time to go over to answer questions every twenty minutes or so. They knew what to do, and the aides took care of the details. There's a big pile of stuff in your "In" baskets, though. Jim was really impressed." I was impressed, too, which only shows how much faith I really had in my own students!

The other incident occurred not long after the first quarter of our grand experiment with Rewrite. As all teachers know, it is de rigueur to circulate through the classroom when students are engaged in seatwork. It was a Friday, a day usually reserved for term project work. A few students had gone to the school library, a couple were working in the class library, some were working alone, others were in research groups, and still others were in editing groups. I was making my rounds, checking with students to see what they were working on and offering help and encouragement, and doing pretty well at it, I thought.

Suddenly, a voice piped up from one of the groups. "Mrs. E., do you mind? We're trying to get some work done here. Don't you have something you could be working on right now?"

"Yeah," said another voice. "We'll call you if we need you, okay?"

BIBLIOGRAPHY

Boyer, Ernest L. *High School: A Report of Secondary Education in America*. The Carnegie Foundation for the Advancement of Teaching. New York: Harper Colophon Books, 1983.

Cox, June, et al. *Educating Able Learners: Programs and Promising Practices*. Austin, TX: University of Texas Press, 1985, 25.

Doyle, Walter. U.S. National Institute of Education. "Effective Secondary Classroom Practices." In *Reaching for Excellence: An Effective Schools Sourcebook*. Ed. Regina M. J. Kyle. Washington, DC: Government Printing Office, 1985.

— 5 —
Nuts and Bolts
Unit Planning for Independence

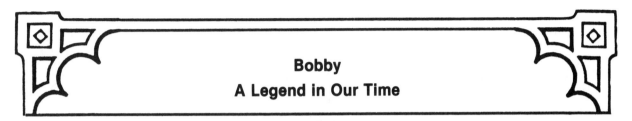

Bobby
A Legend in Our Time

Long ago, so long ago that no one can remember just why or how, our school district divided junior high language arts into two components: English and literature. In the English classes, students were to learn about communication skills such as writing, speaking and listening, grammar and usage skills, and spelling. In literature class, they were to study reading and literary forms. The students were intended to have the same teacher for both classes so that they could get a unified, double dose of language arts every-day. But no one knows the real intent of the planners, and it is unlikely that they would have intended to institute such a logical program. Or so the education anthropologists in the faculty lounge tell us.

In any case all of this was in the "before" time—before the district computer came to make our lives easier and make hash of human considerations like continuity of instruction. The district computer was originally a tool to help with complex but menial tasks such as scheduling and attendance that were too mundane to waste the time of faculty and staff members, or so they tell us. In the end, that which came to serve became that which was served. The noble idea of enriched and unified language arts instruction was cast aside along with so many others so that the needs of the scheduling software could be met.

The net effect of this was that many students had different teachers for English and literature, and the teachers were unable to coordinate the two courses. The result was a complete disconnection between English and liter-ature, reading and writing, and communication skills and forms in both the school curricula and in the students' minds. Students came to believe that they didn't have to spell or use good communication techniques in literature and that they didn't have to read or understand organizational skills in English. Darkness fell upon the land, until one day a tiny ray of light appeared in the person of Bobby.

Everyone has a Bobby in class. Bobby is a pleasant student who always seems tired unless something unrelated to class is going on. This isn't because Bobby needs something to wake him up. He participates in class when called on and does most of his homework, but he just isn't vitally inter-ested in the subject matter. He sees no reason to learn as much of it as he can because he only needs a C to stay out of trouble at home. To Bobby, the meaning of English and literature is that he'd better get a decent grade or he won't be able to go out with his friends on the weekend.

Bobby was in my English class in the mornings and in Debbie's literature class in the afternoons. Debbie and I had been working on the English 7 classes together in developing Rewrite, but since we did not teach the same level of literature class, we had no reason to coordinate our efforts there. We had finished a set of units on process writing the quarter before with our seventh-graders, however, and had emphasized, among other things, grammatical devices for eradicating second-person forms from the description of a process. The earth was spinning on its axis and revolving around the sun as usual. The kids went out of our classes to other classes, and we had no idea what they did there, aside from comments made by other teachers in the faculty lounge about the kids' lousy writing or reading skills. This did not disturb us. These types of snide remarks are part of the territory of the English teacher, just as the response from adults of "I always hated English," is de rigueur when an English teacher is introduced at a party.

But everything was not normal. Debbie was the first to notice. One afternoon she swung around the doorjamb of my room with a smug look on her face and announced, "We did it, Pamela." She always called me that when she was either off-balance or feeling silly. I wasn't sure which it was this time.

"What did we do now?" I asked. If we had accomplished something, I wanted to hear about it; if we were in trouble for something, the sooner I knew about it the sooner I could put together an alibi. My sixth-hour class was on its way in and things did not look particularly promising. One of the boys was pulling a six-foot long piece of string back and forth through his pierced ear and the other students were rapt with admiration.

"You know Bobby, who's in your third-hour English class?"

Sure I knew Bobby. The only way he could sit at a desk without getting a concussion was to prop his head up on his left hand while he wrote with his right.

"Well, I'm standing there in literature class explaining how to do their assignment," Debbie went on, "and I get to the end and ask if there are any questions." Debbie paused dramatically. She is a wonderful storyteller and frequently is the main source of entertainment at the lunch table. "Bobby raises his hand and says, 'Mrs. Robbins, you forgot about the "you" forms. You need to use imperative mood or passive voice to get rid of the "you" forms because they aren't appropriate in this kind of writing.'"

"You're kidding!" I gasped. "Bobby said that? A seventh-grader transferred something like that to another class? It's a miracle!"

"No, it's not," Debbie chortled. "It's learning!"

Moral: It's easier to go downriver if you stop swimming upstream!

HOW TO BE MORE SIGNIFICANT AND LESS TIRED

It seems as though there are always one or two teachers on every faculty who have been teaching enthusiastically and well for years and years and show no signs of flagging in zeal or energy. They spend incredible amounts of time and energy on their work and seem to thrive on it. Their former students always seem to achieve all kinds of remarkable things and owe it all to these significant teachers. The rest of us, however, work hard, work long, and get tired. And somehow, the only kids who say they owe it all to us are the ones who haven't paid their book club bills or lab fees. Should we have to sacrifice even more time and energy to figure so significantly in our students' development? Not necessarily. It is possible to be just as significant as those teachers and still preserve life, limb, and sanity by working smarter instead of harder.

A quick review of the characteristics of the MacArthur Fellows' significant teachers can show us where to start. These teachers encouraged the following items:

1.   Initiative on the part of the student.

2. Exploration of the student's own interests.

3. Working toward the student's maximum capacity.

4. Working at the student's optimum pace.

5. Independence in learning and behavior.

6. Setting of personal and academic goals.

7. Use of higher level thinking skills.

8. Personal application of subject matter.

9. Development of individual styles and abilities.

10. Mastery of the basics in preparation for creative work.

Is all of this too much to keep track of? It might be in a traditional classroom where the very structure of management and instruction run counter to these characteristics. One need only watch a teacher try to achieve them in a traditional classroom to see just how antagonistic the conditions in the classroom are. Except in rare cases, these goals are achieved only through force of will and personality of the teacher, often to the point of exhaustion.

In chapter 3, a procedure is presented for providing a coherent curriculum organized around specific unit task themes and for fostering long-term, personal involvement in the subject area. The curriculum plan created by this process supplies the framework and raw materials of unit planning by organizing unit processes, skills, and knowledge. It also supplies the opportunities for exploration of personal interests through the reading and term project segments. When these conditions are compared to the previous ten items, they match up with at least four:

2. Exploration of the student's own interests.

7. Use of higher order thinking skills.

8. Personal application of subject matter.

10. Mastery of the basics in preparation for creative work.

In addition, when these ten items are examined in light of the management procedures presented in chapter 4, an even larger group of significant characteristics are accounted for. The relaxation of traditional controls on information, on rigidity in time and space use, and on apportionment of responsibility and decision making create an environment in which many of these ten items can take place quite naturally. Students can take the initiative in managing their own behavior, setting their own goals, and working at optimum capacity and pace. Additionally, they can work in ways and time frames that suit their own individual styles and abilities. Against this backdrop, it remains only for the teacher to choose the specific subject matter, materials, and learning experiences of a unit.

GO WITH THE FLOW: NATURAL PREDISPOSITIONS

Rather than fight an uphill battle against the natural proclivities of learners, the teacher in a Rewrite classroom strives to capitalize on them. For the purposes of unit planning, these natural cognitive drives can be distilled into four areas. Learners are predisposed to:

1. Interact with their environments.

2. Make sense of their interactions and observations by constructing meaningful schemata.

3. Become competent in the sphere of investigation.

4. Become autonomous.

These are the things students want to do. If teachers prevent them from doing these things within the sphere of the subject matter, students will find other arenas in which to exercise these drives. For instance, if a gifted student is forced to practice skills that have already been mastered or sit through several more iterations of something already understood, he or she may find another area to investigate and achieve competence and autonomy, such as finding out how long a conversation with a classmate can go on before the teacher reacts.

YABBUT ...

Yabbut you can't tell me it's my fault every time a kid gets off task!

Response: As long as people are people, they will drift or jump off task for any number of reasons. We all do it, even though some of us have more self-discipline than others. But to be successful in managing our own behavior and learning, we must all learn to develop an internal locus of control. A fair, simple disciplinary system in the classroom is helpful in communicating behavior expectations to students. By setting up a system of natural and logical consequences for unproductive or disruptive behavior, teachers can help prepare students for the constraints of living in an adult community. When adults interfere with the regular functions of the community, there are consequences, often both natural and logical. For instance, if a student repeatedly interferes with the work of other students, several things will happen. The student will not be able to complete all of his or her work up to highest standards in the allotted time. He or she will earn a reprimand or other negative consequence from the teacher and will be the focus of his or her classmates' irritation for bothering them and taking away some of their work time. This has its parallel in the adult world when someone disrupts the normal functioning of the community. Not only are there natural consequences like loss of friendly relationships or loss of a job, but there are logical ones such as fines, loss of privileges, and sometimes even incarceration.

The teacher/student relationship should not have to be an adversarial one in which students struggle to behave and learn in ways that are not natural for them and teachers struggle to counteract normal propensities. Instead, by using the naturally occurring predispositions of students, teachers can avoid many stressful confrontations and can enhance the learning process by creating better opportunities for learning and encouraging task commitment. Everyone wants to work toward something they perceive as worthwhile, even students. Problems crop up when learners perceive that they are being prevented from accomplishing something worthwhile. These problems often disappear when the class is structured to "go with the flow." Here are some examples of how traditional and Rewrite procedures combine with the needs of learners.

The need to interact with the environment. In a traditional classroom, students are usually expected to listen to lectures or read about subject matter. Discussions are highly structured according to a lesson plan of strictly sequenced and preplanned questions. Unusual questions or insights from students are discouraged as being "off the track." Students must sit at their desks and listen, read, or work alone and the teacher is the sole audience and point of interaction. Sensory input is limited and so is learning.

When students can work with the methodologies and resources of the subject area, they can get greater sensory input and elaborative processing opportunities. They can discover things in the subject matter that are of personal interest and value to them. They can learn about other viewpoints, ask questions as they surface, and learn how to explore unknown areas of subject matter. This latter benefit can be truly advantageous to a gifted adult investigating a subject area at its cutting edge.

YABBUT ...

Yabbut kids *do* ask questions to try to get off the track and avoid the subject matter and sometimes you really *do* have to make sure you cover everything in a discussion.

Response: Some students are true virtuosos when it comes to pulling teachers off the subject at hand. Others have legitimate questions and concerns. It is often difficult to tell the difference. However, when the teacher is clear on what must be covered and why (as a result of using the procedures covered in this chapter), it becomes easier to tell which questions and comments are truly facetious and which need a serious response. If those questions and comments require a serious response or if the student wishes to pursue them, it is a simple matter to explain that certain material must be covered in a whole-class context and that peripheral concerns can be considered during the unstructured time that is a regular part of class time in the Rewrite classroom. (If the question was not a legitimate one, it will probably not be brought up again!) Students can also be encouraged to devote their reading and project time to a further exploration of their "off-track" questions and comments. Most of the time, if students are really serious about finding answers, they will follow up on them. If they are not, they will generally not bring it up again since it would detract from their regular work time.

The need to make sense of their interactions and observations by constructing meaningful schemata. Knowledge and skills in the traditional classroom are taught in a disconnected fashion as ends in themselves until the true structure and value of the subject area is lost in a haze of minor details and overkill.

Instead of using their mental abilities to accumulate such bits and pieces of knowledge as might be useful on a quiz show or multiple choice test, students can really make the new subject matter their own when classroom activities are structured to enhance their natural learning processes. When these processes are facilitated, students can hook the new knowledge onto existing schemata or create new ones instead of memorizing a paradigm based on someone else's cognitive structures. They can search out patterns and relationships within a given field or between fields that may not have been noticed or explored by anyone else. They are able to see the subject area as an area of inquiry with a structure of its own as they become simultaneously knowledgeable and creative within it.

EMILE.	... Did you study French in school?
NELLIE.	Oh, yes.
EMILE.	Ah, then you can read French?
NELLIE.	No! ... I can conjugate a few verbs.

—Rogers and Hammerstein's *South Pacific* act 1, scene 19

The need to become autonomous. When the teacher is the decision maker of the classroom as in the traditional model, students cannot decide when they have or have not practiced enough. The teacher decides. Students cannot decide how best to hook the new knowledge onto their existing cognitive structures.

YABBUT ...

Yabbut if the students knew when they had practiced enough, they wouldn't need to take the class!

Response: How true! But they are not working in a vacuum. In the Rewrite model, they have several sources of ongoing feedback. If they turn in a substandard support module, they will receive a revise along with a note on what is wrong. If they whip off their support modules without really internalizing the concepts, those deficiencies will show up on their unit tasks. Once their peer editors compare their papers to the evaluation criteria, the editors will point out the errors and the students will have to go back and either remediate themselves or seek help from the teacher or peers for remediation.

The teacher presents the material as it is structured in his or her mind. Students cannot make decisions about when or how long they will work, because the teacher has already scheduled all learning. They cannot set their own goals because the teacher is the sole possessor of information regarding the unit plan, scheduling, and evaluation criteria. Without this information, students cannot make informed decisions regarding the quality and quantity of work required to complete a unit or the level of achievement they wish to obtain. They have no benchmarks along the way to tell whether they are doing as well as they would like to do. They do not know when their efforts have been adequate until they receive a graded paper back from the teacher.

When students are given information on learning activities, schedules, and expectations along with some instruction and modeling on how to use that information, they can become more autonomous. As they are taught strategies and processes for using their new knowledge, they gain more awareness and control over their cognitive processes and the outcomes of those processes. They learn to direct their own learning, not only *in* the classroom context, but *out* of it as well.

The need to become competent. Because everyone in a traditional class must do the same thing at roughly the same time, resources are carefully doled out. Each student can have ten minutes to learn to use the microscopes on Tuesday or twenty minutes to practice the command modes on the spreadsheet software on Friday, regardless of whether some students need five minutes or an hour. The students who pick up the knowledge quickly are not becoming competent at what they are capable of and the slower students are not becoming capable of competence.

YABBUT ...

Yabbut time is not unlimited, particularly in a regular classroom. We can't go on forever while some kids take their time or fool around.

Response: There are deadlines in the real world, too. That's why the teacher sets due dates at reasonable intervals. Students should be given a reasonable amount of time to complete assigned work. If they finish early, fine. If they turn in work on time, fine. The problems start when students fail to meet their deadlines, as some inevitably will. To teach students that deadlines must be met, we do not accept any late work unless the circumstances are extreme. However, we do not wish to discourage students who are having a difficult time with a particular assignment, so we have a revision policy. This policy states that if a student turns in an attempted assignment on time, he or she will then have the opportunity to revise that assignment within two days of receiving it back. But we also limit the student to three tries on any given assignment: first attempt, first revision, and second revision. If the student either does not master the material or does not choose to revise, then he or she receives a zero and must go on to the next unit.

Gifted students have a greater capacity for learning, mastery, and creativity than the general population of students. They often have voracious appetites for new knowledge and skills and apply themselves to the creation of complex and novel products with great dedication. When they are given the opportunity to either demonstrate an already mastered skill or to master it and move on, they are less frustrated and often end up working much harder than the rest of the students because they have set goals for themselves far beyond those of the rest of the class.

They need a larger knowledge base, more highly developed skills, and larger opportunities in order to achieve the competence they will need as adults. These students need to learn how to operate specialized equipment to do more complex research. They need to learn more advanced research methods. And they need to learn to apply their knowledge and abilities in more complex contexts than a classroom set up only for regular students.

But sometimes even gifted students need extra time and opportunities to master a skill or concept, just like anyone else. When time and space use is made more flexible as in the Rewrite model, everybody can have the time and help they need to become competent. It doesn't matter whether they pick up the new knowledge on the first try or on the fifth. They have the opportunity to reach the level of competence of which they are capable.

MAXIMIZING POSITIVE LEARNING FACTORS

There are so many factors that negatively affect the learning and performance of students both in and out of school that it is probably impossible to eliminate them all in a classroom situation. Even if we knew what all of them were and removed them from the equation, we would probably remove much of what makes people human and give a false impression to students of how the real world works. To help balance these negative factors, teachers can try to maximize factors that positively affect learning and performance. As more is learned about the learning processes of human beings, this approach will become even more feasible. An overview of the experiences of Bobby's writing class can show how this is possible.

Bobby and his classmates were certainly able to overcome not only what we, his teachers, had perceived as a lack of interest and ability, but the negative influences of the scheduling software as well. Through the media of the unit structure and activities, they were able to attach meaning to what they were learning. Once the information, skills, and methodologies had become meaningful to them, they were able to retain and transfer what they had learned.

Skills and knowledge were presented to them in a meaningful context, a methodology which included modeling and instruction in a set of problem-solving strategies and processes and student goal setting and participation. They were given time to take the new knowledge and skills and to build them into new and existing schemata in their own ways. They were given the opportunity to work in their own ways and at their own paces within the limits of the classroom to achieve a success about which they cared. As a result, they understood what the skills and knowledge were for and how to apply them in the achievement of a goal. That goal was successful communication of personal expertise and knowledge to teacher and classmates.

Although the academic and management environments were what allowed these things to take place in a regular classroom, it was the curriculum unit itself that dictated just exactly what should be going on there. The curriculum unit in Bobby's class was on process writing. Each student was given the opportunity to invent something, either real or imaginary, and then asked to write an owner's manual for it. There was a great deal of room for variations of complexity and interest both in the inventions themselves and in the composition of the owner's manuals, but the goal of all of them was the same: successful communication of a process through writing. They were taught certain grammatical and organizational skills and shown examples of real owner's manuals. Then they were given the opportunity to work on their own on a project of their own choosing, at their own paces, their own levels of challenge, and in their own styles within the constraints of the scheduling and evaluation criteria of the unit.

They were given unit activity checklists and grading criteria that both allowed and required them to set their own goals and evaluate their own progress. This increased opportunities for elaborative processing. If they took a draft of their owner's manual to a peer response group and it contained you forms, their peers used the evaluation criteria to point out the errors and to help them correct the mistakes. If the organization or diction made it difficult to understand, this, too, was pointed out. In this way, the students discovered their areas of weakness and had ample opportunity to review imperfectly learned skills and knowledge at any time before they had to turn in the assignment without risking a bad grade. They could even begin the actual drafting of a manual and pick up the support knowledge as their own schema-building processes required instead of being required to learn what they needed to know when the teacher decided they needed to know it. At the same time, they were able to observe how other students had applied the knowledge and skills and increase their own audiences beyond the teacher to the whole class. Additionally, by virtue of the variations inherent in the inventions, students could not merely copy a solution from another student. They had to analogize to their own situations. This also required greater elaboration and higher level thinking skills than copying would have. It also ensured greater task commitment because they were working to achieve goals they had chosen for themselves. In short, the construction and execution of the unit purposely and purposefully exploited the natural drives of the learners.

The unit was effective because it sought to increase students' opportunities and motivation to learn. The opportunities to learn were increased in several ways. The scheduling of unit time was loosened to allow for individual pacing and idiosyncratic building of schemata. The unit activities were specifically constructed to force the students, rather than the teacher, to do the exploring and practice. The students had to plan their work; the students had to do all preliminary evaluations; the students had to use the knowledge, skills, processes, and strategies introduced by the teacher to synthesize and evaluate their own, original products. They were the ones doing the elaborative processing; they were the ones taking the class.

YABBUT ...

Yabbut I need all my class time to cover the material!

Response: Particularly in senior high, the material to be covered is greater in volume and complexity than in the lower grades. But also in senior high, students are better able to take their responsibility to complete individual work at home. If the teacher decides that class time cannot be used for some individual activities, these activities should be given as homework and class time reserved for small group or whole class activities.

Teachers should consider the possibility that they are not really covering their material in class if the students are not really attending to it. Some things are best covered in a lecture-discussion format, but it might be a good idea to have students hand in their notes in place of a skill or knowledge module. Most things, though, are best learned when the student can become involved in the material. Whatever the case, the teacher should actively search for ways to convert subject matter presentations from teacher-centered to student-centered activities.

Motivation to learn was fostered by building opportunities for individual choice into the unit activities and scheduling. Students could choose how they would spend their allotted work time as long as they did not disrupt the learning of others and met the deadlines set by the teacher. As long as they used the knowledge, skills, and the methodologies specified by the teacher, they could choose what they wanted to invent and select an acceptable owner's manual format from among the samples provided by the teacher. The invention was theirs. They had a personal investment in it. They cared about it. Because they had access to unit activity calendars and grading criteria, they could exercise some control in goal setting, time management, and academic achievement. Much of what happened in the learning process was under their control and because it was, they could exercise both autonomy and competence. They had an investment in the class and it became their class, not just the teacher's class.

A TEMPLATE FOR UNIT PLANNING

How is all of this accomplished? Is it by hours of complex unit planning? Is it by the perfect mix of teacher and students? Is it by magic? The answer is none of the above. Instead, the application of a basic set of planning heuristics is all that is really needed to construct an effective unit that will function smoothly within the academic and management environments set up in chapters 3 and 4. The unit planning process consists of five basic questions:

1. What do you want the students to be able to do at the end of the unit?

2. How do you want them to do it?

3. What do they need to know to do it?

4. How is the material best presented?

5. What do you expect of a well-done task?

To illustrate how this template is used, let's look at how the process writing unit for Bobby's class was constructed.

What do you want the students to be able to do at the end of this unit? Brainstorming a list of goals and objectives such as that shown in figure 5.1 is a good way to get the answer to this question. In the inventions unit, the students needed to be able to clearly describe a process. In order to do this, they would have to be able to organize information and present it according to the conventions of the process mode of discourse.

How do you want them to do it? There are many different types of process descriptions in the real world. There are how-to books, lab reports, field notes, and user's manuals among other things. But because the students needed an opportunity to invest personally in the unit material and because they were too inexperienced to plunge into anything as lengthy or complex as a book or a lab report, shorter forms were chosen. Owner's manuals can be quite short and comprehensive, depending on their purpose and audience, so their potential for diversity made them an attractive choice for a unit task product. Also, because the students would be describing their own inventions, no additional unit time was needed for instruction in specialized field or lab techniques.

Brainstorm List

Describe a process.

Put it in a correct order.

Make it easy to understand.

Make the directions complete.

Have a diagram or illustration for reference.

Know how to get rid of second-person forms.

Be able to tell good directions from bad ones.

Be able to construct efficient sentences showing cause and effect and chronological order.

Become familiar with different types of owner's manuals.

Learn divergent thinking techniques.

Become familiar with a specialized writing process.

Fig. 5.1.

What do they need to know to do it? This question was the stimulus for another brainstormed list of knowledge, skills, and processes and strategies (see figure 5.2). Students needed to know what an owner's manual was and what formats were commonly used. They needed to know how to gather and organize the necessary data for inclusion in the manual. Finally, they needed to know how to eradicate second-person "you" forms from their writing using imperative and passive sentence construction as well as a repertoire of vocabulary and syntax that could be used in expressing chronological and cause and effect relationships.

 Brainstorm List II

Practice imperative mood.

Practice passive voice.

Practice subordinating conjunctions for cause and effect and chronological order.

Read through some manuals.

Collect data on an invention.

Organize data logically.

Brainstorm with prompts.

Fig. 5.2.

How is it best presented? This is the sorting section of the process. Where among the curriculum categories do all of these things fit in? Obviously the owner's manual goes in the unit task category, but what other objectives should go with it, since all of them are meant to be applied in the synthesis of the manual? A perusal of the types of thinking and evaluation required in each objective and category can help in the sorting.

Passive voice and imperative mood are both grammatical skills used for transforming one form of meaning to another form. Instead of writing, "You should put in the batteries before you turn it on," the form should be, "The batteries should be put in before turning it on," or "Put the batteries in before turning on the machine." These are straightforward applications of a grammatical skill and easily practiced in isolation from the unit task. They are also easily graded on a mastery scale; therefore, they are sorted into the skills category. Imperative mood, a simpler transformation, is scheduled for the first week and passive voice for the second.

Vocabulary items and their usage in sentence constructions expressing chronological and cause and effect relationships are also the type of knowledge easily isolated from process for practice and measured on a mastery scale. They have to do with the building blocks of meaning and fit well into the vocabulary category. Week one could be focused on words, phrases and constructions showing time relationships. Week two could deal with the vocabulary and usages of subordination and coordination showing cause and effect relationships.

This leaves data gathering, organization, and formatting. All of these are processes and strategies for producing the manual and are difficult to isolate from the task for evaluation. They are best included as objectives within the context of the unit task. They are also typical of the type of reasoning most likely to be subject to individual differences and expressions and are consequently less easily measured on a mastery scale. The teacher models the data-gathering processes he or she wishes the students to learn and shows them how to organize the data collected by those processes. The teacher also shows them examples of formats so they will have some idea of what their finished products could be like. If the teacher desires, he or she could assign the study of several manual examples to the reading category, but that is not really necessary because it can also be assigned as part of the unit task process. Thus, a set of mutually reinforcing activities in corresponding categories is created:

Unit Task: Owner's Manual

Divergent thinking exercise

Data gathering

Organizational strategies

Possible formats

Editing and proofreading for potential errors

Skills

Week one: imperative mood

Week two: passive voice

Vocabulary

Week one: chronological vocabulary and usage

Week two: cause and effect vocabulary and usage

Once the subject matter has been sorted into categories, the teacher can decide how each area can best be presented. This involves several considerations. How much time should be allotted to each category relative to the others? What types of presentations and practice are best suited to the category of subject matter? What type of class situation is most efficient for those presentations — whole class, small group, or individualization?

Relative time allotments for different categories of activities are extremely important, more important, perhaps, than most teachers realize. In *Reaching for Excellence*, time was an item of importance that recurred again and again in the findings of educational researchers. The authors of this document recommended as their first principle for instructional decisions that educators pay attention to time: "Students will learn what is included and emphasized in the curriculum, and time allocations reflect the priorities and commitments of a teacher, a school, or a school district."[1] Keeping this finding in mind, it becomes clear that the unit task, the most complex aspect of the unit and the aspect that provides context and meaning for the other aspects, should be given the greatest time priority and commitment of attention. If skills or vocabulary are given more importance than the organizing theme, students will perceive that the support knowledge is more important than its applications. Indeed, they may not even perceive what the applications are. The unit task should take a large amount of time, both to communicate to the students the importance of subject matter application in the synthesis and evaluation of creative work and understanding and to allow the students more time to work at higher cognitive levels than on the lower ones required for drill and practice. The question then becomes, How much time should be allotted for each area? This leads to another interesting question. How does one allot time in a self-paced, flexible environment?

Traditionally, the teacher has had to schedule specific activities for all of the available instructional time. In the Rewrite model, however, the teacher decides what proportion of available time should be used for different curricular categories. In Bobby's writing class, we wished to communicate the overriding importance of the unit task and to help the students see that support knowledge and skills were just that — support. We constructed relatively short skills and vocabulary modules, estimating roughly how much an average student could do in about thirty or forty minutes. We made the explanations as short and straightforward as we could. We also put together work sheets that consisted of the bare minimum of practice and performance necessary to show us whether the student had grasped the target concept. Nothing more was really needed in these categories because these concepts would be actively applied again within the context of the unit task. The unit task was constructed to be lengthier and was scheduled to last for the entire two-week period. We scheduled time for demonstration and direct instruction time, small group, individual, and whole class activities and made as much class and homework time available for those activities as possible. By virtue of the relative lengths and complexities of the support modules and the unit task, relative time allotments and importance of activities and material were communicated to the students.

Once these judgments of relative importance and time allotments are made, it is simpler to decide on the types of presentations and practice best suited for each category of instruction. For support modules, the presentations should be short, clear, direct, and include only as much drill and practice necessary to make the student aware of what is being stressed, to help the student master the concept, and to show the teacher that the concept has been mastered at a specific application level. For unit tasks, the implementation should be deeper and richer in presentations and practice. Certain types of information are best presented by lecture and explanation. In the process writing unit, the explanation of the unit task itself, its processes, and scheduling were best achieved through a whole class lecture period. The invention brainstorming that preceded the data-gathering process seemed to be more appropriate for small groups as did the editing portions of the writing process. The actual data gathering, organizing, and drafting of the manual were individual activities. As a result of this segment of the planning process, a rough unit plan emerged:

Unit Task

Introduction: whole class; show some crazy inventions, explain overview; show some sample formats

Prewriting: small groups; brainstorm on "Inventions we *really* need" or "Somebody ought to invent ... ," individual data gathering and organizing

Drafting: individual drafting of text and illustrations

Postwriting: small groups; use rubrics to evaluate rough drafts; individual revisions

Skills

Whole class introduction and demonstration

Individual practice sheets and possibly quizzes

Peer tutoring or small group reviews where necessary

Vocabulary

Whole class introduction and demonstration

Individual practice sheets and quizzes on sentence combining

This plan can be scheduled by transferring it to a planning calendar such as the one in figure 5.3. Notice that the bulk of direct instruction and teacher guidance comes at the beginning of the unit, but that the schedule becomes more and more open as the students diverge into their individual projects.

	DAY 1	DAY 2	DAY 3	DAY 4	DAY 6
WEEK ONE	Intro. Sk#1 + Vocab. #2 ——— Worktime	Intro Unit Task –show examples –begin pre- writing activities	Finish up Prewriting Activities Worktime	Student Workday	→Due →Due ——— Project Day

	DAY 6	DAY 7	DAY 8	DAY 9	DAY 10
WEEK TWO	Intro Sk. #2 + Vocab. #2 Worktime	←Student Workdays →			→Due →Due Unit Task Due Project Day

Fig. 5.3. Unit planning calendar.

What do you expect of a well-done task? It is at this point that decisions concerning evaluation should be made. Waiting with vague dreams of incredible papers to make these decisions until the students turn in their work only complicates things. Not only are the students left in the dark as to what is expected of them, but the grading process turns into a long, anguished turmoil of comparing papers and deciding what was really important. By going over the earlier brainstorm lists created in the unit planning process, it is easy to set up evaluation criteria. For instance, the main point of the unit was for students to learn the process of process writing. If they can turn in all of their early brainstorming, diagrams, and rough drafts along with the final form, they can receive credit for all their work and the teacher can be sure that they have indeed practiced and mastered the methodology. Also, the students will perceive the relative importance the teacher attaches to the unit task work. Second, data gathering and organizing were points discussed and illustrated by the teacher, so the manual should contain complete, logical instructions. Third, second-person forms should be eradicated by the application of the grammatical skills taught in the skills modules. Fourth, the syntax and vocabulary of the manual should correctly describe time and cause and effect relationships. Finally, the owner's manual should be in a correct format and easy to understand. By combining these concerns into a list (see figure 5.4, "Rough Rubric"), the criteria for grading can be clearly communicated both to the teacher and the students. Once the criteria for an A-level task are set, students can check their work as they go along and teachers need only check papers against the criteria, thus removing much of the time and travail so often put into the grading of these sorts of creative assignments.

◇ *Rough Rubric*

1.   Completed prewriting materials, two rough drafts, and final draft

2.   Complete, logical instructions for care and use

3.   No second-person forms

4.   Smooth syntax in expressing cause and effect and chronological order relationships

Fig. 5.4.

PREPARATION OF UNIT MATERIAL

The preparation of unit materials should use the plans for learning to create tools for learning. The materials should help students exercise their natural learning drives. Whenever possible, they should require a minimum of teacher explanation and allow students to obtain as much information as possible. The lesson plan developed with the unit planning template should be used as a source for developing a "shopping list" of materials for a specific unit.

The unit plan for the process writing unit task contains the following steps:

1.   Explain unit task and materials.

2.   Share examples of owner's manuals with class.

3.   Introduce divergent thinking activity—brainstorming: "Inventions we *really* need," or "Somebody ought to invent...."

4. Have students:

- Choose focus (invention).

- Choose format.

- Gather data using an illustration or diagram or showing the parts and functions of invention.

- Organize data.

- Prepare first draft of manual.

- Send to editing group with grading criteria.

- Prepare second draft of manual.

- Send to editing groups with grading criteria.

- Prepare final draft.

- Turn in work by due date.

By perusing the process, the teacher can decide what kinds of resources, materials, and handouts are needed to complete the task.

An *overview checklist* of the unit (see figure 5.5) would be useful both for explaining the unit task to the class and for student reference during the course of the unit. It would give the students a sense of direction, allow them to go on ahead if they should finish some subtasks early, and give them the autonomy of finding schedule answers for themselves. It would free the teacher from having to jump start the class everyday and from continually having to answer the same questions about "What do we do next?" and "What did I miss?"

Overview checklists can be put together in several ways. They can either include the support module assignments along with the unit task activities or they can cover only the unit task activities. It is often best to let the requirements of the subject matter dictate the form. If, as in the owner's manual, it is not really necessary to master a particular skill before embarking on the unit task process, then it is probably not necessary to include support activities on the checklist. A simple due date notation on the class calendar will suffice to let students know when they need to work on a certain support activity. However, if it *is* necessary to master a certain support area before proceeding to the next unit activity, then the support activities should definitely be included on the checklist. It would be wise, for example, for students to demonstrate mastery of the proper use of a Bunsen burner before they begin to heat solutions in a science class.

A set of sample owner's manuals are also needed for the unit introduction. The teacher can select examples of the types of formats he or she wishes the students to work with and share them with the class, pointing out important aspects of each. Then, the set of manuals can be made available for in-class examination in a resource area so that students can refer to them throughout the course of the unit whenever their schema-building processes require it.

Work sheets to guide in brainstorming, data gathering, and organizing might also be necessary, depending on the age and experience of the students. A small group brainstorming sheet (see figure 5.6, page 80) might have a short explanation of brainstorming rules and the necessary divergent thinking prompts. This could be followed by a convergent-thinking work sheet (see figure 5.7, page 81) to guide students in data gathering and organizing. These types of handouts should be rather sparse in their content and actually serve only as prompts. In this way, the students will be forced to expend more effort and will become more aware of their cognitive processes as well as the heuristic strategies modeled by the work sheets.

(Text continues on page 82.)

◇ *Sample Checklist*

In this unit, we will be learning about a type of writing called *process writing*. Process writing is used to explain processes—how to do something, how to use something, how something works, how something changes over time. These are only a few of the applications for process writing. One of the most common uses is the writing of owner's manuals to go with machines, furniture, pets, clothing, and many other things. This is the type of process writing we will be doing in this unit.

In order to learn how to create a good owner's manual, complete all of the steps below:

_____ 1. Make sure you understand the purpose of the unit as presented in class by the teacher.

_____ 2. Look over some examples of owner's manuals.

_____ 3. Meet in a brainstorming group and complete the brainstorming work sheet.

_____ 4. Choose something from your brainstorm sheet that you would like to invent, even if it is an imaginary invention.

_____ 5. Complete the data work sheet to help you gather and organize your information.

_____ 6. Write a rough draft of your owner's manual and take it to a peer editing group along with the diagram of your invention.

_____ 7. Using your own judgment, the rubric, and your peers' comments, write a second rough draft and take it to a second peer editing group.

_____ 8. Prepare a final draft of your owner's manual. Let the teacher know if you need any special supplies, but don't wait until the last minute.

_____ 9. Turn in your brainstorm and data sheets, both rough drafts, and final draft on or before the due date. Turn in everything so you can get credit for all of the work you did.

Fig. 5.5.

◇ *Brainstorming Work Sheet*

Brainstorming is a technique used to generate a lot of different ideas in a short time. The rules of brainstorming are simple:

1. Think of as many ideas as you can.

2. Record every idea. Don't stop to decide whether an idea is a good one or not.

3. Piggyback ideas on earlier ideas.

4. Never criticize an idea until the session is over.

For this brainstorming activity, each group has been given two prompts. Five minutes will be given for each prompt, with a few minutes in between to jot down any additional notes or ideas. As a group, generate as many ideas for each prompt as possible. Students should write down all of the group's ideas on their own sheets, adding their own ideas on their own sheets if there is no time to share them with the others. Time will be monitored by the teacher.

Prompt 1: Inventions We Really Need

Prompt 2: Somebody Ought to Invent ...

Fig. 5.6.

◇ *Data Work Sheet*

Complete all sections of this work sheet so that you will be ready to start your rough draft.

1. What have you decided to invent?

2. What is the purpose of your invention?

3. What are all the things your invention can do?

4. Draw a picture or diagram of your invention on the back of this sheet and label all the parts.

5. What information will the owner's manual need to include?

6. What needs to be done to care for your invention to keep it in good working order?

7. Put the care instruction items for your invention in a logical order.

8. List the order in which you will explain the functions of your invention.

9. For each function, list the steps for use in the correct order.

10. Write out a short table of contents for your owner's manual.

Fig. 5.7. Convergent-thinking work sheet.

A list of evaluation criteria is also necessary to help students evaluate their work as they go along. One of the most useful formats for this is called a *rubric*. The rubric contains a set of standards for each level of achievement so that students can tell exactly where they stand and teachers can quickly pinpoint the level of student achievement on the unit task. A rubric is constructed in the following manner:

1. Make a list of the requirements for an A paper.

2. Subtract by increments from each category for each level of letter grade.

3. Draw up the sets of grade characteristics on a one- or two-sheet handout and give it to the students at the beginning of the unit along with the checklist and other work sheets.

The rubric for the process writing unit begins with the following criteria for an A paper:

An A paper has all or most of the following:

- All prewriting work, two rough drafts, and a final draft.
- Complete, logical, and clear instructions for use.
- No "you" forms.
- Few or no format, grammar, or spelling errors.

From this starting point, a small amount is subtracted from each category of criteria to arrive at a B set of criteria.

A B paper has all or most of the following:

- All prewriting work, one rough draft, and a final draft.
- One to three errors in completeness, logic, and clarity.
- One or two "you" forms.
- Few format, grammar, or spelling errors.

This process continues until a document similar to the one shown in figure 5.8 emerges. The rubric is now ready for several uses. First, the students working alone can gauge the quality of their work. Second, peer editing groups can use it as a guide in evaluation of others' work. Third, the teacher can use it in grading completed work.

The value of the rubric does not end there. It is a way to provide ongoing feedback to students without continual, one-on-one interaction with the teacher. It teaches students to produce a product to specification, a valuable skill in the adult world. It teaches students that grading is not a capricious process but merely a record of how well they have met the demands placed on them. It also gives them some autonomy in crafting their work, shows them where their weaknesses are, and eliminates much of the fear of risks involved in trying to complete a task. As an additional bonus to the teacher, it allows students to catch most of their own mistakes before the final draft and communicates the message that students, not teachers, bear primary responsibility for error correction. In the initial stages of rubric use, some teachers like to include an additional reaction sheet or comment sheet for student editors to fill out as they evaluate a paper. Later on, as students become more experienced, they will not need such prompts.

◇ **Sample Rubric**

An A paper has all or most of the following:

1. All prewriting, two rough drafts, and a final draft
2. Complete, logically organized, clear instructions for care and use of the invention
3. No you forms
4. Few or no errors in format, grammar, or spelling

A B paper has all or most of the following:

1. Prewriting, one rough draft, and a final draft
2. A few minor errors in instructions for care and use due to incompleteness and/or organization problems
3. One or two you forms
4. A few minor errors in format, grammar, or spelling that do not interfere with understanding

A C paper has all or most of the following:

1. Prewriting *or* rough draft with final draft
2. Three to five errors in completeness and organization
3. Several you forms
4. One to three serious errors in format, grammar, or spelling that interfere with understanding

A D paper has all or most of the following:

1. Only a final draft
2. Many errors in completeness and organization which make it difficult to understand
3. Many you forms
4. Many errors in format, spelling, and rammar that make it difficult to understand

An F paper has all or most of the following:

1. Only a final draft
2. Little or no organization and is seriously incomplete
3. Difficult or impossible to understand

Fig. 5.8.

All of this creates a list of needed unit materials for this unit task:

1.   Unit checklist/overview

2.   Sample manuals

3.   Divergent thinking work sheet

4.   Convergent thinking work sheet

5.   Rubric

6.   Editing comment sheets

These materials encourage and allow students to take the initiative in managing their own learning by letting them pace themselves, make decisions about their goals, and revise less-than-desirable work before their grades are indelibly inscribed in the gradebook. They also promote autonomy and responsibility by sharing information with the students in a static rather than consecutive manner.

All that is needed to complete the shopping list now is an inventory of support module materials for skills, vocabulary, and reading. If the teacher is fortunate enough to have good texts or deep file cabinets loaded with tried and true activities, little preparation may be necessary in these areas. For skills in the process writing unit, materials providing practice in imperative mood and passive voice are needed. This can either be exercises from an available text or a set of teacher-made materials. Ditto for vocabulary. For reading, the teacher can provide a set of owner's manuals for classroom use or require students to go out and find some on their own to read. The students can then be given some reaction forms to fill out on the manuals they have read. The shopping list now looks like this:

1.   Unit checklist/overview

2.   Sample manuals

3.   Divergent thinking work sheet

4.   Convergent thinking work sheet

5.   Rubric

6.   Editing comment sheets

7.   Imperative mood exercises

8.   Passive voice exercises

9.   Chronological order exercises

10.   Cause and effect exercises

11.   Reading reaction sheets

Eleven items may look like a lot, but traditionally, teachers do a lot more than they should. These eleven items will be used to shift a large measure of that work and responsibility over to the students where it will do the most good. By sharing information and responsibility with students, teachers involve students more deeply in their own learning. By involving students more deeply, they become better, more significant teachers. The reason there are so many materials to prepare is that the teacher is actually transferring most of the traditionally teacher-held responsibilities to the students. By creating these materials, the teacher actually relieves himself or herself of the work and responsibility that rightly belongs to the students. But lest this planning process seem too intimidating, let's sort the materials into curriculum categories to see how onerous their preparation really is:

Unit Task Student Materials

Checklist/overview

Divergent thinking prompt

Convergent thinking prompt

Rubric

Editors' comment sheets (optional)

Teacher Materials

Sample manuals

Skills Materials

Imperative mood exercise

Passive voice exercise

Reading Materials

Reaction forms

Vocabulary Materials

Chronological order exercise

Cause and effect exercise

Skills and vocabulary exercises may be no more difficult to assemble than assigning certain sections of a textbook to the students. Sample owner's manuals are no more difficult to find than a trip to the school industrial arts shop, the home economics room, the office, the janitor's office, and one's own home. A master editor's sheet, if it is constructed flexibly, can be used again and again for many different unit tasks. The same can also be true of the reading reaction forms. It is a matter of how much form the teacher wishes to impose on the students' activities.

A FINAL BIT OF ADVICE

It is true that planning and constructing a unit in this way requires forethought and nearly complete preparation of all materials prior to the beginning of the unit. For some people, this may be a mental and emotional stumbling block because they may feel pressured by an apparent mountain of work for which they have little time. For others, all of this early preparation may make them feel as though they will be robbed of the freedom to respond flexibly to students' needs. These are valid concerns shared by the author as well as many other teachers using Rewrite.

> I know my students are working more than they ever were before, but I feel kind of funny having so much time to do my own work ... sort of guilty, I guess.
> —TAG teacher, Colorado Springs, Colorado

As far as being buried under a mountain of preparation paperwork is concerned, the preparation would have to be done sooner or later anyhow. Preparing all of the materials before the unit starts frees the teacher from having to rush around on an almost daily basis to have masters reproduced and collated. The effect of this is that the teacher is freed up to be a resource to the students during and between classes. If no students require that time for interaction with the teacher, then class time can be spent preparing the materials for the next unit. The teacher is not the only beneficiary of early preparation. If all of the materials are assembled for the beginning of the unit, students who are able to can go on ahead instead of waiting for the next set of materials to be produced.

Sometimes, despite the most careful planning and preparation, things do not go exactly as desired. A large segment of the students may not grasp the target concepts of a particular support module or they may race through the entire unit so quickly that they are suddenly left with nothing more to do. This is where the flexibility of time use that was built into the management system comes to the rescue. Because so much of the unit time is loosely structured, it is no scheduling disaster if more class instruction is needed on a particular concept. There is plenty of time available for flexibility according to student need, whereas in a traditional classroom the entire unit schedule would be thrown off for days. Likewise, because of the multiple activity types and categories planned into the course, students will always have something of interest and value to work on, whether it be reading or working on a term project or revising substandard work.

The important thing to remember in constructing unit activities and materials is that the purpose of the unit is to involve students with subject matter so that teachers can involve themselves with students. It is difficult to encourage all of the attitudes and behaviors valued by significant teachers if one is pressed into being the sole source of information and the chief clerk and manager of the classroom. It is impossible to provide ongoing guidance and feedback to each and every student as needed in a classroom containing more than a few students. But by planning ahead and making information and feedback available in the form of written or recorded documents, teachers can make themselves more available and less exhausted when they are needed—when the students are in the classroom.

NOTES

1. Walter Doyle, U.S. Department of Education, "Effective Secondary Classroom Practices," in *Reaching for Excellence: An Effective Schools Sourcebook*, ed. Regina M. J. Kyle (Washington, DC: E. H. White, 1985) 67.

BIBLIOGRAPHY

Doyle, Walter. U.S. Department of Education. "Effective Secondary Classroom Practices." In *Reaching for Excellence: An Effective Schools Sourcebook*. Ed. Regina M. J. Kyle. Washington, DC: E. H. White, 1985.

— 6 —
Term Projects
Learning to Inquire

The Big Deal
A Teacher's Memoir

Linda taught English in the same department with us when Debbie and I were developing Rewrite. She had encouraged us in our work and experimented extensively with the program herself. She had taken it with her to the high school the year our gang at the junior high had broken up, all of us heading in different directions. Linda had a wonderful capacity for encouraging the best in people, so it seemed appropriate to call her up to brag about my latest accomplishment. I had just finished my semester project, and it was nearly sixty pages long—longer than anything I had ever written. It felt so good to have finished something so substantial, that I quite naturally wanted to enlarge upon the experience. Accolades from Linda seemed just the ticket. Or so I thought. Linda, it seemed, had other things on her mind.

"Linda, it's Pam! How're you doing?" Feigned selflessness seemed only polite for someone fishing for compliments.

"Awful! I'm buried in papers and grades were due in three days ago, and I haven't been to the gym in weeks." Linda is a very busy person. She is the one about whom the phrase "The hurrieder I go, the behinder I get" was written. It is possible to gauge Linda's busyness by how often she gets to go to the gym for her "daily" workout.

"Oh. Then I won't keep you long." This was really quite a vain hope. I don't call Linda very often because once we start talking, my long-distance budget collapses. "I just finished my curriculum course project, and I wanted to brag about it to somebody. It's a handbook of Rewrite units and it's almost sixty pages long! How about *that*?" I waited for Linda's cry of admiration.

"That's nothing," she answered. It didn't look as though I was going to get minimal approval, let alone an accolade. "My sophomores just turned in their term projects last week, too. Some of them are eighty to one hundred pages long, and the presentations last week were incredible! It's so amazing to see what they'll do when you let them do something they're interested in. They have no idea they're doing scads more than I would have ever asked for."

"Oh," I said, wondering if this was worth wrecking my phone budget. "That sounds great."

Linda loves nothing better than to see her students blossom. Anything that lets her do that is a-number-one in her book. "You bet!" she went on. "And I can really tell which kids have been doing term projects since you and Debbie had them in seventh and eighth grade. Their projects are the longest, the most original, and the most detailed. Remember Jarilynn? You had her for seventh and eighth grade? Her project was on poisons. She's writing a mystery novel this year and the murderer uses poison, so she needed to learn all about poisons. She researched and wrote a seventy-page handbook on poisons and how to make and use them. There wasn't anything anyone asked her during her presentation that she didn't know."

"How about that?" Sure, I remembered Jarilynn. The first quarter of seventh grade had been a real trial for her. She had been smaller than most of the other kids, completely intimidated by the Conan-like ninth-graders who smashed her against the lockers as they boiled down the halls. She had what I would call an actual talent for leaving things behind in classrooms. She had gradually overcome these handicaps. She had developed the habit of always wearing her purse slung over one shoulder and carrying everything she owned with her wherever she went, even if it was only up to my desk to ask me a question. She grew about nine inches between seventh and eighth grade and learned that the rules about walking on the right side of the hall were universally ignored by everyone. "Seventy pages, huh? Sounds like she's still indulging her taste for the morbid," I observed. Her first report for me had been on ghost stories of our local area. The report hadn't been very long because Layton, Utah, doesn't have the same traditions of Salem, Massachusetts, but a reporter from the Ogden paper had wanted a copy of it for his files for the Halloween feature the following year. My project booklet began to look rather insignificant there on the kitchen table.

"Well, yeah," Linda admitted, "but I don't think it's pathological. She's more like a budding Agatha Christie. She's only fourteen, but she's on her second novel and plans to write more. All of the Rewrite kids you and Debbie taught are like that. They chomp at the bit for new projects to start. It's great. The other English teachers here mention it, too. They can always tell a North Layton kid from the rest of them."

"Oh, really?" I was beginning to gain a new understanding of "ambivalent." This call wasn't at all what I had expected it to be. I was getting complimented on the wrong thing. At least I thought I was. It was getting harder to be sure. Linda has that effect on people sometimes. "Well, that's nice to hear. It really is. Any other students I would know in your class?"

I listened to Linda's update on my old students with half of my attention. The other half was focused on Jarilynn. The kid was fourteen, had written a seventy-page project in eight weeks, and was on her second novel. I, at age thirty-six, had written a sixty-page handbook in twelve weeks and hadn't even conceived of writing anything more ambitious than that. I remembered Jarilynn, alright, and it felt good to know she had already surpassed me.

Moral: Teach them what they need to know, and they'll do the rest.

REWRITING SOME DEFINITIONS

In researching the topic of research and independent study, I discovered some interesting definitions and biases of the education community. Research is something students do for teachers for course credit. It is something that students have to learn to do to succeed in school. Research is a forced activity. Research papers and other products such as science fair projects are the things that are supposed to come out of student research. Teachers assign research papers to students so they will learn to use the library and write papers for more advanced classes in school. It is up to students to find out what will satisfy the teacher and then to do it. One need only look at the volume of literature on how to interest students in research to see that it is often regarded by students and teachers as something any normal person would naturally want to avoid.

Independent study, on the other hand, is usually regarded as something for students to do who have too many questions or who know too much about what the teacher is teaching. It is a program that is set up for those gifted students who want to go on to learn more than is available in the usual school program. It is an activity to keep them busy and happy, apart from the rest of the students. For some schools and districts it also fills the requirement for gifted programming.

These two sets of attitudes would seem to present a paradox of sorts. Students without a natural desire to do research are considered normal and are prodded into doing it, while those students with the curiosity to do it willingly must be "banished" from the regular program with an alternative activity. Research and independent study then, instead of appearing to be exciting opportunities to meet the human need to learn and know, is made to appear as something abnormal, while those who enjoy investigation are seen as weird students or mad scientists.

Of course, there is no malice on the part of teachers who have these kinds of things happening in their classes, no conspiracy to squash curiosity in the abler students or to whip regular students into submission with punitive research reports. In fact, teachers are struggling to meet the needs of both sets of students by preparing the "normal," research-hating students to succeed in future school situations and providing opportunities for the "abnormal," overly curious students to learn all they can.

Oddly enough, these attitudes have resulted in an interesting phenomenon in adult education. Independent study has become an important focus in adult education programs because it seems that somehow almost everybody got out of "real" school without learning how to find out about what they need or what to know. They didn't learn that research is a normal, human activity that every adult needs to be able to do to adapt and learn. They have learned that independent study is done for extra credit or when the real course isn't offered and that it is something one does under a teacher's supervision. What the adult education programs are trying to teach them (or unteach them) is that independent study is a way to learn on their own and that it is not a program; it is a capability. In their book, *Independent Study*, written for educators of adults, Paul L. Dressel and Mary Magdala Thompson describe this capability:

> We prefer the term *independent study* as describing an ability to be developed in some measure in every student. It means motivation, curiosity, a sense of self-sufficiency and self-direction, ability to think critically and creatively, awareness of resources, and some ability to use them.[1]

Probably all teachers who set up research units or independent study programs want to develop these qualities and abilities in their students. But when the traditional hidden curriculum of over-dependence provides the context, the result is quite the opposite. However, when research is presented within the context of independent study and independent study is presented within the context of the Rewrite hidden curriculum of independence and responsibility, these qualities and abilities can be gradually nurtured and directed throughout the period of formal schooling to produce adults who are capable of self-directed inquiry.

WONDERING COMES FIRST

From the beginning, children question, observe, hypothesize, experiment, and then question some more. They wonder about things. If they don't, they are considered abnormal and are steered toward medical and psychological help. Later on, though, wondering seems to become an artificial activity and finding out a passive one.

A quick survey of the materials available to help students and teachers with research projects and units provides some revealing clues as to what happens. Nearly all of these materials begin with such questions as "What are you supposed to research?" followed by "How long does your report have to be?" and "Are there enough books and articles available to fill up that many pages?" These are hardly the type of questions one would ask of someone who is excited about finding out something new. Instead, it implies that research is something done at the teacher's instigation, that it is done on a page-quota system, and that if there isn't enough information sitting around for the researcher to regurgitate onto a certain number of typed pages, the topic isn't worth attacking.

None of these attitudes are what teachers usually want their students to assimilate. They want their students to wonder about things, to look for answers, to find answers, and then wonder some more. How can this type of motivation and capability be developed? By changing the values that are communicated to students about research and independent study through the traditional hidden curriculum. When wondering and searching are valued and nurtured ahead of writing a research paper of a minimum number of pages, the basis for motivation changes from external to intrinsic reward. Then normal proclivities for curiosity and exploration can blossom.

RELEARNING LEARNING

All of the elements of the Rewrite model are aimed at increasing intrinsic student motivation, independence, and responsibility, but the categories of shorter activities are still structured with definite criteria for performance and focus. Originality, initiative, and creativity are particularly encouraged in the unit task category, but still within the limits of the curricular needs of the students. The term project category, however, is meant to provide a much freer environment for student questioning and learning. There is, of course, still a general focus on the subject area, but instead of requiring students to cover certain specific material, the emphasis in term projects is to push the student out to find his or her own areas of interest within the area of study. In term projects, students are expected to wonder about things beyond what is covered in the regular class activities. In doing so, they can find their own reasons for learning about the subject matter and learn how to explore the field on their own.

YABBUT ...

Yabbut what about kids who aren't interested in anything?

Response: This is always a tough problem. Sometimes students are so far gone that they have given up. I once had a student who combed his hair for 50 minutes a day, everyday for an entire school year despite my best efforts to interest him in something. I came to the conclusion that for some students, nothing short of a divine epiphany will shock them out of their apathy.

However, for most students who moan and groan about not knowing what to do for a project, a teacher/student conference and some surreptitious observations on the part of the teacher can help a student focus on an interest. For many students who have been given little opportunity for choice or who have had their interests ridiculed in the past, sharing their private avocations is a risky proposition. They must be reassured that risks are safe in this class and are even encouraged. They will gradually pick this up from the general organization of the class, but often need a strong dose of encouragement direct from the teacher in a teacher/student conference. By asking some strategic and prodding questions and making a brainstorm list of suggestions, a reluctant student can learn how to wonder and focus again.

This is not to say that this is a panacea for every student who doesn't have the foggiest notion what to do for a project. Sometimes they still need to be "assigned." But if the teacher can observe the student's interests through conversation or reading and listening material, favorite movies, and other overt expressions of interests, the teacher can often come up with a suggested list of projects. This list can then be the subject of a conference in which the teacher makes suggestions and the student improves on them.

These are valuable goals for teachers to pursue in nurturing all of their students, but they are particularly valuable when working with gifted students. These students are often characterized by what seems to many to be a surfeit of curiosity, which is one reason they are often put in pullout and independent study programs, but many gifted students give up on ever being able to learn what they want or feel they need to learn in school.

By allowing quick completion of support modules and variable complexity in unit tasks, tendencies toward boredom and despair can be minimized. Providing gifted students with opportunities to go beyond the course material and to learn how to explore and learn prepares them for roles they will fulfill as gifted adults. As adults, it is likely that they will at some point surpass their available teachers and have to proceed on their own. They will need to know how to question productively, how to plan and carry out investigations, and how to communicate their discoveries to others. They can begin to gain some of the necessary knowledge, skills, and experience to do this while still students through the term project segment of the Rewrite model.

The term project also attempts to encourage affective as well as cognitive development in a manner that is valuable to students both in the present and the future. Through the term project segment of a course, gifted students can learn to inquire without existing as outcasts from human society. By having all students working on their own individualized investigations as part of regular class activities, gifted students can be part of the group while working at their own advanced levels and regular students can learn that investigation and creative work are normal activities. When all students are researchers, the classroom becomes a community of scholars, each investigating an area of personal interest. This is important because much of the work done in our society requires group cooperation or at least coexistence with other workers. Isolating these gifted people from their chronological and/or intellectual peers by putting them in separate independent study programs while they are students reinforces the perception that they are strange or different in a negative way. It also sends a subliminal message to the rest of the students that being curious enough to engage in independent study is abnormal and therefore warrants separation from the rest of the class. It also deprives gifted students of experience in interaction and communication with their peers. One of the conclusions of the survey of MacArthur Fellows was that, "sometimes as important as good teachers was the opportunity to be with supportive and challenging peers."[2] Working with and alongside other students in an open, interactive atmosphere allows these experiences to take place.

> I liked doing the interviews, the presentation, and working with my partners. We have worked well with each other. We have picked really good and knowledgeable [sic] subjects.
> — Utah high school student

PLANNING TERM PROJECTS

Term projects, by definition, last an entire quarter or term. They are not short tasks that are easily or quickly disposed of. Rather, they are investigations that are carried out by students over an eight- or nine-week period. Most of the specific planning for these projects is done by the students so that they will learn how to set up investigative projects for themselves, but certain elements must be planned by the teacher to shape the experience. In this way, the accumulation of investigative knowledge and experience will not be haphazard but can follow a logical progression.

Several things should be considered in planning the goals, objectives, and subtasks of the term project category. While it is not necessary for teachers to know everything about everything to oversee term projects, it is necessary that they be clear in their own minds about what is expected from this activity.

YABBUT ...

Yabbut what if a student wants to do something I know nothing about? How can I help that student and evaluate the project?

Response: More than anything else, this one worry kept me from embarking on term projects for quite a while. I felt that if my students were working on something I didn't understand, then I had lost control of the classroom and could not function as their teacher. Fortunately for me and my students, a wise professor of mine pointed out that I only needed to know how to find things out and how to teach students how to find out. He also showed me that if I could not function as guide and mentor for a particular student, then I could still find someone else I trusted who could function as guide and mentor.

The expectations are shaped by the following considerations, which will be expanded upon:

1. The larger purposes of the course.

2. The typical methodologies, investigative skills, and products of the subject area.

3. Opportunities for varied interests and abilities.

4. The need to keep track of student progress.

Larger purposes of the course. Showing students how to connect their personal interests with the subject matter at hand is a good way to increase their involvement in the study of that subject matter.

> Love the project! Never had so much fun in an English class!
> — Utah high school student

The larger purposes of the course should dictate the general areas of investigation. In most cases, for instance, it would not be appropriate for a student to investigate the life cycles of crustaceans in a physics class or the cuisine of Pakistan in an American history course. However, the dynamics of crustacean propulsion or the influence of Pakistani immigrants in North America would be quite reasonable. Possible exceptions to this would be in a foreign language or English class or an art class where the subject matter is a means of expression. In these cases, the actual subject matter covered in the project is not as important as the opportunity for students to use and discover uses for the medium. See figure 6.1 for some ideas on refocusing student interests.

◇ *Refocusing Student Interests*

One of the brightest students I ever taught was a junior high girl in my Sunday school class. She had a wonderful mind that was utterly consumed with her clothes, her hair, and her general appearance. Her life was dedicated to shopping. When I put a question box on the table and passed around pieces of paper for the students to write whatever question they would most like to ask God, she wrote, "How is the best way for me to wear my hair?" Luring her into topics of more lasting importance was frustrating to say the least.

This happens to every teacher, and when students are told they can do anything they want for their term projects they often come up with something totally unrelated to the subject area. So what's a teacher to do with a student who loves mystery novels and has to do a geography project? Refocus, that's what. Have the student survey a cross section of mystery novels and put together a set of criteria for ideal mystery settings. Then let the student do a geographic survey of a hemisphere or other division of the world and put together a directory of ideal mystery novel settings.

What about a fisherman in German class?

Plan a fishing vacation in the German-speaking countries.

A carpenter in chemistry class?

Investigate the properties of different bonding materials used in carpentry.

A martial arts buff in literature class?

Survey and evaluate martial arts films as a genre.

A violinist in biology class?

Compare and contrast stringed instruments and human speech apparatus.

A baseball fan in math class?

Use statistical records to see if baseball players are any better today than in the past.

A horseback rider in shop class?

Find out how modern blacksmiths are trained and how they do their work

Fig. 6.1.

Typical methodologies and strategies. Term projects consist of eight subtasks, one per week for the eight-week period of planned work. These sets of subtasks are used to guide students through problem-solving and/or investigative processes common to the subject area. Through careful choice of the subtasks, teachers can influence the structure of the activity unobtrusively without unduly affecting the choices of topics, products, and complexity for students. The choice of subtasks is based on student experience levels and investigative and problem-solving methodologies of the subject area (see figure 6.2, pages 94-95, for a list of sample methodologies). For a science class, these subtasks could be based on the scientific method or engineering and inventions processes, for a writing or art class the processes of creative composition, and for a computer programming class the steps of a top-down problem-solving algorithm.

◇ *Sample Methodologies*

A heuristic is a plan that can be applied in the solution of a problem. Heuristics are different from algorithms in that they are not hard and fast formulas and can be altered to suit the needs of the problem solver.

Invention

1. State your goal.
2. Research existing and analogous products.
3. Sketch out your ideas and try to solve trouble spots.
4. Select an idea to develop and draw plans for a breadboard.
5. Build and test the breadboard.
6. Solve the problem areas using problem-solving strategies.
7. Design, build, and test the prototype.
8. Present the prototype to the public.

Business Planning

1. State your objective.
2. Research the competition.
3. Develop your product.
4. Research the market.
5. Develop a marketing plan.
6. Plan the financing for development and marketing.
7. Carry out the marketing plan.
8. Report on the results and project improvements.

Discovery

1. Observe and search for existing patterns.
2. Compare and identify similarities and differences.
3. Measure and record your actual observations.
4. Classify your data to create order and structure.
5. Identify your variables.
6. Infer a conclusion based on your observations.
7. Formulate your hypothesis.
8. Experiment and test your hypothesis.
9. Analyze and report your discoveries.

Top-Down Computer Problem Solving

1. Identify your problem.
2. Sketch out an outline of a solution.
3. Figure out the details of the solution.
4. Write out your computer program.
5. Type the program into the computer.
6. Run the program.
7. Debug the program.
8. Check to see that the problem is really solved.

Fig. 6.2.

Fig. 6.2—*Continued*

*Four-Step Problem-Solving Process**

1. Analyze the solution.
2. Gather facts that are pertinent to the problem.
3. Reason logically with theses facts and the original certainty.
4. Look back. Does the solution make sense? Is there an easier way to solve the problem?

Creative Problem-Solving Process (CPS) by Sidney Parnes

1. Fact finding
2. Problem finding
3. Idea finding
4. Solution finding
5. Acceptance finding

The Scientific Method

1. Recognize your problem.
2. Define your problem.
3. Develop your hypothesis.
4. Select or develop techniques for gathering data.
5. Gather the data.
6. Analyze the data.
7. Draw conclusions from the data.

---

*From Harry Bohan, "Free Rides for Kids," *The Arithmetic Teacher*. November 1990, 11.

How closely these subtasks resemble the actual complexity of those performed by professionals depends on the abilities and experience of the students. If most of the students in a class have never had any serious exposure to the subject area before, the subtasks should be simplified and the emphasis put more on basic processes and skills used in the field rather than on more complicated ones. For classes or individuals with greater experience in the field, such as might occur in advanced language or math courses or when a gifted student is a member of a regular class, however, the goal should be to let the students stretch and extend their basic knowledge to more esoteric or complex areas and products that approximate the work done by professionals. For a gifted student, this might mean that the work done in a particular subtask would be more demanding or complex than that required of less able students.

Opportunities for varied interests and abilities. Term projects are purposely less specific than unit tasks and support modules in order to encourage greater variability in subjects and difficulty. When teachers assign specific topics and parameters for individual research and study, they are usurping the prerogative of the student to wonder and discover. When the interests of students are not allowed reasonably free rein in the forum of the classroom, the message is sent that their interests are not valued. If their interests are not valued, then the students' own value is diminished. But if their interests are considered, even in just this one segment of the course, students are much more likely to feel that their contributions are valuable and their questions appreciated. In such an atmosphere, it is more likely that their contributions and questions will be freely offered.

> What I liked the most about doing a project is the research, where I in fact learn about things I didn't know.
>
> —high school sophomore

Another finding of the Richardson survey of the MacArthur Fellows was that in setting goals, gifted students "preferred to participate in determining how to reach or go beyond those goals."[3] But to do this effectively, gifted students must also receive instruction in how to focus on goals and direct their efforts to reach them. To accommodate this need and provide an atmosphere that encourages individual curiosity and investigation, guidelines for term projects should be kept as general as possible. It is not usually necessary to assign topics for term projects. In fact, assigning topics is probably more of an impediment than an aid to fostering open inquiry and curiosity. Instead, a good project plan and set of subtasks provide all the structure necessary to teach students about inquiry processes without impinging upon student selection of topic (see figure 6.3 for a sample project plan).

A good project plan involves two main considerations. First, the teacher should decide what type of methodological experience should be provided for the students. Do they need experience in finding and solving problems? Do they need experience in historical research or descriptive or experimental research? Do they need experience in composing a product from start to finish? By deciding on the type of experience the students need, the teacher can craft a set of general subtasks to guide the students through their projects.

> It helped me *tons* to get where I want with the point of the project I am doing.
>
> —A.G., Utah high school student

The second consideration involves encouraging individuality. If every student has to complete an identical product through an identical set of skills and processes, individuality will be stifled. However, if there are several ways students can fulfill the requirements of the subtasks through choice of subject, resources, methods of data location and recording, products, and presentations, then individual variability can be accommodated more easily. If a term project plan does not allow for variability in most of the subtasks, then the project plan is probably too rigid and should be redesigned.

As the project plan provides an external structure, so subtasks provide an internal structure. Good subtasks have five characteristics, each of which contribute to the effectiveness of the subtasks individually and the term project as a whole:

- They provide practice in a step of the process.

- They are logical divisions in the process.

- They are manageable chunks of work in the process.

- They provide opportune moments for teacher/student interaction.

- They allow several ways to satisfy requirements.

◇ *Sample Project Plans*

The project plan described in the text is only one example of a plan. There are as many possibilities for plans as there are teachers and ideas. Here are a few variations on the basic plan based on the heuristics from figure 6.2:

An Invention Project Plan

1. Write out your invention proposal and get approval on it.
2. Research existing and analogous products.
3. Sketch out your ideas and work on the trouble spots.
4. Select one idea to pursue and draw plans for breadboard.
5. Build and test your breadboard.
6. Try to solve trouble spots with problem-solving strategies.
7. Design, build, and test a prototype.
8. Present your prototype to the class.

A Business Project Plan

1. Write a proposal for your business and get approval on it.
2. Research the competition and the market.
3. Develop a financing plan for development and marketing.
4. Develop a prototype of your product line.
5. Test consumer reaction to your product.
6. Refine your product.
7. Carry out your marketing plan.
8. Report on your results and further goals.

A Computer Programming Project Plan

1. Identify the purpose of your program and get approval on it.
2. Outline your basic solution.
3. Write in the details of the solution.
4. Write out the entire program.
5. Run and debug the program as far as you are able.
6. Take the program to an editing group.
7. Improve the program using editors' feedback.
8. Demonstrate your program for the class.

A Science Project Plan

1. Fill out the proposal sheet and get approval for your project.
2. Conduct your experiments.
3. Record your data in a field or lab notebook.
4. Analyze the data and draw conclusions about the hypothesis.
5. Write out a rough draft of your process and conclusions.
6. Take your rough draft to an editing group.
7. Revise your report into a final draft.
8. Present results and proposals for further research to the class.

Fig. 6.3.

Practice. Most students are not stupid; they are merely inexperienced in the conventions of the subject area. Subtasks help them gain needed experience by giving them both the reason and the opportunity to learn and use specific skills and strategies common to the methodology at hand. Students who have little experience in library research, for example, can learn to use both traditional and innovative means of locating materials in a library media center in the sources and bibliography subtask of a term project. When introducing this subtask on a project day, the teacher can demonstrate how to use an electronic data base and/or a card catalog or *Readers' Guide* to find materials, depending on the experience of the class members. More advanced methods for locating data can be covered in subsequent quarters or on an as-needed basis for those students wishing to go beyond the rudiments of data location. By teaching a skill and requiring its use in the investigation of a personal interest, teachers can give students real and reasonable practice in a part of a process that both teacher and student regard as valuable.

Logical Divisions. Our first term project plan was divided into eight subtasks so that it would fit comfortably into our quarter schedule and our record sheets, but even then we made the effort to divide the subtasks logically. Logical divisions typically fall at points where the type of work involved in the project changes in some way. There is a natural break between getting approval on a project and beginning to put together a working bibliography. Likewise, there is a natural break between finishing a rough draft or prototype of a product and getting preliminary feedback in a peer editing group.

YABBUT ...

Yabbut what if I can't fit my project plan into eight subtasks?

Response: No problem! Nowhere is it carved in stone that project plans *must* be eight subtasks long. Eight is just a convenient number for a quarter based on eight full weeks of class time with a record sheet already handily divided into eight squares on the skills and reading bars. Particularly for teachers and students just starting out on term projects, it is easy to keep track of one subtask a week. However, if the inquiry process needed by a particular class doesn't lend itself to eight subtasks, any other manageable number is workable.

Manageable Chunks. Students need help in learning to manage their work, particularly if they are involved in a complex or lengthy process. Cutting the project process into manageable chunks helps students plan their work by seeing the composition of the process and keeps them from bogging down at one stage to the detriment of the entire process. One of the premier pieces of advice given by Alden Todd, a teacher of research, in his book, *Finding Facts Fast*, is to "be realistic about purpose, time and cost of your research,"[4] and while most students don't need to be concerned about the monetary cost of their research, they should learn to be concerned about how they spend their time and energy in achieving a goal. Having a set of subtasks that in effect divides the project into almost weekly steps helps students learn to keep a perspective on what they are doing. If a student has not done enough work to go on to the next step, the teacher can show him or her what must still be done. If too much work has been undertaken, the teacher can likewise help that student to pare down or refocus the project before things go too far.

> I, as an appreciative scholar, really feel that the procedure of spacing the different requirements (notes and research, outline, rough draft) at intervals really is an adequate system.
> —concerned scholar, high school sophomore

Points of interaction. Fortunately, most logical and manageable divisions occur at opportune points for teacher/student interaction. These points can be defined as those points in the process at which disaster can most easily be averted. Getting approval on a project before starting it is a good way to avert disaster. So is making sure that one's bibliography isn't inadequate or that one has done enough background study to begin working on a rough draft or prototype. Subtask divisions allow teachers to keep tabs on each student without having to maintain a stranglehold on individuality.

Flexible requirements. Finally, subtasks should allow for more than one method of fulfillment. If students are assembling a set of sources, can they use human sources and interview them? Can they also use television shows, apprenticeship experiences, and computer data bases in addition to or instead of more traditional sources? Does everyone have to give a speech to present a project or can some students use graphic media or other means of publication? Does everyone have to give a presentation to the class or can some students give their presentation to a professional group or prepare an article for publication in a professional journal or newsletter? Even though there must be certain specific requirements to help students through their projects, the availability of options can offset any sense of unnecessary rigidity and allow students some freedom of choice. If too much freedom of choice is withheld from students and replaced by teacher decrees, the projects cease to belong to the students. When this happens, there is no basis for intrinsic motivation or for taking ownership or responsibility. A list of project suggestions is shown in figure 6.4, page 100.

◇ *Project Suggestions*

Here are a few suggestions for project products to help teachers and students start their project planning:

1.   Activity books for children and shut-ins
2.   Advertising campaigns
3.   Anthologies of poems, stories, artwork, and multimedia themes
4.   Books: novels, nonfiction, biographies, autobiographies, childrens' books
5.   Business plans for real or imaginary ventures
6.   Comic and cartoon books
7.   Community service projects
8.   Computer programs with user's guides
9.   Consumer reports on dream purchases
10.   Costuming: historical, contemporary, imaginary, theatrical
11.   Cycles of poems, stories, songs, sketches, etc.
12.   Entertainment and sporting guides
13.   Family histories and genealogies
14.   Field books and field guides
15.   Greeting card and gift item product lines
16.   Interior design and architectural plans and models
17.   Investment plans
18.   Magazines, newsletters, and newspapers
19.   Model machines
20.   Practicum and apprenticeship journals, written or filmed
21.   Scientific research
22.   Scripts: television, theater, movies, radio, speeches
23.   Simulation games
24.   Static and bulletin board displays on research topics
25.   Translations of foreign works
26.   Travel guides and plans

Fig. 6.4.

Keeping track of student progress. Subtasks are graded on a pass/fail basis to allow individualized evaluation of each student's work according to his or her ability and the complexity of the project. They are also set up so that the teacher can check on the progress of each student at crucial points in the term project process. There must be an initial exchange between teacher and student when the project is being planned, intermediate points of contact to allow the teacher to interject

YABBUT ...

Yabbut then there are no standards for performance, and it's not fair to all the students!

Response: In fact, there *are* standards of performance and they are even fairer than standards that are the same for the entire class. Teachers usually know the capabilities and problems of their students in the subject area better than almost anyone else because teachers have the opportunity to observe their performance on a daily basis over a long period of time. Because of this, they are able to look at a subtask turned in by a student and tell if it is representative of the best that student should be doing. If not, they return the subtask for further work. If the subtask seems to be too hard for the student, they can return it with directions for simplifying the work. If the subtask is representative of a student's best work, then the student receives a "Pass" on the work and is cleared to go on with the next subtask.

This is really much fairer than requiring everyone to turn in work of the same level of difficulty because every student is able to work at his or her own best level for learning. It is not fair to expect a low-achieving student to produce work of the same complexity as a highly gifted student. Instead, in the term project, both students are expected to work at the same level of challenge not difficulty.

assistance at crucial points in the investigative process when necessary, a point of contact between the investigator and other students, a chance for the investigator to share what has been learned, and an opportunity to evaluate the completed work. These needs are of great help in dividing methodological processes into logical subtasks.

The initial exchange of ideas accounts for the first two subtasks: the *project proposal* and the *project approval*. Rather than the teacher assigning a research topic, the responsibility is placed on the student to wonder, question, and plan a way to find out about these wonderings and questions. This is not only important for sending a message to students about responsibility; it is also important for ensuring student interest and involvement in a long-term activity. The freedom to choose a subject and a means of investigation is particularly important in dealing with gifted students. As C. June Maker explains in her book *Teaching Models in Education of the Gifted*: "Whenever possible, gifted students should be given the freedom to choose what to investigate and how to study. Their interest and excitement in learning will be increased by such techniques. However, not all gifted students are independent learners, so they may need assistance in making and executing their choices."[5]

The proposal sheet is set up to help students plan their investigations and inquiries and to help the teacher find weaknesses in the students' abilities to do so. Each student is required to fill out a term project proposal sheet explaining the purposes of the project, a rough plan of attack, a means of communicating findings, and a reasonable schedule for completion (see figure 6.5, page 102).

◇ *Proposal Sheet*

Name _____ Course _____

Partners, if any (limit 3)_____

Period_____   Quarter _____   Date_____

Approved _____   Not approved_____   (see comments below)

You *must* get your project approved *before* beginning work on it!

Title of project _____

1. Briefly describe your project, including its length, the amount of time it will require to complete, and what you intend to cover or do for the project.

2. List the kinds of sources you can use for research and note-taking. Include *all* types of sources, including nonprint.

3. Describe your project in its final format. What will it look like? Will you have illustrations, charts, graphs? Will it be in a report format, a booklet, a videotape and program guide, or an original work of art?

4. What will you do for a class presentation? Will you need any special equipment or props?

5. Set reasonable due dates for each of the required subtasks. Fill in the dates below:

   Approval _____

   Working bibliography (at least three sources) _____

   Notes and organizing _____

   Rough draft _____

   Editing group _____

   Final draft turned in (*before* presentation) _____

   Presentation to class (*before* Drop Dead Day) _____

   All term projects are due in this class by _____

Fig. 6.5.

The proposal sheet should contain questions that will help the teacher to see any potential trouble spots and the student to think through the entire project. Potential trouble spots include such things as an inappropriate choice of subject or complexity, inadequate preliminary surveys of resources, inadequate or overblown plans of attack, and unrealistic time frame, product, or presentation plans. Not all of the trouble spots inherent in a given term project will turn up on the proposal sheet, but a good measure of the likely ones will. In any case, the proposal/approval process presents the teacher with a chance to exert individualized quality control without having to explain differences in requirements, because they are private and everyone is working on something different. It also introduces students to one of the conventions of adult inquiry and investigation, seeking a sponsor for original work. A shrewd teacher can spot a project that needs to be divided in two or one that is too simple for a student or is inadequately or unrealistically planned. When the teacher shares his or her expertise in troubleshooting, students have the chance to learn firsthand about problem solving. Students also have an opportunity to learn how to think through their ideas by following the implied heuristic of the form and to learn how to communicate their intentions to a sponsor.

The third subtask involves students' *working bibliographies*. Locating data is an important part of every type of inquiry. Even those students who choose to work on an original work of art will need to locate some sort of background information for process, skills, and content involved in the work. Our art museums are filled with sketches and studies done by famous artists such as Rembrandt and Breughel in preparation for major works. Assembling a set of resources or a working bibliography is a crucial step for a young investigator. By turning in a copy of this, the student can gain the benefit of the teacher's or other mentor's experience in locating sources which may enable that student to find additional or better sources than those found to date. By looking over the working bibliography of a student, a teacher or mentor can spot weaknesses in the student's research abilities or knowledge, maintain a certain measure of quality control, and root out any adolescent laziness before a student gets too deeply into the project to make adjustments.

Notes and organization is the fourth logical step and must be completed before beginning work on the product itself. Gathering, recording, and organizing data is an important stage in an investigative process. Quite often, inexperienced students will not be aware of strategies and conventions for taking notes accurately, recording necessary reference information, or organizing their notes into a coherent plan or outline. This fourth step, then, would require students to turn in their notes and outlines or other organizational plans to their teachers or mentors for checking. Teachers and other mentors, who have more experience with these things, can point out holes in students' data bases or illogical organizational plans before students begin rough drafts of their project products.

Once all of the preliminary steps have been checked off as satisfactory and students know they are well-prepared to begin the actual creation of their product, students can begin the fifth step, *rough drafts*, with a good measure of confidence. They know that their background inquiries have been adequate, they have enough information to complete the product, and they have a concrete plan and schedule for doing so. Teachers can relax because they know that they have kept tabs on their students' work through all of the preliminary stages. When students have finished their rough drafts, they turn them in so that the teacher can make sure they have done enough to proceed to the next step, *peer editing*.

> I liked the writing and presentation. These projects give one a chance to learn about something.
> —D.L., Utah high school student

The completion of a rough draft prepares students for an exercise in audience analysis, evaluation, and revision. This exercise takes place in a *peer editing group*. Up to this point, students have had their primary input from the teacher, and the peer editing group allows them to try out their products and ideas on a larger audience as they prepare a product for presentation. Only one editing group is required, and it consists only of students sharing term projects. Other editing or peer review groups for unit tasks are separate from term project groups. This is because term projects are usually lengthier, less uniform, and more complex than a unit task, and the time and involvement needs of the two types of review groups are different. Asking a student to go through an entire project when he or she is working only on a unit task is an inconsiderate abuse of that student's daily work time.

With the comments and suggestions of the editing group to add to prior input from teacher or mentor, the student is ready to proceed with the *final draft* of the project product. In this seventh step, the student concentrates on creating a polished product to share in a public presentation. Careful preparation for a specific audience and mode of presentation is the emphasis here as the student comes to closure on all the answers and new questions gained in the inquiry process.

The eighth and final step, *presentation*, has several purposes. Students learn that their knowledge and expertise is of value to the group at large and they learn valuable communication skills in audience analysis and public speaking and publication. They also receive positive feedback from a larger audience of their peers, whether chronological or intellectual, and possibly spark new questions or interests in their audience. It is always exciting to see students cook up an original project of their own based on an idea from another student's work. It truly takes the responsibility for posing questions and designing projects away from the teacher and creates a community of creativity.

> It was fun to tell everyone what I learned. I liked the satisfaction from [sic] the audience.
> —J.P., high school student

MANAGING TERM PROJECTS

Term projects take away many of the common headaches associated with daily classroom control and management, but they can contribute a few headaches of their own. For the most part, term projects do not require a great deal of oversight or tricky scheduling. In fact, because they do not, they are wonderful for filling in those times when students have finished unit assignments early, when they feel they need a break from unit work to work on something more to their liking for awhile, and on Fridays when no one feels like doing much of anything except waiting for Saturday. Still, there are several special sorts of problems that can crop up if plans have not been made for dealing with them ahead of time. Some of these problems stem from scheduling term project work time or setting up group and class projects, and still others involve helping individual students dissolve unexpected glitches.

Scheduling

On the surface, term project scheduling looks neat and tidy. There are eight subtasks to last eight weeks. Every Friday is term project day. Everybody has a nice set of subtasks and a specific product in mind for completion by a certain date. But there are always "buts." Not every subtask takes a week to complete. Not every subtask can be completed in a week. Some students, usually the bright ones who find the regular work easy enough to finish early, get extra time to work on their projects on regular class days when other students don't. Any one of these problems can disturb the tidiness of the eight-week schedule. Taken together, they would seem to disrupt the entire segment of the course. However, this need not happen.

First of all, teachers need to remember that inquiry is often an untidy process. If it weren't, the detective novel genre would not even exist and there would be a cure for the common cold. Realistically, one cannot expect students to conduct investigations on eight-week schedules. One can, however, expect them to complete projects by posted due dates. They may need help to do so, but that is why subtasks are set up to allow for teacher/student interaction at critical points in the process. If a teacher finds that there simply are not enough resources available for a student to complete a project as originally planned, the two of them can modify the project plan to something that can be accomplished. If a teacher finds that a student has overestimated what can be accomplished in one quarter, then the two of them can examine the total investigation and divide it into manageable pieces, stretching the investigation out over two or three term projects, with each term project making up one segment of the total inquiry. For instance, if a student is interested in veterinary science, he or she may wish to find out about what vets do by serving an apprenticeship with a local vet and writing about or filming the experience one quarter, inquire about veterinary careers and training another quarter, and a particular branch of veterinary science the third quarter.

On a smaller scale, some students may find that they can get approval on their project and find their resources within the space of one week, but need two or three weeks to complete taking notes and organization. Others may find that they are ready to give their presentations by the end of the sixth week instead of the eighth. All of these situations can work, as the term project category is flexible. As long as the student completes the entire project by the end of the quarter and still fulfills the requirements for quality of work, there should be no altercations between teacher and student.

YABBUT ...

Yabbut what about kids who procrastinate? They'll always get caught rushing around at the last minute to finish.

Response: These are often the same students who have trouble staying on task for regular unit assignments, but sometimes they are the students who do fine on a daily basis where work comes in small increments but who can't keep themselves on track over a longer period of time. Whatever the case, it is often helpful to remind the class at large where they should be on their term projects and to take a moment alone with those students whose gradebook record is glaringly empty in the term project category.

The schedule planning section on the proposal sheet is mainly to help the student set benchmarks for completing certain segments of the project, not concrete due dates. However, to spare the teacher the agony of a tidal wave of several stacks of term project subtasks and unit assignments at the end of the quarter, it is often a good idea to set early due dates for final drafts and to insist each student turn in subtasks one at a time throughout the quarter instead of all together at the end of the quarter on presentation day.

Many students will find that they have extra time to work on their term projects if they finish their other work early. Because they want to work on their projects, this provides an incentive for them to complete their classwork as quickly as possible and a ready-made sponge activity for students who do finish early. However, not all students will be able to do this. For this reason and to communicate the value of individual research and creative work, weekly project days must be given, no matter how attractive that "empty" day looks as an opportunity to make up for lost time on unit activities. Particularly for those students who need more time to complete their unit work and reading and for those who have limited resources outside of school for accomplishing their investigations, the project day is an absolute necessity if they are to be able to pursue their projects. In fact, sometimes unit time should be sacrificed to project time, such as when a student wishes to schedule a short presentation on some day other than a project day. Most unit schedules can accommodate minor intrusions such as this and project days can remain open for research, editing, and conferences.

Types of Projects

Group projects. Most projects will be individual ones, but quite often at least one group of students will approach the teacher about doing a term project together. Sometimes this may take the form of a newspaper or a piece of descriptive or experimental research. There is no real reason why group projects cannot take place if certain modifications in requirements are made. First, the group size should be limited to two to four students. Anything more than this in a secondary classroom quickly turns into a crowd. Too large a group can result in distracting noise levels during work time or can make it difficult or impossible for group members to find time to meet together to work. Second, the scale of the project should be increased so that, instead of three people splitting the work of one, three people are doing the work of three. Finally, each group member should turn in a proposal sheet that outlines the group's work in general and the student's work in particular so that it is clear how the work is to be divided up right from the start.

Class projects. Another type of project is most valuable for classes with little experience working on their own. Quite often, students in these classes need the security of having everyone working on similar projects so that they can share ideas and support more easily. An example of this type of project would be a situation in which every student is required to write and illustrate a children's book (see figure 6.6). The subtasks and products would be fairly clearly defined, but the content and appearance of the books would be highly individual. Working on class projects helps provide a sense of community for many students and makes it easier for students to transfer the solutions of others to their own work. These are valuable commodities when one is teaching a class that is extremely dependent and inexperienced. As soon as possible, however, students should be weaned away from these types of projects into more individual ones. The time frame from this process, as always, is a matter of the classroom teacher's judgment, since no one knows a class as well as the teacher.

Three-ring circuses. A third type of project is the three-ring circus project. This is a project that involves the entire class in achieving a goal of such large proportions that it must be divided into segments and shared by the entire class. A science or Renaissance fair would be an example of this type of project. The sponsors of the fair decide what types of work must be accomplished at all levels and have students sign up for the type of work they wish to do. For a fair, there might be a publicity group, a props and scenery group, a programming group, and a personnel group among others. Each of these groups would have a set of subtasks to complete to receive credit for a term project. As in a regular term project, the subtasks should provide internal structure and definite requirements while allowing groups and group members to place their individual stamp on the

◇ *Storybook Project Plan*

This project plan was developed by Debbie Robbins for a low-skills English class. Many of the students habitually cut classes and were chronic underachievers; they had little or no self-management abilities and little interest in school or school activities. But when they were working on this project, there was 100 percent attendance on project days.

1. Go to the elementary school and meet the student for whom you will be writing.

2. Interview the student to find out what kind of books he/she likes to read and why.

3. Write a book proposal.

4. Get approval.

5. Write a rough draft of book.

6. Take draft to editing group.

7. Revise draft and prepare final draft copy.

8. Return to elementary school to present books to students and to participate in story hour.

Fig. 6.6.

projects. Three-ring circus projects require a great deal of careful planning on the teacher's part and can easily cause disorientation as the great day approaches. They also require a great deal of self-discipline and group interaction ability on the students' part. This type of project is best reserved for classes with plenty of experience in self-management, cooperation, and term project work.

Individualized Assistance

For most students, the project plan and subtasks will provide more than enough guidance as they work on their projects. But sometimes students get themselves into unusual situations that require some additional, individualized assistance from the teacher. This assistance is easy to give, however, because the teacher has more open time to work with individual students. Individualized assistance can run the gamut from making peace with an offended school staff member to getting permission for special privileges such as using a school telephone, finding a mentor with specialized knowledge, or simply sitting down with a student to hash out a trouble spot.

It is unusual for young people to conduct original investigations, create original work, or make inquiries beyond the traditional school or library arena. Many adults, who have all been to school and know exactly what ought to be going on there, have difficulty accepting requests and inquiries from students. They just do not understand why a student, a minor, a *kid* is asking questions out of school. (Where are the teachers, for heaven's sake, and what are they paid for, anyhow?)

Deciphering Linear B

Linear B was a mysterious script found at Knossos on Crete and at Pylos on the Greek mainland. Only seventy-three symbols of the script were available to aid linguists in their efforts to break the code of the script, and nobody even knew what language the symbols represented. For many years the key to deciphering this script eluded professionals, but it was found by a young British architect named Michael Ventris. Ventris adopted Linear B as a hobby when he was still a young teenager and began to learn everything he could about decipherment and Linear B on his own. He made original contributions to the decipherment when he was still a teenager, but he had to conceal his age to get his work published in professional journals. After all, everybody knows that kids can't do original research!

Because they do not understand, they will often become suspicious of a student who claims to be doing original research and will refuse the use of special resources out of hand unless the teacher steps in to mediate. Most people are happy to help students in their work, but every once in a while, some intransigents crop up. When this happens, there is an excellent opportunity to teach students about good manners and ways to make formal requests. They can be coached in how to explain their project needs and how to request assistance in person, over the telephone, or by letter. Role-playing is good practice for personal interviews and telephone calls in particular. Usually this is enough to break down barriers of adult prejudice, but occasionally the teacher, as a certified adult and school official, has to intercede. Even this situation can be turned to an advantage, though, because in acting as an intercessor, the teacher provides one more basis for a positive relationship with the student and demonstrates one more way to find out.

As stated earlier in this chapter, students are often quite inexperienced in the structure and customs of the adult world and are therefore ignorant of many of the opportunities and resources available outside the classroom. When a student comes up with a project that is unusual enough that the usual resources are not adequate, the teacher can use his or her greater experience to help that student find a mentor or alternative source of information. There are many places to search for mentors and sources, but a set of three questions suggested by Alden Todd's book are probably the best place to begin. They are as follows:

1.   Who would know?

2.   Who would care?

3.   Who would care enough to put it in print?[6]

It may not always be necessary to ask all three questions, but a telephone book, a set of good community contacts, and a detective's instincts can help teachers track down mentors and special agencies and resources for those students who need them.

Finally, some students do not have the experience to successfully take responsibility for their project process. These students need some extra reminders and some special help made available to them. For these students, it may be necessary for the teacher to check with them every few days to find out where they are in completing their subtasks and to articulate for them where they need to be and how they can get there. It may be necessary to give them extra encouragement to push on and extra feedback on how they are doing. It is often a good idea to make as many of their resources as possible easily and readily available right in the classroom, if at all possible. These students are often overly passive and dependent and need to be pushed out of the nest a bit at a time. Over time, though, the need for this extra attention should diminish as these students gain self-confidence and skills in self-management.

On the other side of the coin, there are some students who need some help reining in their ambitions a bit so that they can achieve their goals. These students usually require a few short conferences to help them in their planning and to keep them in step with their plans. They are often the same students who require special additional resources and mentors for their projects, and their needs can often be met simply by finding them what they need.

CONCLUSION

The beauty of term projects is multifaceted. They are easily managed because students want to do them. Because students want to do them, they minimize boredom and aggravation in the classroom and provide incentive for students to involve themselves in the subject matter. Because they are loosely structured, it is relatively easy for teachers to give timely help to those students who really need it and for students to express and develop their own individuality in style and knowledge. They encourage students to become self-starters who can initiate and manage their own learning, which prepares them not only for more advanced study, but for life outside of school as well. And after all, isn't that what school is about?

NOTES

1. Paul L. Dressel and Mary Magdala Thompson, *Independent Study* (San Francisco, CA: Jossey-Bass, 1973) 7.

2. June Cox et al., *Educating Able Learners: Programs and Promising Practices* (Austin, TX: University of Texas Press, 1985) 24.

3. Ibid., 26.

4. Alden Todd, *Finding Facts Fast: How to Find Out What You Want and Need to Know* (Berkeley, CA: Ten Speed Press, 1979) 14.

5. C. June Maker, *Teaching Models in Education of the Gifted* (Rockville, MD: Aspen Publishers, 1982) 6.

6. Todd, 10.

BIBLIOGRAPHY

Anderson, Margaret A. "Assessing and Providing for Gifted Children with Special Needs in Reading and Library Skills." In *Teaching Gifted Learners in Regular Classrooms*. Ed. Roberta M. Milgram. Springfield, IL: Chas. C. Thomas, 1989.

Barzun, Jacques, and Henry F. Graff. *The Modern Researcher, Fourth Edition*. San Diego, CA: Harcourt Brace Jovanovich, 1985.

Bohan, Harry. "Mathematical Connections: Free Rides for Kids." *The Arithmetic Teacher* 38 (3) (November 1990): 10-14.

Boyer, Ernest L. *High School: A Report of Secondary Education in America*. New York: Harper Colophon Books, Harper & Row, 1983.

Cox, June, et al. *Educating Able Learners: Programs and Promising Practices*. Austin, TX: University of Texas Press, 1985.

Dressel, Paul L., and Mary Magdala Thompson. *Independent Study*. San Francisco, CA: Jossey-Bass, 1973.

Everly, Pamela. "The Kid Is the One Taking the Class." *Middle School Journal* 21 (3) (January 1989): 33-35.

Krapp, JoAnn Vergona. "Teaching Research Skills: A Critical-Thinking Approach." *School Library Journal* 34 (January 1988): 32-35.

Maker, C. June. *Teaching Models in Education of the Gifted*. Rockville, MD: Aspen Publishers, 1982.

Parker, Jeanette Plauche. *Instructional Strategies for Teaching the Gifted*. Boston: Allyn and Bacon, 1989.

Polette, Nancy. *The Research Books for Gifted Programs*. O'Fallon, MO: Book Lures, 1984.

Polette, Nancy. *Three R's for the Gifted: Reading, Writing, and Research*. Littleton, CO: Libraries Unlimited, 1982.

Rogers, Carl R. *Freedom to Learn*. Columbus, OH: Merrill Publishing, 1969.

Settle, Mickey, and Michel Boillot. *Turbo and Apple Pascal: Programming and Problem Solving*. St. Paul, MN: West Publishing, 1987.

Todd, Alden. *Finding Facts Fast: How to Find Out What You Want and Need to Know*. Berkeley, CA: Ten Speed Press, 1979.

Part 2
Applications

— 7 —
A First Quarter in Language Arts

INTRODUCTION

The fact that there are six chapters preceding the "Applications" part of this book should be a clue to the reader that switching from a traditional classroom model to a Rewrite model is not something to be done hastily. Not all of the suggestions and techniques described in the first section will be applicable to every classroom. Some may have to be modified or even discarded to fit the particular needs of teacher, students, subject matter, and physical resources. Careful consideration of these elements must be weighed against the value of the procedures and techniques in the model classroom of part 1.

It is best to make the switch at a natural break point in the school year—at quarter midterm or at the beginning of a new quarter—to avoid the problem of combining two different methods of record keeping. Any teachers wishing to revamp their traditional classrooms would do well to start planning a few weeks ahead of time and set a date for changeover at the beginning of the next quarter or just after midterm grades have gone out. This planning period gives teachers the opportunity to work out most potential problems ahead of time. The planning period also provides time for teachers to accustom themselves to the new system so that they will be relatively comfortable with it from the start. It may even be possible to field test certain procedures and techniques before the changeover. It is important that the teacher be as familiar and comfortable with the new model as possible from the start since there will be some rough moments, particularly at the beginning, and students will automatically look to the teacher for an instant solution. There may not be an instant solution, but the more familiar the teacher is with the new model, the easier it will be to adapt and modify it as needed.

The following four units are intended as an example of how to ease a class into the new system over the course of one quarter. By the time the quarter is over, both teacher and students should be quite comfortable with the Rewrite model and should be able to begin modifying it even further to fit special needs. The subject matter in these units has been kept deliberately simple—junior high language arts—so that no one need have specialized knowledge to understand the content of the units. This is important so that the reader will be able to look beyond the actual subject matter and concentrate on how the model has been applied. It should be easy to see how different types of activities and procedures can be managed in the Rewrite context and to analogize these applications to other subject areas and situations.

In figure 7.1, page 112, the quarterly planning grid for this section summarizes the course structure and the assignments and activities of each unit. Notice that the first two units, the mini-unit and the biographical sketch unit, are not two-week units. This is to allow the teacher to quickly introduce the new course structures in the one-week mini-unit and to provide extra guidance through modeling and teacher-student interaction in the three-week biographical unit when students are learning to actually apply what they learned in the mini-unit. The last two units are standard two-week units that will help both teacher and students accustom themselves to a new routine. Once this is accomplished, more liberties can be taken in planning future unit schedules and activities.

UNIT TASK #1 Mini-Unit Test on Procedures	SKILL#1a Procedures, Roles, Information Sources	VOCAB #1a classroom Terminology	READING-WK #1 Reference Sheet	TERM PROJECT SUBTASK #1 Proposal
UNIT TASK #2	SKILL#2a Introductions	VOCAB #2a Honey + vinegar Questions	READING-WK #2 Sample Articles from Current	TERM PROJECT SUBTASK #2 Approval
Autobiographical Sketches	SKILL# 2b The writing Process	VOCAB #2b Writing Process Terms	READING-WK #3 Biographies, People, interviews, obits, +	TERM PROJECT SUBTASK #3 Sources + working Bibliography
	SKILL#2c Effective Editing	VOCAB #2c Constructive Editors' Comments	READING-WK #4 Who's Who	TERM PROJECT SUBTASK #4 Notes + Organizing
UNIT TASK #3 Narration I: Personal Experience	SKILL#3a Sentences as Whole Thoughts	VOCAB #3a Thesaurus Skills #1	READING-WK #5 Charles by Shirley Jackson +	TERM PROJECT SUBTASK #5 Rough Draft
	SKILL#3b Paraphrases and Partial Quotes	VOCAB #3b Thesaurus Skills #2	READING-WK #6 outside recreational reading	TERM PROJECT SUBTASK #6 Editing Group
UNIT TASK #4 Narration II: Excuses, Excuses!	SKILL#4a SCAMPER Thinking Strategies	VOCAB #4a Similes	READING-WK #7 Tall tales, legends + other types	TERM PROJECT SUBTASK #7 Final Draft
	SKILL#4b Reported Speech	VOCAB #4b Thesaurus Skills #3	READING-WK #8 of exaggerated literary forms	TERM PROJECT SUBTASK #8 Presentation

Fig. 7.1. Quarter planning calendar.

MAKING THE SWITCH: AN INTRODUCTORY MINI-UNIT

For most, if not all students, this model will be an entirely new experience. They will probably feel somewhat uncomfortable within its constraints and demands and try to fall back into the traditional roles to which they have been accustomed. This unit is intended to give an example of how to make the transition smooth and nonthreatening. Some teachers may decide to take the material in this unit verbatim and use it in their classes, but it is intended only as an example for those teachers wishing to construct an introductory unit for their particular versions of the model.

The introductory unit is a mini-unit in the sense that it lasts only one week and requires students to complete one skill and one vocabulary module, a sample reading assignment, a term project proposal, and a unit task. The introductory unit gives students an experiential way to learn about their new type of classroom as well as an object lesson on how much they can achieve when they apply themselves. It lays a positive foundation for the rest of the school year by making sure that students know how to operate on their own within the environment and how to find out on their own what they need to know.

This may seem to be a rather large chunk of a quarter grade to devote to what appears to be a classroom management system, but to quote Jean Hopper, a high school psychology teacher who has used Rewrite for several years, "The interaction in the classroom is at least as important as the subject. Learning to take responsibility, get along with others, and become an adult in our culture is what we are learning."[1] By taking the time to teach students what is expected of them and giving them the basic skills and information to begin to achieve it, the teacher is laying the foundation for better learning not just for the rest of the school year, but for a lifetime. Also, seeing how quickly that first record sheet fills up can be quite a shot in the arm for even the most passive student.

For some teachers, even this one week may seem like too great a sacrifice of valuable subject matter time, so they may choose to compress it into two or three days. Many teachers opt for this variation, particularly when they are starting to use the new model at the beginning of the year since many school districts schedule only a partial week for the first week of school. Many times this partial week is followed by a long Labor Day weekend which is a real speed bump when a teacher is trying to get some momentum going at the beginning of a new year. The mini-unit makes productive use of those few, odd days and helps orient students more thoroughly at a time when they are often overwhelmed by a collection of new teachers, classes, rules, and procedures. Even if they don't retain all of the specifics from the mini-unit, they will have at least internalized and/or collected enough information on how the classroom runs to be able to review the procedures and terminology for themselves when there is a problem. If they are unable to find the information for themselves, they will at least be able to ask the teacher specific questions to find out what they need to know.

Because the mini-unit runs so quickly, it is a good idea to prepare all of the materials ahead of time and have them available in the current handouts file. The teacher will not be constantly besieged by students needing the next handout, and the students will get the idea that they need to take the initiative to get up and go get what they need. Among the materials needed for this unit are reference sheets containing information on the material covered in the skill and vocabulary modules, the support modules themselves, a unit checklist, a term project proposal sheet, and a reading response card or sheet. Class job descriptions and applications could also be included with the handouts. These materials can either be given out as they are assigned and explained or collated and distributed all at once at the beginning of the unit. It is often a good idea to have several extra mini-units on hand for new students who come in during the course of the school year. These can be used as orientation packets for new students.

The materials in this mini-unit are based on the hypothetical class used as an example in the first chapters of the book. Included are a unit task checklist and a sample unit test. The skill and vocabulary modules are not included because they are merely shorter versions of the unit test. The goals and objectives are listed here and are followed by the unit calendars and materials (see figures 7.2 through 7.5, pages 115 through 121).

Goals

1. Students will become familiar with the classroom environment including paper flow, teacher and student roles, and record keeping.

2. Students will learn where to find information on classroom procedures.

3. Students will begin to take an active role in their learning, behavior, and time management, and in the daily running of the classroom.

4. Students will find a topic of long-term interest to pursue for a term project.

Objectives

1. Students will achieve 80 percent mastery on the skill work sheet to demonstrate a working knowledge of classroom procedures and record-keeping techniques.

2. Students will achieve 80 percent mastery on the vocabulary work sheet to demonstrate their understanding of classroom terminology.

3. Students will achieve at least a C on the unit test to demonstrate their ability to apply their knowledge of classroom procedures and personnel in hypothetical situations.

4. Students will read a short story or article of at least fifteen pages and complete a reading response card.

5. Students will choose a topic for a term project and properly complete a proposal form.

6. Students will practice personal time and behavior management by completing all of the steps on the checklist and using their in-class work time successfully.

Content

Unit Task

Test on classroom procedures and terms

Skill Module

Procedures, personnel, record-keeping and information sources

Vocabulary Module

Classroom terminology

Reading

Read an article or short story pertaining to course subject matter and fill out a response card

Term Project

Fill out and turn in a term project proposal

This unit is scheduled for five days, but can be compressed if desired.

(Text continues on page 122.)

DAY 1	DAY 2	DAY 3	DAY 4	DAY 5
- Introductions - Class Orientation - Set up Student Files - Go over Syllabus - Pass out Checklists - Pass out Job Applications	- Review from yesterday - Post the due dates - Introduce Skill #1 & Vocab #1 - Introduce Term Projects - Worktime	- Return Graded Work - Review Revision Policy - Mark Recordsheets - Hand out Reading Response Cards - Worktime	- Return Graded Work - Review Recordsheets Worktime	All work due in —— Unit Test —— Project Day

Fig. 7.2. Mini-unit calendar.

Mini-Unit Activities Plan

Day One

    Teacher and student introductions

    Orientation on class rules, jobs, and procedures

    Orientation on classroom use and materials

    Pass out student files and record sheets

    Staple in record sheets and color-code files

    Brief overview of quarter syllabus

    Pass out unit checklist and store in folders

    Make job applications available all week

    No homework

    Collect files

Fig. 7.3.

(Fig. 7.3 continues on page 116.)

Fig. 7.3.—*Continued*

Day Two

Pass out files

Review unit checklist and post due dates

Pass out skills and vocabulary modules

Pass out proposal sheets and explain term projects

Student work time

No specific homework

Collect files

Day Three

Pass out files

Hand back graded work

Demonstrate how to mark record sheets

Answer questions

Pass out reading response cards and explain

Student work time

No specific homework

Collect files

Day Four

Pass out files

Return graded work

Review record sheet procedures

Answer questions

Student work time

Homework: study for unit task test

Collect files

Day Five

Pass out files

All unit work due in

Administer unit test

If possible, grade as a class to review

Mark record sheets

Extra time may be given for reading or project work

No homework

Collect files

◇ *Language Arts*
Orientation Unit
Student Checklist

This sheet is a checklist to help you keep track of where you are in the orientation unit. I will go over it with you in class to answer any questions you may have, but you may also use it on your own so that you will know what to expect during this unit. If you finish an item on the checklist ahead of time, please feel free to go ahead with the next items if at all possible. If it is not possible, you may use the extra time to work on your term project or on your reading.

_____ 1. Attend the class orientation session on the first day of class. Make sure you understand the parts of the reference sheet that are covered in class. If you have any questions, please ask.

_____ 2. Set up your student file with your record sheet and name in the proper places.

_____ 3. Get a job application if you are interested in being an aide. Fill it out and turn it in to the "In" box.

_____ 4. Complete the vocabulary module and turn it in to the in box on or before the posted due date.

_____ 5. Complete the skill module and turn it in to the in box on or before the posted due date.

_____ 6. Fill out the term project proposal sheet and turn it in on or before the posted due date.

_____ 7. Complete the reading assignment and fill out a reading response card. Turn in the card on or before the posted due date.

_____ 8. Record all of your earned credit on your record sheet and store your returned work in your file.

_____ 9. Take and pass the orientation test. Record your credit on your record sheet.

Fig. 7.4.

Language Arts
Orientation Unit
Unit Test

Part I: What's wrong with this picture?

In this section, you will find short descriptions of common classroom situations. In each situation, the student involved has misunderstood one or more classroom procedures. Read through each scenario and tell what mistake the student has made and what he or she should have done. Keep your answers as short as possible, but be clear in your explanations.

1. Sam has just finished his skill module a day early. He puts it in his file folder so it will be ready when the teacher collects the assignment tomorrow.

2. Georgia didn't get her student file this morning. She immediately went to the library aide to find out what happened to it.

3. Lisa got an R on her vocabulary module. She isn't happy with the grade so she throws the paper away.

4. Russ got his paper back four days ago and is just starting to revise it.

5. Max's project presentation is ready. He shows up to give his presentation and asks the teacher for a videocassette recorder so he can show the videotape he made.

6. Sue's unit task paper isn't done and the due date has arrived. She keeps the paper to work on it so she can turn it in tomorrow.

7. Pat's been absent for two days. He asks the teacher, "What did I miss? Can I get the handouts for the days I missed?"

Fig. 7.5.

Fig. 7.5.—*Continued*

8. Anna turned in her skill module four days early and wants to see what she got, but the management aides haven't passed any papers back today. She asks the teacher to find out where her paper is.

9. Paul is making a bulletin board display for his project presentation. He's scheduled the bulletin board with the teacher, but needs supplies to make the display. He asks one of the management aides to help him get the paper and markers he needs.

10. Jackie just got back her unit task graded B on it. She fills in two squares on her record sheet.

Part II: Matching

Listed below you will find a set of classroom terms and a set of definitions. Match each definition with the correct item from the terms list by writing the letter of the term in the blank beside the definition.

a.	management aide	k.	"In" box
b.	absent eyes aide	l.	"Out" box
c.	vocabulary aide	m.	reading points
d.	bulletin board aide	n.	response card
e.	attendance aide	o.	term project
f.	library aide	p.	proposal
g.	unit task	q.	approval
h.	skill module	r.	notes and outline
i.	vocabulary module	s.	presentation
j.	current handout file	t.	student file

_____ 1.   information from project research

_____ 2.   someone who gives makeup vocabulary quizzes

_____ 3.   a quarter-long activity

_____ 4.   someone who maintains classroom displays

(Figure 7.5 continues on page 120.)

Fig. 7.5.—Continued

_____ 5. something you fill out to tell about your reading

_____ 6. someone who keeps track of absences and tardies

_____ 7. someone who gets handouts for absent students

_____ 8. a weekly assignment to help with your word power

_____ 9. someone who checks out books from the class library

_____ 10. an assignment that receives a letter grade

_____ 11. a weekly assignment that teaches you a skill

_____ 12. the place where you get a new work sheet

_____ 13. a description of a prospective term project

_____ 14. the way you share your term project with others

_____ 15. where you keep your record sheet

_____ 16. credit that is earned at the rate of one point per page

_____ 17. someone who passes out and collects student files

_____ 18. where you turn in an assignment

_____ 19. where you pick up a graded assignment

_____ 20. how the teacher lets you know you can do your project

Part III: Record Keeping

On the next page, you will find an empty record sheet. Use the grades below to fill it in correctly, then tell what grade the student has earned for the quarter.

Unit tasks: A,A,B,A

Skills: 7 passed

Vocabulary: 8 passed

Reading points: 388 pages

Response cards: 5 completed

Term project: all but presentation

Grade for quarter _____

Fig. 7.5.—*Continued*

UNIT TASKS	SKILLS	VOCAB	READING	PROJECT	
16 / 15	8	8	351-400pp.	PRESENT PBLCATN	A
14 / 13	7	7	301-350pp.	FINAL DRAFT	B
12 / 11	6	6	251-300pp.	EDITING GROUP	B
10 / 9	5	5	201-250pp.	ROUGH DRAFT	C
8 / 7	4	4	151-200pp.	NOTETAKE & ORGANIZE	C
6 / 5	3	3	101-150pp.	WORKING BIBLIO.	D
4 / 3	2	2	51-100 pp.	TEACHER APPROVAL	D
2 / 1	1	1	1-50 pp.	PROP. SBMISTN	F

RESPONSE CARDS

ESTABLISHING COMFORT ZONES: AUTOBIOGRAPHICAL SKETCHES UNIT

If students are to have positive attitudes toward the processes of the subject area, they must be given the opportunity to manipulate it in as comfortable an environment as possible. In this unit, this comfort zone is established and maintained by keeping the task deliberately short (no more than one side of one page per sketch), showing students several examples of professionally written auto-biographical and biographical sketches, allowing them to share ideas, insights, and solutions in the prewriting groups, the editing groups and the revision groups, giving them frequent feedback on their performance through rubrics and editing groups, and giving them the opportunity to correct and improve their work several times during the unit, both before and after they turn in their work for grading.

If students are to develop positive attitudes about their relationships and roles in the classroom, they must also be given the opportunity to do this in an encouraging and comfortable atmosphere. Several activities provide this. The brainstorming session allows them to contribute in a constructive manner, the interviewing session to get acquainted legitimately with a classmate, the introduction to practice a valuable social skill, and the small group sessions to get to know other students as friends and colleagues. The assignment itself gives them the opportunity to introduce themselves as they wish to be introduced.

It looks like a lot for students to learn in three short weeks, but nearly all of their class time will be spent in active interaction with the subject matter (see the calendar in figure 7.6, page 124). They will be learning several things at once all through the unit. For instance, when they are working in their prewriting groups choosing formats, they will be learning about the prewriting stage of the writing process, a strategy for prewriting, how to get along in a group, and how to accomplish a specific task in a group. They will also be getting acquainted with several of their classmates at once. This type of parallel instruction is easily accomplished within the Rewrite model because its flexibility allows for experiential learning and multiple, simultaneous activities.

In planning the actual daily schedules and management of the unit (see figure 7.7, pages 125-27), the teacher should take several things into consideration. Don't ask students to undertake a task without giving them the tools for it. Introduce the skill module on introductions and the vocabulary module "Honey and Vinegar Questions" before actually asking them to interview a live subject. Brainstorm with them on questions that are both appropriate and revealing so that they will have a data base of questions to use when they interview their classmates and model an introduction for them before asking them to get up and introduce another student in front of the class. Remember that in most cases, students are not incapable, they are merely inexperienced.

The unit is three weeks long instead of the usual two so that there will be time for extra direction and modeling from the teacher and correction of any problems encountered in balancing time and behavior against the demands of the unit. The unit ends at quarter midterm, which gives teacher and students a chance to walk through a small-scale Judgment Day process in preparation for figuring quarter grades at the end of the quarter.

The goals, objectives, and content of the unit follow. Notice that there are several intermediate due dates for the unit task on the unit calendar. This is to allow the teacher more opportunities to provide extra guidance and modeling during the transition from a traditional classroom to a Rewrite classroom and to spotlight the various stages in the writing process.

Goals

1. Students will learn the basics of the writing process.

2. Students will become acquainted with their classmates both as friends and colleagues.

3. Students will learn to use the classroom procedures and resources they learned about in the previous unit.

Objectives

1. Students will write a short autobiographical sketch in a format of their own choosing to introduce themselves to their classmates.

2. Students will demonstrate their ability to introduce someone to a group by introducing a classmate to the rest of the class.

3. Students will practice simple group processes by participating successfully in small groups with specific activity instructions.

4. Students will demonstrate their understanding of higher order writing concerns by successfully editing their peers' papers using a rubric.

5. Students will demonstrate their understanding of lower order concerns by assisting their peers in proofreading their second drafts in an editing group.

6. Students will demonstrate their understanding of the editor's function by writing constructive comments on the papers they edit.

7. Students will demonstrate their mastery of the basic writing process by successfully completing all steps on the unit checklist.

8. Students will demonstrate their understanding of revision and the class revision process by revising their graded papers.

9. Students will become familiar with at least three different forms of autobiographical and biographical writing.

Content

Unit Task

Write a short autobiographical sketch using one of the suggested formats.

Skill Modules

1. "Interviews and Introductions"
2. "The Writing Process"
3. "Effective Editing"

Vocabulary Modules

1. "Honey and Vinegar Questions"
2. "Writing Process Terms"
3. "Constructive Editor's Comments"

Reading

Sample articles from *Current Biography*, *People*, newspaper and magazine interviews, obituaries, *Reader's Digest*, and *Who's Who*.

Term Project

Students should be able to complete their note-taking and get a start on their rough drafts by the time this unit is ended.

Not all of the unit materials are included in this section. Only those materials that illustrate a particular solution to a problem or that provide context for the unit content are given (see figures 7.8 through 7.13, pages 127-33). This includes the unit task checklist (figure 7.8, pages 127-28) and rubric (figure 7.11, page 131) for context and the first skill and vocabulary modules (figures 7.12 and 7.13, pages 132 and 133). The first skill module, "Introductions," is an example of an open-ended activity used in the skill category. Criteria for grading are set in two ways. A numerical requirement for the quantity and types of questions required for interviewing are specified along with time constraints and requirements for a public introduction are enumerated. The vocabulary module, "Honey and Vinegar Questions," shows how vocabulary practice can draw on personal experience and allow for individual creativity while still having specific requirements for mastery. Both units taken together show how skills and vocabulary/knowledge modules can be scheduled for mutual reinforcement of concepts.

(Text continues on page 134.)

	DAY 1	DAY 2	DAY 3	DAY 4	DAY 5
WEEK 1	Intro Sk. #1 — Intro Vocab #1 — Student Worktime	Intro Unit Task - Brainstorm Questions - Interview Pairs	Find focus for introductions Compose + practice introductions Classmate Introductions Assign Prewriting Groups	Prewriting Groups Meet Worktime	→ Due → Due Project Day
	DAY 6	**DAY 7**	**DAY 8**	**DAY 9**	**DAY 10**
WEEK 2	Intro Sk. #2 — Intro Vocab. #2 — Worktime Homework: Rough Draft	Editing Groups Rubric Practice Worktime. Homework: Second Rough Draft	Student Workday	Editing Groups Worktime Homework: Final Drafts due on day 11	→ Due → Due Project Day Homework: Final Draft due on day 11
	DAY 11	**DAY 12**	**DAY 13**	**DAY 14**	**DAY 15**
WEEK 3	Intro Sk #3 — Intro Vocab #3 — Final Drafts due Worktime	Workday	Repair Groups revise papers + work on publishing	Workday	→ Due → Due Revision + Publishing due Project Day

Fig. 7.6. Sketches calendar.

Sketches Activities Plan

Day One

Introduce skill module 1: "Interviews and Introductions." It may be helpful to play a tape of a radio or television interview for the students. Talk shows are full of them.

Introduce vocabulary module 1: "Honey and Vinegar Questions."

Use the rest of the class time for student work time.

Homework: work on assignments, reading, or term projects.

Day Two

Introduce unit task to class.

Brainstorm interview questions on the board or overhead.

Divide students into interviewing pairs and give students 25 minutes to complete their interviews.

Day Three

Ask students to go over their notes and find a focus for a two-minute oral introduction to be given the next day in class.

Ask students to work in their pairs to put together and practice the introductions.

Have students introduce their partners to the class.

If there is time, assign students to prewriting groups. Instruct them to look over the various biographical formats and choose which one they would like to use to publish their autobiographical sketches at the end of the unit.

Day Four

Allow prewriting groups to finish their work. The rest of the hour should be used for student work time.

Remind students of the upcoming due dates for skills and vocabulary and of the term project work time tomorrow.

Day Five

Vocabulary and skill modules should be in the in box by the end of the hour.

Give vocabulary quiz if desired.

Term project work day.

Day Six (Week Two)

Introduce skill module 2: "The Writing Process."

Introduce vocabulary 2: "Writing Process Terms."

Student work time.

Homework: have a rough draft of sketch ready for tomorrow.

Fig. 7.7.

(Figure 7.7 continues on page 126.)

Fig. 7.7.—*Continued*

Day Seven

Divide students into editing groups. Hand out rubrics and explain their use. Review the higher order concerns, go over a simple editing group procedure of your choice, and let students work in their groups.

As groups finish editing, students should go to work on skills, vocabulary, a second rough draft, reading, or term project work.

Homework: have a second rough draft ready by day nine.

Day Eight

Student work day.

Homework: second rough draft due tomorrow.

Day Nine

Second editing groups meet. Review lower order concerns with them as well as the editing procedure. As groups complete their editing work, students may choose from individual activities.

Remind students that skill and vocabulary modules are due tomorrow and that Friday is a term project day.

Homework: final drafts due on day eleven.

Day Ten

Skill and vocabulary modules are due today. Give vocabulary quiz if needed. Term project work day.

Homework: final draft due at next meeting.

Day Eleven (Week Three)

Introduce skill module 3: "Effective Editing" and vocabulary module 3: "Constructive Editor's Comments."

Final drafts are due in.

Student work day.

Day Twelve

Student work day.

If students are finished with the modules, they may work on reading or term projects while the teacher is involved in grading the sketches.

Day Thirteen

Return graded sketches.

Review the revision policy and explain how revision is a part of the writing process.

Fig. 7.7.—*Continued*

Return students to original prewriting groups, now repair groups. Have them repair their papers together and transfer them into the final format they had planned on for publishing as a small magazine, tabloid, or bulletin board. These should be turned in by day fifteen.

Day Fourteen

Student work day. Repair groups are still meeting or students are working on modules, reading, or projects.

Remind students that publishable sketches are due tomorrow along with modules and that tomorrow is a term project work day.

Day Fifteen

Skill and vocabulary modules are due. Give quiz if needed. Term project work day. Meet with management and bulletin board aides to plan publishing of sketches so that everyone can read about everyone else.

Today is quarter midterm. Either today or at the next class meeting, go over the record sheets with the students to make sure they are accurate for midterm grading. Explain how midterm grades are estimated on the record sheet by compressing the total points by half.

 Language Arts
Autobiographical Sketch
Unit Checklist

Now that you've had the chance to learn about the course, it's time to learn about the class. In this unit, you will have the opportunity to introduce yourself to the rest of the class by writing an autobiographical sketch. An autobiographical sketch is a *short* way of telling about yourself and your experiences. Since everyone in the class will be writing and publishing a sketch about themselves, you will have the opportunity to find out who your classmates are and what their interests and talents are. In this way, you will be able to find some new friends and become more comfortable with your classmates. You will also be learning about one of the basic processes we will be studying this year, the writing process. This is a method of writing that you will be able to use in all of your classes whenever there is a written assignment. Complete all of the steps below to be eligible for full credit in this unit.

_____ 1. Attend the introductory session on interviewing and finding a focus or get notes from someone who did.

_____ 2. Use the brainstorm list of interview questions from the introductory session along with any other questions you think would be valuable and interview one of your classmates. Keep the interview *under ten minutes* and take notes on your classmate's answers.

Fig. 7.8.

(Figure 7.8 continues on page 128.)

Fig. 7.8. — *Continued*

_____ 3. Use your notes to help you put together a *two-minute* oral introduction of your classmate. In order to do this, you will have to boil down all of your notes into a basic focus so that you can give the class a reasonably accurate impression of your interviewee. Then, introduce your subject to the class.

_____ 4. Meet in a prewriting group and choose a format for the sketches you will be doing on yourselves. Choose from among the options I have provided for you or come up with one of your own. Here are some possibilities for you to choose from:

> *Who's Who in the Student Body*
>
> *Current Teen Biography*
>
> *People Magazine — Teen Edition*
>
> *Dream On: Don't You Wish You Were Me*
>
> *New York Times Obituaries*
>
> *Reminiscence: Looking Back*
>
> *Fantastic Journey: Life Stories*

_____ 5. Use your interview questions to interview yourself. Take notes. Mark the items you want to be sure to include in your sketch. Look them over and choose a focus for your paper. Then put the notes in a logical order. Write your first rough draft.

_____ 6. Take your rough draft to a peer editing group and use the rubric to edit for higher order concerns only.

_____ 7. Look over your editors' comments. Decide which ones you think are most helpful and try to revise your sketch using their advice. Take this second rough draft to a peer editing group and use the rubric to edit for both higher and lower order concerns.

_____ 8. Once again, check over your editors' remarks. Use them to improve your paper. Make any spelling, grammar, or format changes on your second rough draft and then write your final draft. Your final draft should be as error-free as you can make it. It should be either typed or clearly handwritten in ink and handed in on or before the due date.

_____ 9. When you receive your paper back, meet once again in your original small groups. Help one another to repair any errors in your papers and then prepare your papers for publication. When your group decides that their papers are ready for publication, turn them in to the "In" box. The bulletin board and management aides will help me display them.

Language Arts
Autobiographical Sketch
Prewriting Work Sheet

Prewriting is the first stage in the writing process. For this unit, you will do some of your prewriting in a group. In this group, you will share ideas and make choices about how you will publish the material you write for this unit task. When you receive your graded autobiographical sketch back, you will meet with this group again to prepare it for publishing. Here are the directions for your group's prewriting work.

1. You will be able to share the group's autobiographical sketches with the rest of the class at the end of this unit. To do this, you need to decide on a way to present, otherwise known as publish, your sketches so that the rest of the class can learn about each of you and you can learn about each of them.

2. Look over the examples of written sketches provided for you in the unit introduction and share any other ideas you may have for publishing sketches in other formats or media. List your group's ideas below.

3. Decide as a group what your most important considerations should be in choosing a format. List those considerations below.

4. Compare your brainstorm list and your considerations list. Cross out any brainstorm ideas that absolutely will not work for your group and then list the remaining ones here.

5. Once again, share your opinions on which ideas would work best for your group. Using any fair method, take a vote on the remaining ideas and choose your publishing format. Write the format below along with any items that will be necessary for your group to be able to do this. If you need to order special supplies from the teacher, do so as soon as possible. Turn in this sheet along with the rest of your prewriting, rough drafts, and final draft.

Fig. 7.9.

Language Arts
Autobiographical Sketch
Interview Work Sheet

1. In order to introduce someone, you must know who they are. As a class we will brainstorm a set of questions you could use to find out about one of your classmates. Write down the class's set of questions below.

2. Now put a check next to the questions you would like to ask a classmate when you interview him or her. Add any other questions that occur to you in the space below.

3. You will have ten minutes to interview a classmate. Use the space below to take notes on the information you get from asking your questions.

Fig. 7.10.

◇ *Language Arts*
Autobiographical Sketch
Rubric

An A paper has all or most of the following:

1. Prewriting, two rough drafts, and a final draft

2. Basic facts about you

3. At least five things about your interests, ambitions, and accomplishments

4. Simply organized so that it is easy to follow

5. Written in ink with margins and has few or no errors in grammar or spelling

A B paper has all or most of the following:

1. Prewriting, one rough draft, and a final draft

2. Basic facts about you

3. Three or four things about your interests, ambitions, and accomplishments

4. Reasonably easy to follow

5. Written in the correct format with a few minor errors in grammar or spelling

A C paper has all or most of the following:

1. Prewriting or one rough draft with a final draft

2. Two or three basic facts about you

3. Only two things about your interests, ambitions, and accomplishments

4. Some parts that are difficult to follow

5. A few errors in format, grammar, or spelling that interfere with understanding

A D paper has all or most of the following:

1. Only a final draft

2. Only one basic fact about you

3. Difficult to follow due to disorganization

4. Several errors in format, grammar, or spelling that make it difficult to understand

An F paper has all or most of the following:

1. Only a final draft

2. No basic facts about you

3. Difficult or impossible to understand

Fig. 7.11.

Language Arts
Autobiographical Sketch
Skill 1: Introductions

Introducing someone is a common activity. There are several types of introductions, some more formal than others. The one used most often is the social introduction in which names and basic information is exchanged. In this module, you will learn how to perform a more formal and detailed type of introduction used by public speakers.

For this public introduction, you first need to find out how much time you will have to do your introduction and what things your audience would find interesting about that person. Finally, you will need to get to know something about the person you will be introducing. These things include the following:

1. Basic personal information such as name, age, residence, etc.

2. Interests and accomplishments

3. Ambitions and goals

4. Unusual and interesting aspects of your subject

5. What the subject wishes people to know about

This last item is important if you are to avoid embarrassing the person you introduce.

A good way to find out the necessary information is to interview the person you are to introduce. This is done by asking your subject questions about all of the five areas listed above. Once you have gotten all the information you need, look over your notes and choose what you will share with your audience. Be sure to go over your introduction with your subject to check for accuracy.

For this skill module, you will need to interview and then introduce one of your classmates. You will have ten minutes in class to interview your classmate and two minutes to introduce them to the rest of the class. You will be given a short time to practice your introductions privately with your partner before you get up in front of the class.

Write down your set of questions on a separate sheet of paper. Make sure that you include at least two questions from each category of questions listed above. Leave room for notes so that you can write down your partner's answers. Use the notes to help you prepare your introduction. You may write out the introduction to take with you before the class or you may just write out a few notes, whichever makes you more comfortable with the situation. When you have finished your introduction, hand in your skill module to the in box for grading.

Fig. 7.12.

◇ *Language Arts*
Autobiographical Sketch
Vocabulary 1: Honey and Vinegar Questions

You can catch more flies with honey than you can with vinegar!

You may not be interested in catching flies, but when you're interviewing someone, you are interested in getting as much information from them as possible. Barbara Walters, one of the most gifted interviewers of our day, has a knack for asking difficult questions without offending her subject.

Ten rude questions are written below. Find a way to rewrite each question so it is polite enough to get the information you desire.

1. You've really gotten fat this year. Why? Problems at home?

2. Why do so many people hate you?

3. You're a lot younger than you look, aren't you?

4. You have a lot of weird interests, don't you?

5. Are you always such a motor mouth?

6. Is there anything useful you can do?

7. Your friends say you're really strange. Why?

8. Why do you wear such dopey clothes?

9. Is it true you have hardly any friends?

10. I heard you want to be a sculptor when you grow up. Why in the world would you want to do something like that?

Fig. 7.13.

ESTABLISHING THE ROUTINE: PERSONAL EXPERIENCE NARRATION UNIT

So far in this hypothetical first quarter, both teacher and students have been working hard to overcome old habits of role definition and dependence and to replace them with new expectations, roles, and procedures. This unit establishes a basic two-week unit routine that will provide the typical schedule for subsequent units in the course (see figures 7.14 and 7.15, pages 136-37). Once this basic schedule is internalized by teacher and students, a set of predictable expectations is in place that allows everyone to relax a bit and concentrate more on what they are doing and less on how they are doing it.

Skill and vocabulary modules are not supplied for this unit because they consist of generic types of grammar and thesaurus practice, but readers should note the importance attached to these concepts in the unit task rubric. The materials that are included in this unit are the unit task checklist and rubric (see figures 7.16 and 7.17, pages 138-40) and examples of two prewriting strategies. Often it is not possible to cover every support skill or knowledge area in a separate module. Putting this instruction within the process of the unit task provides a solution to this problem, particularly when the skill or knowledge area is directly related to the process itself. In this example, the prewriting strategy instruction in clustering and free writing (see figures 7.18 and 7.19, page 140) are worked into the unit task instruction, thus increasing the total number of skills presented in the unit. The goals and objectives for personal experience narration are listed as follows:

Goals

1. Students will learn about the narrative mode of discourse.

2. Students will learn about the concept of the sentence.

3. Students will learn about some new prewriting techniques.

4. Students will become familiar with a standard unit schedule.

5. Students will explore a personal experience and express it in written form.

Objectives

1. Students will participate in a class analysis of a short story about a personal experience that is appropriate to age levels and interests of the class.

2. Students will demonstrate their mastery of the clustering prewriting technique by producing a cluster on the phrase "school starts."

3. Students will demonstrate their mastery of free writing as a prewriting technique by producing three free writing samples of five minutes each.

4. Students will practice analysis and evaluation of prospective foci for their story by choosing a subject from their free writing, producing a set of five potential first lines, and then choosing a first line from that group.

5. Students will demonstrate their understanding of the narrative form by producing a short narrative of a personal experience using one of the format options given in the unit task.

6. Students will demonstrate mastery of basic sentence structure by passing the skill module with 80 percent correct.

7. Students will demonstrate mastery of indirect and partial quotations by passing the skill module with 80 percent correct.

8. Students will demonstrate understanding of the use of variety in word choice by passing the vocabulary modules with 80 percent correct.

9. Students will demonstrate their ability to use a thesaurus by passing the vocabulary modules with 80 percent correct.

10. Students will demonstrate their ability to apply their skill and vocabulary knowledge in their narrative piece by using a variety of "tags," having few or no errors in sentence structure, and successfully using the prewriting techniques to get ideas for writing.

11. Students will demonstrate their understanding of a standard Rewrite schedule by successfully completing all assignments on time.

Content

Unit Task

Tell the story of a personal experience from the first weeks of the school year.

Skill Modules

1. "Sentences as Whole Thoughts"
2. "Paraphrases and Partial Quotes"

Vocabulary Modules

1. Thesaurus skills: "Synonyms and Antonyms"
2. Thesaurus skills: "Choosing Thesaurus Categories"

Reading

A short story about a personal experience that is appropriate to age levels and interests of class.

Term Project

Students should be finished with their rough drafts and have attended a term project editing group by the end of this unit.

(Text continues on page 142.)

◇

	DAY 1	DAY 2	DAY 3	DAY 4	DAY 6
WEEK ONE	*Intro Sk #1* *Intro Vocab #1* ――― *Worktime*	*Intro Unit Task* *-Clustering* *-Freewriting* *worktime*	*Workday*	*Workday*	→ *Due* → *Due* *Project Day*

	DAY 6	DAY 7	DAY 8	DAY 9	DAY 10
WEEK TWO	*Intro Sk. #2* *Intro Vocab #2* ――― *worktime*	← *Student Workdays* →			→ *Due* → *Due* *Unit Task Due* *Project Day*

Fig. 7.14. Narration I calendar.

◇ *Narration I Activities Schedule*

Day One

Introduce skill module 1: "Sentences as Whole Thoughts."

Before assigning the work sheet portion of the module, have the students perform or read through the courtroom scene together and see if they can spot the fragments in Goldilocks' speech.

Introduce vocabulary module 1: "Synonyms and Antonyms."

Use the remainder of the period for work time.

Homework: skills and vocabulary are due Friday. Work on modules, reading, or projects.

Day Two

Introduce the unit task. Read personal experience short story aloud to the class and complete item 1 on the unit checklist.

Demonstrate the clustering technique for the class using a word or phrase of your choice. Have students do a cluster on the phrase "school starts" to complete item 2 on the unit checklist (see figure 7.18, page 141).

Fig. 7.15.

Fig. 7.15.—*Continued*

Demonstrate the free-writing technique for the class using an idea from your demonstration cluster. Have students try free writing to complete item 3 on the unit checklist (see figure 7.19, page 141).

Have students choose a topic from their free-writing samples to use as a focus for their narration to complete item 4 on the unit checklist.

Go over the rest of the checklist with the class to see if there are any misunderstandings about the assignment. Then give students the rest of the class time to work on their narratives.

Day Three

Remind students of approaching due dates and list the menu of activities they may engage in for the day. Let them use the rest of the class for individual work.

Day Four

Student work day.

Skill and vocabulary 1 are due tomorrow.

Day Five

Skill and vocabulary 1 are due in the in box by the end of the hour.

Term project work day.

Day Six

Introduce skill module 2: "Paraphrases and Partial Quotes."

Introduce vocabulary 2: "Choosing Thesaurus Categories."

Student work time.

Day Seven

Student work day.

Day Eight

Student work day.

Day Nine

Student work day.

Skill and vocabulary 2 are due tomorrow.

Unit task is due tomorrow.

Day Ten

Unit task, skill 2 and vocabulary 2 due today and should be in the in basket by the end of the hour.

Term project work day. Students should begin scheduling their project presentations if they have not already done so.

Language Arts
Narration: Personal Experience
Unit Checklist

In this unit, we will begin learning about a type of writing called *narration*. Narration is a common form of writing and speaking. It is, quite simply, storytelling. The story can be true or imagined. It can be exciting, dull, funny, sad, scary, comforting, or anything the author wants. In narration, it is important to get all of the facts and feelings of the story in the proper order so that the reader or listener can follow the story more easily.

A good place to start in practicing narrative writing is telling about a personal experience you have had. Now that you have made it through the first few weeks of school and can look back on them calmly, choose a personal experience from that time and tell the story of how it all happened.

To learn more about using the writing process in narrative writing, complete all of the steps below.

_____ 1.   Listen to the story selected by your teacher or read it on your own. As a class, make a list of the experiences the main character had and describe how they were pulled together into a unified story. How did the author maintain suspense and keep the story interesting?

_____ 2.   Do a cluster on the phrase "school starts."

_____ 3.   Choose one to three items from your cluster and do five minutes of free writing on each.

_____ 4.   Now look back over our free-writing samples and choose the topic that seems most interesting to write about.

_____ 5.   List all of the elements you want to include in your story on a sheet of paper and then number any items that must be presented in a certain order.

Fig. 7.16.

Fig. 7.16. — *Continued*

_____ 6. Write at least five different first lines for your story and then choose the one you like best. Save your list; you may choose wrong the first time.

_____ 7. Choose among the following formats for your story.

Short story	Play script
Diary entry	Television script
News article	Radio script
Letter to Ann Landers	Song or ballad
Epic poem	Other poetic form

_____ 8. Write your first rough draft and take it to a peer editing group. Go over your story with your editors and gather their suggestions for improving it on the next draft.

_____ 9. Write a second rough draft that uses the best suggestions from your editors. Then take it to another peer editing group.

_____ 10. Prepare your final draft. Turn it in on or before the posted due date to the "In" box along with the following items:

Cluster

Free-writing samples

First lines

First rough draft

Second rough draft

This way you will get credit for *all* the work you did and not just the end product. I'm looking forward to some interesting stories. Have fun!

◇ **Language Arts**
Narration: Personal Experience
Rubric

An A paper has all or most of the following:
1. All prewriting, two rough drafts, and a final draft
2. One incident or experience as the clear focus of the story
3. Interesting beginning
4. Meets the requirements of the chosen format
5. Logically organized and easy to follow
6. Few or no errors in format, spelling, or grammar

A B paper has all or most of the following:
1. Prewriting, one rough draft, and a final draft
2. One incident or experience as the focus
3. Average beginning
4. Few problems with the chosen format
5. Only minor errors in organization
6. Few, minor errors in format, spelling, or grammar

A C paper has all or most of the following:
1. Prewriting or a rough draft with final draft
2. Minor problems keeping one focus
3. Poor beginning
4. Several problems with the chosen format
5. Organization problems that interfere with understanding
6. Several errors in format, spelling, or grammar

A D paper has all or most of the following:
1. Only a final draft
2. Lacks a focus on one incident or experience
3. Poor beginning
4. Lacks the requirements of the chosen format
5. Errors in organization that interfere with understanding
6. Serious errors in spelling grammar or format that interfere with understanding

An F paper has all or most of the following:
1. Only a final draft
2. Lacks a focus
3. Poor beginning
4. Lacks a clear format choice
5. Difficult or impossible to understand due to organizational, grammar, spelling, or format errors

Fig. 7.17.

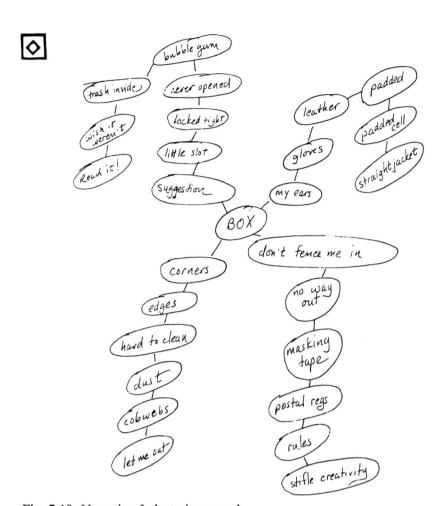

Fig. 7.18. Narration I clustering sample.

What's freewriting? When you just write whatever comes into your head without thinking about it whether it makes sense right away or not. Spelling, grammar not important. Just spill out ideas on paper and look back later to see if they make sense. Helps break writer's block & gets everything out where you can see it. And if you get stuck you just keep writing the same word over & over & over & over until your brain finds another direction & you go that way. You can go for a certain amount of time or just until you finally get a good idea for writing about. Then you quit. That's all.

Fig. 7.19. Narration I free writing sample.

WRAPPING UP THE QUARTER: "EXCUSES, EXCUSES!" NARRATION UNIT

This unit is the final unit of the quarter, so there will be several things happening at the end of this unit that do not occur in the other units. Quarter grades will need to be calculated, term projects completed, and all work graded and returned to the students before Judgment Day.

Quarter grade calculation and Judgment Day procedures will not be entirely new to the students, thanks to the midterm grade procedures of the second unit, but the scale of the operation will be somewhat larger because all of the work for the entire quarter is involved. Also, where there may have been some amount of leeway for incomplete work at midterm, there can be no such leeway at this time except in extreme cases. District data bases wait for no man, woman, or bubble sheet. Therefore, Drop Dead Day is an important date on the quarter calendar. This deadline should allow for the usual revision time of two days after the graded work is returned. For this reason, the teacher may want to encourage students to turn in unit work early so that they can receive graded work back sooner. But if the teacher chooses not to do this, there is usually time during the ninth week of the quarter for both Drop Dead Day and Judgment Day.

During this ninth week, students can give term project presentations and work on project proposals for next term. The latter activity is often popular with students once they have had a chance to comprehend the possibilities inherent in the term project category. They are usually quite content and often eager to get started investigating an area of personal interest to them, leaving the teacher with ample time to prepare materials for next quarter, fill out forms, and serve as a resource person for term projects in an atmosphere that is more relaxed than that of the more heavily scheduled days in the quarter. Since Judgment Day is scheduled for this week and a few days may have been lost during the quarter to school closures, absences, or assemblies, this ninth week is often quite full. No new course work is planned for it and it is left open for end-of-term activities.

This particular unit is intended both to extend what the students learned about narration and its supporting skills in the last unit and to encourage creativity and risk taking in the subject area (see the calendar and activities schedule in figures 7.20 and 7.21, pages 144-46). The unit task, like the task in unit 3, is a narrative based on a personal experience, but instead of accurate storytelling, the students are expected to create an explanation or excuse of truly gargantuan proportions. To help them in this, they are introduced to a new prewriting strategy in the unit task, attribute listing, and a set of productive thinking strategies called SCAMPER[2] in a skill module:

S - Substitute

C - Combine

A - Adapt/adjust

M - Magnify, minify, modify

P - Put to other uses

E - Eliminate or elaborate

R - Reverse or rearrange

The skills they learned in reported speech and thesaurus use are also expanded in this unit.

Only the unit task checklist and rubric (see figures 7.22 and 7.23, pages 147 and 148) are included here to give context to the support modules and activities. The skill and vocabulary modules are not included for three reasons. First, the SCAMPER productive thinking strategies are readily available through many creativity training resources. Second, an example of an open-ended exercise used as a skill module was provided in the introductions module of the "Autobiographical Sketches" unit and the inclusion of a second example would be redundant. Third, the remaining support modules are easily filled by any number of favorite activities and resources already available to most language arts teachers and would be of little interest to teachers in other areas. The goals and objectives for this unit are as follows:

Goals

1. Students will obtain more practice in the narrative mode of discourse.

2. Students will learn additional invention strategies for prewriting as well as other productive thinking tasks.

3. Students will learn the conventions of reported speech through observation, analysis, and summarization.

4. Students will learn about storytelling techniques.

5. Students will learn the procedures for meeting end-of-quarter deadlines and calculating quarter grades.

Objectives

1. Students will demonstrate their understanding of the storytelling technique of exaggeration by writing a tall tale based on an excuse for a real situation.

2. Students will demonstrate their mastery of the productive thinking technique of clustering by making a cluster of their own on the word *trouble* and using it to choose a topic for their tall tale.

3. Students will successfully participate in a group activity by helping to produce a brainstorm list as a prewriting activity and selecting a leader to share the list with the class.

4. Students will demonstrate their understanding of evaluation by criteria by rating the excuses according to the criteria developed by the class.

5. Students will demonstrate their mastery of the free-writing technique by producing a free-writing sample and using it to choose a subject for their narrative.

6. Students will demonstrate their mastery of the SCAMPER strategy by successfully completing the skill module on the technique and by using the technique in generating material for their narrative.

7. Students will demonstrate their mastery of writing dialogue by completing the skill module with 80 percent correct and by including at least three correctly punctuated quotations in their narratives.

8. Students will demonstrate their understanding of the simile by completing the vocabulary module on similes with 80 percent correct and by using the technique in their narrative.

9. Students will demonstrate their ability to use the thesaurus to find more descriptive tags for dialogue by completing the vocabulary module on thesaurus use with 80 percent correct and by minimizing the number of trite dialogue tags in their narratives.

10. Students will turn in all work by Drop Dead Day and will successfully participate in Judgment Day festivities.

Content

Unit Task

Write a tall tale based on an actual situation for which you needed an excuse.

Skill Modules

1. SCAMPER productive thinking technique
2. Reported speech

Vocabulary Modules

1. Similes
2. Thesaurus: descriptive tags

Reading

Tall tales, legends, or any other appropriate material to illustrate the technique of exaggeration.

Term Project

Final draft

Presentation

	DAY 1	DAY 2	DAY 3	DAY 4	DAY 6
WEEK ONE	Fairy Tale or Tall Tale Intro Sk #1 Intro Vocab #1 Worktime	Intro Unit Task -Prewriting Groups -Brainstorming -share excuses -evaluate excuses -share evaluations	Freewriting & SCAMPER strategies Worktime	Workday	Skill & Vocab due Project Day
	DAY 6	DAY 7	DAY 8	DAY 9	DAY 10
WEEK TWO	Intro Sk #2 Intro Vocab#2 Worktime	← Student Workdays →			due due Unit Task due Finish all Project work

Fig. 7.20. Excuses unit calendar.

◇ *Excuses Unit Activities Schedule*

Day One

Read aloud a short fairy tale or tall tale to illustrate the concept of exaggeration.

Introduce skill module 1: "SCAMPER Strategy."

Introduce vocabulary module 1: "Similes."

Student work time.

Homework: skill and vocabulary modules due Friday.

Day Two

Introduce the unit task, "Excuses, Excuses."

Divide students into brainstorming groups and give them twenty minutes to produce their lists of excuses.

Have groups share their excuses with the class.

Develop a set of evaluation criteria as a class and have students rate their excuses in their groups.

Have groups share their evaluation conclusions.

Day Three

Have students do a free-writing sample to choose a topic for their narrative.

Have students apply the SCAMPER strategy to their chosen topic when they have completed skill module 1 and then allow them to continue through the unit checklist on their own.

Day Four

Student work day.

Homework: skill and vocabulary modules due tomorrow.

Day Five

Term project work day.

Skill and vocabulary modules due today.

Day Six

Introduce skill module 2: "Reported Speech."

Introduce vocabulary module 2: "Descriptive Tags."

Student work time.

Fig. 7.21.

(Figure 7.21 continues on page 146.)

Fig. 7.21.—*Continued*

Days Seven and Eight

Student work day.

Day Nine

Student work day.

Homework: skill and vocabulary modules and unit task due tomorrow.

Last term project work day tomorrow.

Day Ten

Term project work day.

Unit task, skill and vocabulary modules due.

Term project work finished up.

Presentations may either begin today or may be scheduled for the ninth week before Judgment Day.

Language Arts
Narration: Excuses, Excuses
Unit Checklist

Everyone has recurring nightmares. A nightmare often experienced by teachers is that they are out enjoying themselves somewhere and they realize that it is a school day and they have somehow forgotten to go to work. Worse yet, they have forgotten to call a substitute and the day is too far gone to come in late and plead car trouble or any other excuse to the principal. Every excuse they can think of is too lame to be believed, particularly by someone like the principal who has years of practice seeing through excuses.

In this unit, you will learn to use your imagination and some creative thinking strategies to invent bigger and better stories to further improve your narrative writing. You will choose a true experience of your own when you needed a really good excuse and tell the story of that experience. But you will blow the story and the excuse out of proportion and turn it into a tall tale. Complete all of the steps below to be eligible for an A.

_____ 1. Make a cluster on the word "trouble."

_____ 2. Divide into prewriting groups of three to five students each. Compile a list of situations with excuses for escape. Then make up as many different excuses as you can for at least three of the situations on your list.

_____ 3. Appoint a group leader to share the excuses your group liked the best with the rest of the class.

_____ 4. Return to your class seats. With your teacher, compile a set of criteria for evaluating excuses. Make it into a chart and rate the excuses your group shared with the class.

_____ 5. Now do a five-minute free-writing session on times when you needed a good excuse. Use the free-writing text to choose a focus for your story.

_____ 6. Apply the SCAMPER strategy you learned in skill 1 to your subject and make a list of ways to make your story into a tall tale.

_____ 7. Write a rough draft of your story using any point of view you like, but make sure that you have at least two speakers in your story.

_____ 8. Take your rough draft to an editing group. Then revise your paper to improve it.

_____ 9. Take your second rough draft to an editing group. This time concentrate on lower order concerns as well as higher order concerns. Make sure that you have at least three direct quotations and that they are properly punctuated.

_____ 10. Prepare your final draft and hand it in on or before the due date.

Fig. 7.22.

◇ *Language Arts*
Narration: Excuses, Excuses
Unit Task Rubric

An A paper has all or most of the following:
1. Prewriting, two rough drafts, and a final draft
2. A specific event as its focus
3. An organizational plan that makes it easy to follow
4. Use of at least five SCAMPER techniques to blow the story out of proportion
5. Four correctly punctuated, direct quotations
6. Few or no errors in format, grammar, or spelling

A B paper has all or most of the following:
1. Prewriting, one rough draft, and a final draft
2. A specific event as its focus
3. A logical organizational plan
4. Use of at least four SCAMPER techniques to blow the story out of proportion
5. Three correctly punctuated direct quotes
6. A few minor errors in format, grammar, or spelling

A C paper has all or most of the following:
1. Prewriting or a rough draft with final draft
2. Loss of focus no more than twice
3. A faulty organizational plan that interferes with understanding
4. Three SCAMPER techniques
5. Two direct quotes with minor errors in punctuation
6. No more than three errors in format, grammar, or spelling that interfere with understanding

A D paper has all or most of the following:
1. Only a final draft
2. Loss of focus more than twice
3. Little or no logical organization
4. Use of one or two SCAMPER techniques
5. Only one quote with punctuation errors
6. Many errors in format, grammar, or spelling that make it difficult to understand

An F paper has all or most of the following:
1. Only a final draft
2. No definite focus
3. No apparent organizational plan
4. No use of SCAMPER techniques
5. No direct quotations
6. Serious errors in format, grammar, and spelling that make it difficult or impossible to understand

Fig. 7.23.

NOTES

1. Jean Hopper, psychology teacher, Layton High School, Layton, Utah, HiPath Research Project log entry, week of September 12-17, 1988.

2. The SCAMPER diagram is found in J. D. Flack, *Once upon a Time: Creative Problem-Solving through Fairy Tales* (East Aurora, NY: D.O.K. Publishers, 1985): 19.

— 8 —
That's Fine
for English But ...

ADAPTING REWRITE TO
SPECIAL NEEDS

Even though Rewrite was developed for language arts classes, the model is easily adapted to other subject areas. These subject areas are defined by their special types of instructional and management needs and cluster into sets that often have little to do with their academic relationships. The clusters dealt with in this section center around three basic types of situations: laboratory-type courses, group performance-type courses, and student aide assignments.

The laboratory courses account for those courses which involve a great deal of hands-on work with specialized equipment, supplies, and facilities. Some examples of these courses are vocational education courses such as home economics, shop, keyboarding, art, drafting, physics, chemistry, computer science, and some types of physical education courses. Sometimes, depending on available resources and teacher preferences, foreign language classes may also fit into this category.

Group performance courses include those courses that prepare students for public group performances while teaching them the subject matter of the subject area. They require a great deal of group rehearsal time that must be closely managed by the director of the performance group and they allow only minimal time for individual discovery work. This course cluster is represented by such classes as choir, band, and drama. They may also include some types of speech classes and some physical education classes that emphasize team sports.

Student aide assignments often fall to gifted students because teachers tend to choose those students who have shown a particular facility in their subject area to be their aides. These assignments are usually listed as credit courses and should be an opportunity for learning as well as for contributing to the running of a particular classroom or department. This can often result in an apparent conflict of interests, since the idea for having student aides is to use their aide time to *aid*, not to add to the instructional duties of the teacher. Time constraints seem to interfere with instructional ones, but this need not be the casse if the Rewrite model is adapted to these situations.

The following three units provide specific suggestions for adaptation of the Rewrite model to these special clusters of subject areas as well as an example unit for each cluster. For laboratory courses, a physics unit in aerodynamics is presented. In the group performance category, choral music will serve as the example, and in the student aide area, a suggested plan for library science is included.

LABORATORY COURSES

When we developed Rewrite, we believed that one of the most serious problems with traditional English classes was that the students were not spending enough time experimenting with and analyzing the language. Since this is the way they had originally acquired their native language as young children, we felt it was important to foster that same kind of investigative activity. In short, we wanted to turn our classrooms into laboratories for the study of language. Because this was the original goal of Rewrite, the model has many aspects and variations that serve the concerns of laboratory courses.

What makes laboratory courses different from history, math, or English courses? They require students to engage in a great deal of hands-on activity with specialized equipment, supplies, and facilities. These items are often costly components of any school's budget and require extra care in their use. Sometimes these materials and facilities are dangerous when improperly used. In either case, students cannot be simply turned loose to discover proper uses as in a course where the materials of study are written or recorded and the most dangerous thing in the room is a sharpened pencil. This situation breeds a special set of needs that must be addressed before the Rewrite model can work in such a classroom.

Student knowledge and skill are mandatory prerequisites for gaining the privilege of working with lab equipment and facilities. It is extremely important that students understand the necessity of responsible and cautious behavior in these settings. Because of these, teachers must work out ways to ensure that only those students who have mastered the prerequisites use the equipment, supplies, and facilities, and to communicate to students the value placed on responsible and safe behavior in such settings. This can be done by changing the categories of activities and scheduling of unit support modules, by creating some specialized student roles, and by carefully allotting space for different simultaneous activities.

Activity categories are addressed at the curriculum planning level and can include many different types of categories. Since context is important, there should always be some sort of unit task to give meaning to the unit goals and objectives. However, skill modules can either be divided up into two types, subject area and laboratory technique skills or both of these types can be grouped under a simple *skills* heading, with the teacher judging which types of skills need to be learned when. Another category can be set up pertaining to the expectations regarding responsible laboratory behavior. This bar on the record sheet could either be filled by weekly evaluations of how well each student performed in the laboratory setting or it could be "emptied" by subtracting a certain amount of credit each time a student is found deviating from the standards of behavior, depending on the work load and preferences of individual teachers. A record sheet for a lab course might include the following categories:

1. Unit tasks

2. Academic skills

3. Lab skills

4. Knowledge/vocabulary

5. Lab management

6. Term project

7. Reading

Scheduling of unit support activities can also be varied to serve the necessity of ascertaining prior student knowledge before allowing students to begin lab work. This is analogous to the need in a literature or history course for students to be familiar with assigned reading materials before other classroom activities can begin. Rather than assigning a lab skill module at the beginning of the unit and giving the students a week to complete it, it is often more appropriate to assign the lab skill module and require that it be successfully passed before students can begin the lab work required to complete their unit task. This practice accomplishes several things. First, it enables the teacher to make sure that every student who begins lab work has demonstrated an understanding of how that work is to be performed safely and efficiently. Second, it teaches students that they must acquire the necessary knowledge and skills before embarking on a project with unfamiliar materials, equipment, or facilities. Finally, it provides a natural staggering of students using lab facilities because students will not all master the material in the support module at the same time. As students pass the module, they may sign up for lab space, gather their materials, and go to work. This also can provide an added incentive for students who dislike structured learning activities to finish the module, because they will not be able to begin the "fun" part of the class until they have passed the module.

Lab skill modules can also be used to create an extra level of student roles in the classroom. Teachers can accumulate a set of student lab specialists by requiring that specialists attain a score of 90 or 95 percent instead of 80 percent on the skill module. These specialists can be listed on rosters posted in the classroom or in a file kept in a readily accessible place. When a student has a question about lab work and the teacher is busy with another student, he or she can look up a list of student specialists under the appropriate skill module category on the rosters or the file. The question can be asked of the student specialist and if the answer is still not forthcoming, the questioner can wait for the teacher. Student specialist status should be given to every student who attains the necessary mastery of a module, regardless of that student's general academic status. We have found that it is enormously encouraging to learning disabled students or students who have not been academically successful for other reasons to achieve this type of leadership role. Quite often, it is the first chance they have had in a long time to be an expert on something valued at school and helps to build their self-esteem and strengthen their feelings of cohesiveness with the class.

Because lab work is often incompatible with less physically dynamic activities such as reading, writing, calculating, and editing, the classroom space should be apportioned by activity. In nonlaboratory courses like English and history, students can work on different things in the same space without getting in one another's way, but in a lab course this is rarely the case. For this reason, whenever possible, there should be a place in the classroom for those students who need to work individually or in pairs on support modules, reading, or writing lab reports as well as a place for small groups to meet for editing or group projects.

Finally, as all good laboratory-course teachers have, there should be clear, simple procedures for setting and cleaning up lab areas. The procedures should be conspicuously posted and all students should be well acquainted with them. This item would be a valuable one to include in the introductory unit of the course. Management aides or perhaps a group of special lab managers could oversee these procedures each day, reporting in to the teacher before students can be dismissed from class. These lab manager positions would be especially valuable for gifted students. In functioning as managers, they would gain valuable experience in laboratory management, interpersonal and communication skills and could list this experience on a job application for similar work in a specialized lab or shop, thus contributing to their career opportunities and education.

All of these adaptations are assumed to be in place in the implementation of the unit that follows. Reading assignments are omitted since textbooks vary from school to school. Term projects are not discussed as they are covered in chapter 6.

A SAMPLE UNIT IN AERODYNAMICS

The following unit is an elementary physics unit in aerodynamics that focuses primarily on the application of Newton's laws of motion and Bernoulli's Principle to flight and engineering test designs. Students embarking on this unit need prior knowledge of Newton's laws of motion and how they relate to solids, liquids, and gases, the different properties of liquids and gases as fluids, and how to formulate a scientific hypothesis. (Knowing the differences between null, alternative non-directional, and alternative directional hypotheses would be helpful, but it is not really necessary.) In addition, students need to have an understanding of velocity, speed, acceleration, force, and mass. This is a two-week unit with the following goals and objectives.

Goals

1. Students will learn how engineers apply theory to practice in the design and testing of model gliders.

2. Students will learn to formulate a test design.

3. Students will learn to communicate their findings.

4. Students will learn to identify and operationalize experimental variables.

Objectives

1. Students will participate in a laboratory demonstration of Bernoulli's Principle, Newton's laws of motion, how they govern airflow around an airfoil.

2. Students will demonstrate their ability to follow written directions by constructing balsa glider with proper dihedral angle to the wings.

3. Students will demonstrate their understanding of Bernoulli's Principle, airfoil parts and functions, relative wind, laminar and turbulent flow patterns, angles of attack, weight, thrust, drag, induced and dynamic life, and glide ratios by passing the knowledge and vocabulary modules with 80 percent mastery and by correctly using these terms in their test reports.

4. Students will demonstrate their understanding of types of variables by passing lab skill module 2 with 80 percent mastery.

5. Students will demonstrate their ability to identify and operationalize experimental variables by correctly describing and identifying the variables in their test designs and reports.

6. Students will demonstrate their ability to collect data in tabular form and interpret that data graphically and verbally by passing academic skill module 1 with 80 percent mastery and correctly describing their data collection and interpretation in their test reports.

7. Students will demonstrate their understanding of the parts and function of a test report by passing academic skill module 2 with 80 percent mastery.

8. Students will demonstrate their understanding of the methods and purposes of engineering test reports by successfully completing the unit task with a grade of C or better.

9. Students will demonstrate their ability to plan a flight test series and report by successfully completing the test design work sheet.

Unit Content

Unit Task

Choose one of three flight test options, design and conduct a flight test series, and communicate your results in a formal engineering test report.

Laboratory Skill Modules

1. Build and learn to fly a model glider

2. Types of experimental variables

Academic Skill Modules

1. Collecting and interpreting test data

2. Elements of test reports

Knowledge/Vocabulary Modules

1. Definitions of terms

2. Use of terms to describe physical manipulations and phenomena (application)

Lab Management

Good use of time, equipment, and materials, consideration for other experimenters, thorough cleanup

Term Project

1. Data collection

2. Data analysis

Reading

Textbook or other appropriate materials relating to topic

Unit Calendar

Because there are three types of support modules for this unit, one of which *must* be completed before the unit task can begin, the unit schedule is somewhat more structured than in the language arts units (see the unit calendar and activities plan, figures 8.1 and 8.2, pages 155-56). There probably will not be enough time in class for all students to complete the assigned support modules and reading, so students should expect to complete much of their module work at home and use class time mainly for flight test and group work. Physics is usually a course reserved for high school students, so homework expectations should not be as much of a problem as for younger students. However, the design and editing group time should not be diminished because this allows the students more time and opportunity for elaborative processing of the material. In planning, discussing, verbalizing, and evaluating one another's work, they will be much more actively involved in the subject matter than if they were reading, listening, or working alone. They will also be able to benefit from being able to see how other students are solving the unit problems, receive peer tutoring, and correct careless errors that would detract from their grade and increase the amount of time needed to evaluate their work. Only the unit task checklist (figure 8.3, page 157), work sheet (figure 8.4, page 158), and rubrics (figures 8.5 and 8.6, pages 159-61) are supplied in this unit, because the specifics of the support modules can vary widely depending on the prior knowledge of the students, the textbooks in use, and facilities and equipment available.

(Text continues on page 161.)

WEEK ONE	DAY 1	DAY 2	DAY 3	DAY 4	DAY 6
	Lab demo Intro Kn #1 + Lab Skill #1 Worktime	Intro Acad Sk #1 → Due Worktime	Intro Unit Task - Test Design Worksheet Worktime	Intro Lab Sk #2 Worktime	Due Due → Due Project Day
WEEK TWO	**DAY 6**	**DAY 7**	**DAY 8**	**DAY 9**	**DAY 10**
	Intro Acad. Sk #2 Intro Kn #2 Worktime	Flight Tests Worktime	Rough Drafts + Editing Worktime	Rough Drafts + Editing Worktime	→ Due → Due Project Day

Fig. 8.1. Aero unit calendar.

Aero Activities Plan

Day One

Laboratory demonstration on Bernoulli's Principle, airflows, airfoils, and the phenomenon of flight.

Introduce knowledge and vocabulary module 1: "Unit Terms."

Introduce lab skill module 1: "Glider Kit and Flying Practice."

Student work time.

Fig. 8.2.

(Figure 8.2 continues on page 156.)

Fig. 8.2.—*Continued*

Day Two

Lab skill 1 due by end of period.

Introduce lab skill 2: "Experimental Variables."

Introduce academic skill 1: "Collecting and Interpreting Data."

Student work time.

Day Three

Introduce unit task.

Test design groups: test design work sheet.

Student work time.

Day Four

Student work time

Lab skill 2, academic skill 1, and knowledge and vocabulary 1 due tomorrow.

Day Five

Project Day.

Lab skill 2, academic skill 1, and knowledge and vocabulary 1 due today.

Day Six

Introduce academic skill 2: "Elements of Test Reports."

Introduce knowledge and vocabulary 2: "Application of Terms."

Student work time.

Day Seven

Flight tests.

Student work time.

Day Eight

Work on rough drafts and editing.

Day Nine

Work on rough drafts and editing.

Test reports due tomorrow.

Academic skill 2 and knowledge and vocabulary 2 due tomorrow.

Day Ten

Project day.

Test reports due.

Support modules due.

◇ *Physics*
Aerodynamics 1: Lift and Drag
Unit Task Checklist

In the last unit, you learned about how Newton's three laws of motion affect the movement of solids, liquids, and gases. In this unit, you will have a chance to see how those laws can be applied in aeronautical engineering to design structures that fly. You will also learn something about how engineers test their designs and communicate their findings by conducting a series of flight tests of your own and writing a test report. Complete all of the steps below to be eligible for an A.

_____ 1. Choose one of the following options:

   a. Put together a commercial balsa glider and determine its maximum and minimum glide capabilities by manipulating the angle of attack.

   b. Put together two or three different glider kits and compare their maximum and minimum glide capabilities by manipulating their angles of attack.

   c. Design your own glider or gliders from the materials of your choice and compare their maximum and minimum glide capabilities by manipulating their angles of attack.

_____ 2. Build and learn to fly your plane(s).

_____ 3. Design your flight test series using the test design work sheet and meet with a test review group to be sure it meets the test requirements on the test design rubric.

_____ 4. Conduct your tests and collect your data.

_____ 5. Analyze and graph your data.

_____ 6. Describe your test design, procedures, and results in a rough draft of a test report. Be sure you describe your observations in terms of induced and relative lift, relative flows, the four forces of flight, and laminar and turbulent flow patterns.

_____ 7. Take your report to an editing group and have your editors check it over using the test report rubric.

_____ 8. Revise your test report into a final draft and turn it in on or before the posted due date. If your report is late, you will lose your contract with the buyer.

Fig. 8.3.

◇ *Test Design Work Sheet*

Now that you have built and learned to fly your glider, you are ready to test some of its flight capabilities. Before you test anything, you must develop a test or research design. Use this work sheet to work with your fellow group members to develop a good test design. When each of the group members has a correctly planned design, your group can adjourn and you may begin your research and support work. Keep this sheet with you so that you will be sure to complete all of your plans and have all of the background information you will need to write your test report. Keep your answers short.

1. What are you supposed to find out with your experiments?

2. What predictions can you make about the outcome of your experiments? Why?

3. State your predictions in the form of a scientific hypothesis.

4. What variable(s) will you manipulate? These are your independent variables.

5. What variable(s) should change as a result of your manipulations? These will be your dependent variables.

6. What variables will you try to keep constant so that they will not interfere with your results? These will be your control variables.

7. What variables will probably affect your results in some way that you will not be able to control very well? These will be your confounding variables.

8. What procedures will you use to manipulate your independent variable and how will you measure the results of your tests?

9. What procedures will you use to record your test data as they are collected?

10. How will you analyze your data? What formulae and graphic techniques will you use?

11. How will you summarize your findings for your readers?

Fig. 8.4.

◇ *Test Design Rubric*

Note to the teacher: Rubrics can come in different formats. Here is an alternative to the format presented thus far in the text.

As you go over one another's test designs, ask yourselves the following questions. If the answer to any of these questions is "no" or "sort of," make a note of the problem on the design sheet or on a separate sheet, depending on the researcher's desires.

1. Does the test design have a clearly stated purpose?

2. Is there a clearly stated hypothesis based on sound scientific reasoning?

3. Are independent, dependent, control, and confounding variables correctly defined?

4. Are the procedures for experimentation and data collection clearly described?

5. Does the researcher have a way to analyze the data that makes sense?

6. Does the researcher have a plan for presenting the plan to a reader?

Fig. 8.5.

◇ *Test Report Rubric*

An A report has all or most of the following:

1. Edited test design and rough draft with a final draft

2. An introduction section with clear statements of purpose and hypothesis and a thorough explanation of reasons for the hypothesis

3. A methods section that correctly identifies all variables, and clearly describes all equipment and procedures for experimentation, measurement, collection, and analysis

4. A results section that analyzes the data according to planned procedures and presents the results graphically and verbally

5. A discussion section that clearly states the test findings, explains possible reasons for the findings, and suggests new procedures and/or questions for further research

6. Few or no errors in format, spelling, or grammar

A B report has all or most of the following:

1. Edited test design and rough draft with a final draft

2. An introduction section with a purpose statement, hypothesis, and some explanation of reasons for predictions

3. A methods section that identifies the variables correctly, but has some weaknesses in description of equipment or procedures

4. A results section that correctly analyzes data but has minor errors in graphic and/or verbal summaries

5. A discussion section that states the test findings and possible reasons for the results, but no suggestions for further research

6. A few minor errors in format, spelling, or grammar

A C report has all or most of the following:

1. A final draft and an unedited test design or rough draft

2. An introduction section with a purpose statement and hypothesis, but little or no explanation of reasons for predictions

3. A methods section with an incorrectly identified variable and some weaknesses in equipment and procedure descriptions

4. A results section that has errors in data analysis and summaries

5. A discussion section that states only the test findings

6. Several errors in format, spelling, or grammar that interfere with understanding

Fig. 8.6

Fig. 8.6.—*Continued*

A D report has all or most of the following:

1. An unedited test design *or* rough draft with a final draft

2. An organizational plan that does not include all four designated test report sections

3. Poorly defined purpose, hypothesis, and procedures

4. Incorrectly analyzed data

5. Little or no summarization of findings

6. Many errors in format, spelling, or grammar that interfere with understanding

An F report has all or most of the following:

1. Only a final draft

2. No discernible organizational plan

3. Sketchily defined purpose, hypothesis, and procedures

4. No real analysis of data or reporting of results

5. So many errors in format, spelling, and grammar that it is difficult or impossible to understand

WHEN AIDES ARE STUDENTS

Many schools have programs for student aides in which students can earn credit while helping a faculty or staff member to manage a particular department, teaching assignment, or facility within the school. It is hoped that both faculty and students will benefit from this arrangement, as specialized school personnel are relieved of less specialized tasks while the student aides learn more about the area in which they are working. Unfortunately, student aide programs often devolve into either free menial labor or dead time in which student aides can fool around without getting into too much trouble. In either case, the outcome is a reduction in opportunities for students to learn. This need not be the case, because student aides are often those students who have shown themselves to be more capable or to have a greater interest in the work area than most students. Because of this, the time students spend as aides should not only be used to contribute to the running of the school, but should also be of real benefit in broadening the student aide's knowledge and experience within the area.

Cries of protest are no doubt arising as those faculty and staff members who have student aides consider the implications of this last statement. Why have a student aide if the presence of that aide only adds to the mentor's instructional load and cuts back on the actual time the aide can put into helping out? If the student aide becomes one more teaching assignment for the teacher or staff member, then the student is no longer an aide. However, if the work time is structured and accounted for positively, then the aide can be both student and aide.

Certain basic adaptations can be made in the Rewrite model to make it easier to structure the aide's experience to be beneficial to both mentor and aide. The primary adaptations must be made in the use of time. These modifications in time use prompt certain types of changes within the structure of the rest of the model to allow time and opportunity for both assigned duties and instruction.

The first major set of decisions affected by the difference in time use is in curriculum activity categories. In curriculum planning, the teacher makes general decisions about which categories of activities will constitute the bulk of the students' time. This is an important consideration, since the teacher's emphases are often communicated to the students subliminally by the amount of time allotted to different categories of activities. If an aide mentor only stresses the completion of menial tasks and does not provide opportunities for the aide to extend knowledge or capabilities, then the aide will learn to become dependent on the mentor for direction, see little value in learning more about the field than is absolutely necessary to complete assigned duties, and do little more than engage in irresponsible behavior when there are no specific tasks to complete. To prevent this and to develop aides who are increasingly valuable by virtue of their training and experience, the teacher can create a set of categories that require not only the faithful completion of aide duties, but that build knowledge and experience in the specialty area and encourage student aides to take initiative in exploring more deeply than would be possible in the regular course offerings of the school.

If the usual curriculum category of unit tasks is retained, there will be little time left for aide duties because unit tasks take up most of the students' work time. However, in an aide assignment, such as a library media center (LMC), the bulk of the aides' time should be spent performing assigned duties. To reflect this difference, a different category, "Aide Work," can replace the unit task category. The working situation itself provides meaning and context for successful learning of the skills and knowledge needed by student aides. "Knowledge" and "Skills" can constitute two more categories of activities, "Knowledge" involving learning about facts and resources used by library media center specialists, and "Skills" involving the mastery of the procedures and techniques used in the running of an LMC. These knowledge and skill items can be organized into modules that support the "Aide Work" category and a term project. These modules can be ordered and presented so that the most necessary ones for working in the LMC are learned first and aides can become assets at some level as quickly as possible. As the aide becomes more comfortable with the simpler functions, more specialized ones can be taught, making the aide more and more valuable. By establishing a support module curriculum and preparing the materials for it ahead of time, the LMC specialist can offer training on a rotating basis. In this way, new aides can join the staff at the beginning of any quarter. Each quarter, every aide can continue to progress through the curriculum. New aides begin with the most elementary modules and more senior aides continue at their own levels of instruction and each aide completes a given number of support modules each quarter to receive an A. The aides do not need to have simultaneous levels of expertise. In fact, the more experienced aides can serve as mentors to the newer ones, thus relieving the faculty/staff mentor from some training duties.

The aide mentor should keep in mind that one of the reasons aides are selected is that they are either more enthusiastic or more capable (or both) and that simply becoming a cog in an organization designed by someone else may not provide the ongoing motivation to continue as an aide. To maintain student motivation through presentation of appropriate and meaningful challenges to the aides and to broaden the aides' contribution to the school, two more categories can be added to the curriculum activities: term projects and book talks. Term projects allow students to explore their own interests within the context of the subject area. In this situation, the context becomes a paraprofessional one and should reflect that emphasis. An appropriate student aide project should require that the student produce something of real value to a real audience. For an LMC aide, this might include a bibliography of available resources on a specific topic for a teacher or department in the school, assembling those resources for use by a group of students and/or teachers, and presenting an overview of them for an appropriate audience. Term project work can be done whenever an aide has completed his or her assigned duties. This prevents the ubiquitous "I'm-an-aide-this-hour-I-don't-need-a-pass" syndrome as well as gives the aide something to do of real value, both personal and public.

The bibliographic work involved in the term project can also provide the data base for the book talk category. In this category, the LMC aide presents a given number of short reports on a particular source or set of sources he or she found interesting. In this way, the amount of time needed to complete both the term project and book talk requirements is compressed together and does not detract from aide work time. These reports can be oral or written, but oral reports to either the rest of the LMC staff or to a particular group of teachers or students who would find the source(s) of interest would probably be of greater real value. Not only does this activity add to the knowledge and experience of the LMC aides, but also impresses upon them the public service nature of the library science field. A simple rubric describing the requirements for a successful book talk, distributed at the beginning of the quarter along with a sample book talk either live or video-taped can give most aides all of the information and guidance they need to complete this activity successfully.

The following sample materials (see figures 8.7 through 8.11, pages 164-69, which present respectively an orientation sheet, term project requirements, a term project proposal, book talk requirements, and a sample LMC aide record sheet) are based on a Rewrite LMC student aide program with the following categories:

1. Aide work time

2. LMC knowledge

3. LMC skills

4. Term project

5. Book talk

A sample gradebook record is also included. LMC knowledge and skills support modules are not included since the content of these areas can be highly variable depending on the preferences and needs of individual school LMC specialists.

(Text continues on page 170.)

*School Media Center
Orientation Sheet
First Quarter*

Welcome to your new position as a student aide in our school media center. The media center staff hopes that you will gain as much from working here as we will by having you here. To this end, we have set up a program to help you progress as a media center aide and to enable you to pursue some of your own goals in the process. Your responsibilities will have five areas.

1. Aide Work Time

    Most of your time here will be spent completing your assigned aide duties. Each day, you will sign in and out in the aides' work record and make a note of the duties you were assigned and completed that day. For each day of successful work, you will receive one unit of credit on your record sheet. Excused absences will not count against you, but if you must be absent for a long period, it may be necessary to make some alternative grading arrangements with the LMC director.

2. LMC Knowledge Modules

    As part of your training here, you will be instructed in the types of resources used by people in running or using a media center. You will need to successfully complete five of these modules to receive an A in this area.

3. LMC Skill Modules

    To help you become a more effective media center aide, you will learn the procedures used in this media center as well as more general procedures and problem-solving strategies used by media center specialists in the performance of their work. You will need to successfully complete five of these modules to receive an A in this area.

4. Term Project

    We would like you to be able to learn about something that interests you personally while you are an aide here, so you will be asked to complete one term project each quarter. Please see the term project sheet in this packet for more information.

5. Book Talk

    We know that you will be a great help to us here in the LMC, but we would like the rest of the school to benefit from your specialized skills and knowledge. Therefore, you will be asked to share five books or other resources you discover in the course of your term project with either the rest of the LMC staff or with some teachers or students who would also find it valuable. Please see the book talk sheet in this packet for more specific information.

Fig. 8.7.

◇ *School Media Center*
Student Aide Program
Term Project Requirements

The following term project description and requirements are general. If, after reading over them, you can think of an alternative, equivalent project, please do not hesitate to discuss it with the LMC director. New ideas are always welcome.

The term project for this course will help you develop your media center skills and extend your knowledge of the library science career field. It will also give you a chance to share your new knowledge and abilities with the faculty, staff, and student body of the school. You are to *choose a topic of interest to you and develop a bibliography and a list of holdings to be assembled for a class or research team to use in their work*. This project consists of eight parts. You must complete all eight of them to be eligible for an A in this area. We will schedule you for one day each week to work on your project when you will not have to perform any other aide duties. You should not need to spend more than one or two hours a week on this project to complete it satisfactorily, but if you wish to spend more time on it, you are welcome to do so as long as it does not detract from your regular duties. Listed below are the requirements for each of the eight project sections. If you have any questions about them at any time, please ask them at once so you will not lose valuable time.

1. *Proposal.* You must first submit a proposal for the work you wish to do. To choose a topic, you must first find a sponsor on the faculty or staff who will be able to use the bibliography you build, either for themselves or for a class they are teaching. Fill out the proposal form and put it in the aides' "In" box.

2. *Approval.* Your proposal must be approved by the LMC director before you begin working on it. This is so that the LMC director can help you find potential trouble spots and show you ways to deal with them.

3. *Search Strategies.* This task consists of two parts—descriptors and non-LMC resources.

    a. Descriptors are the terms you will use to search the card catalogs, periodical guides, and computer data bases for sources. Begin by asking your sponsor to help you develop a list of possible descriptors. Then add to the list as you find alternate entries in the card catalog, periodical guides, and data bases. Record your descriptors neatly and logically so that someone else can make sense of them.

    b. Non-LMC resources are people, businesses, organizations, newsletters, government offices, and any other community resources that might have information on your topic. You may also begin by asking your sponsor for suggestions in this area, but the yellow pages, advertisements in magazines, local specialists and scholars, and local and state government offices will also be useful to you in compiling a list of potential sources. Record your list of these resources neatly and logically.

Fig. 8.8.

(Figure 8.8 continues on page 166.)

Fig. 8.8. — *Continued*

4. *Search*. Conduct your survey of available sources using the descriptor and non-LMC resource lists you compiled in step 3. Choose only those resources that are truly valuable to a researcher in your topic area. Bibliographies should be comprehensive in their coverage of the topic whenever possible, but they should not be inflated with items that are actually of little use. Remember, you are putting this bibliography together so that someone can use it. As you find sources for the bibliography, record the following information:

PRINT AND AUDIO-VISUAL MATERIALS

Subject or topic area   Location of source (Call #)
Author(s)/editor(s)
Title
Publisher, location of publisher, and copyright date
Number of pages, number of minutes, or RAM requirements
A *short* description of what the researcher can expect to find in the source
Reading level: easy, average, difficult

OTHER RESOURCES: SPEAKERS, ORGANIZATIONS, ETC.

Subject or topic area
Name of source
Address and phone number
Type of assistance available
Special notes

5. *Organization*. Sort your entries into categories of type (books, periodicals, speakers, films, etc.). Then sort the entries in each category alphabetically.

6. *Rough Draft*. Prepare a rough draft of a bibliography handout on your research area.

7. *Editing*. Have at least two other aides or professionals in your topic area (faculty or staff members) proofread it for you. Make sure their written comments accompany the rough draft when you hand it in.

8. *Final Draft*. Correct any errors or weaknesses found by your editors and prepare four final copies of your bibliography. They may each be prepared separately or three may be copies of an original. Hand all four copies in for grading. You will receive three of your copies back: one for your own files, one for your sponsor, and one for the LMC reference files.

School Media Center
Student Aide Program
Term Project Proposal Sheet

Name_____Hour_____Quarter_____

Project topic area _____

Faculty/staff sponsor_____

1. Briefly tell why you and your sponsor have chosen this topic area. What is your interest in it and how will it be of use to your sponsor?

2. What obvious descriptors and non-LMC sources can you use to start your search?

3. Set up a rough calendar for yourself to schedule your bibliography work. Remember, you will have one class period off per week to work on your project during school hours.

    Proposal turned in by _____

    Approval obtained by_____

    Descriptor list completed by _____

    Non-LMC resource list completed by _____

    Search completed by _____

    Entries sorted by _____

    Rough draft prepared by _____

    Editing completed by _____

    Final draft turned in by_____

4. Do you foresee any difficulties in creating your bibliography? If so, please describe them below so that one of the LMC staff members can help you with them. Use the back of this sheet.

Fig. 8.9.

School Media Center
Student Aide Program
Book Talk Requirements

Library media center specialists are often asked to share their knowledge and resources with center clients. For a center that caters to young children, this might include reading stories at a regular story hour or creating displays of new or related books. For our center, which has secondary school students and teachers as its clients, sharing knowledge and resources usually means telling clients about good books, periodicals, audiovisual resources, and reference sources. To give you experience in this area and to give the rest of the school a chance to benefit from your knowledge, you will be asked to share five books or other resources you located in your term project work with an audience. Here are the requirements for a successful book talk.

1. Choose a source to share from your term project bibliography.

2. Choose the most appropriate audience for your talk. If it is a reference work or unusual community resource, it may be more helpful to the LMC staff or a faculty department than to a group of students.

3. Schedule your talk with the appropriate LMC staff member, faculty member, or department chairperson. All book talks must be completed by the end of the eighth week of the quarter.

4. Give your talk to your chosen audience. Have the LMC staff member, faculty member, or department chairperson who scheduled your talk fill out a critique form.

5. Turn in your critique form to the aides' "In" box.

Fig. 8.10.

NAME _____

AIDE WORK TIME	LMC KNOWLEDGE	LMC SKILLS	TERM PROJECTS	BOOK TALK
A (31, 30, 29, 28)	5	5	8	5
B (27, 26, 25, 24, 23, 22, 20, 19)	4	4	7 / 6	4
C (18, 17, 16, 15, 14, 13, 12)	3	3	5 / 4	3
D (11, 10, 9, 8, 7, 6, 5)	2	2	3 / 2	2
F (4, 3, 2, 1)	1	1	1	1

Fig. 8.11. Sample LMC aide record sheet.

GROUP PERFORMANCE COURSES:
A CHORAL MUSIC EXAMPLE*

What makes group performance courses different from English, math, or history? The end product or unit task is produced jointly by the entire class. Instead of biweekly unit tasks, one performance at the end of the term provides the context for learning. Skills and knowledge can be attained by individuals, but the methodologies or processes are group processes that leave little opportunity for individualized discovery learning. Besides finding opportunities for discovery learning, performance teachers must seek out ways to foster a sense of individual ownership in each of their students, ways to make the group experience meaningful to the individual.

The methodologies in the group performance course, since they are all tied to performance preparation, are more akin to a term project in the English curriculum. These processes sometimes engage only the teacher, as in making repertoire choices; sometimes engage both teacher and student, as in score analysis and practicing strategies; and sometimes only the student, as in execution and evaluation of individual effort. Students will have a greater investment in the experience if they are able to enter at the foundation level of reading and interpreting the score as the conductor does and progress upward through the subsequent levels of understanding. This can prevent students from entering the experience on the top floor, not realizing and fully experiencing where they are. Responsibility for the nonmusical factors of a performance can also be shared by teacher and students. Delegating many of these nonmusical responsibilities to capable students is a good way to let individuals within the group entity shine and relieve the teacher of a few details. Figure 8.12 shows a list of hooks on which music students can hang their ownership. These hooks involve the whole experience of the music performance course, musical and social.

 Integrating Ownership and Discovery Learning

1. Allow student input whenever possible.

2. Allow for experimentation and discovery learning in teaching skills and knowledge.

3. Prepare students for more responsibility for reading and analyzing the score by building foundational skills.

4. Give students more responsibility.

5. Foster a group psyche by allowing for social interaction and encouragement of public praise of one another.

6. Show respect for students.

7. Express genuine interest and concern.

8. Solicit opinions and feedback.

9. Be an example of commitment to the subject area.

10. Apply knowledge of text and/or historical context to help students get more emotionally involved in the product.

11. Give students the opportunity to declare their commitment.

12. Play a recording of the performance and discuss its strengths and weaknesses.

13. Give students opportunities to watch and listen to rehearsals rather than sing in them.

Fig. 8.12.

---

*This unit was developed and written by Jean Simons.

As in almost any course, skills in the music performance class are easily definable. The choral music class calls for reading, hearing, applying vocal technique, and evaluating. Where reading trains the eye to recognize the symbols of musical language, hearing trains the ear to recognize the sounds represented in the score. Vocal techniques enable the singers to control and improve their own sound production, and the evaluation process is vital in helping students perceive which of the criteria are or are not being met for quality sound production. Figures 8.13, 8.14, and 8.15 illustrate options for evaluative activities. Figure 8.13 is based on criteria for evaluating a singer's individual performance and figure 8.14, page 172, shows the specific criteria that can be made constantly available to the class with a posted rubric.

◇ *Personal Evaluation Calendar*

Rate your performance on a scale of 1 to 6 based on the criteria below for each day of rehearsal. At the end of the week, total your points and figure out your weekly average.

6 = outstanding effort and success with all six criteria

5 = very good effort and good success with criteria

4 = good effort and moderate success

3 = average effort and some success

2 = below average effort and little success

1 = poor effort and little or no success

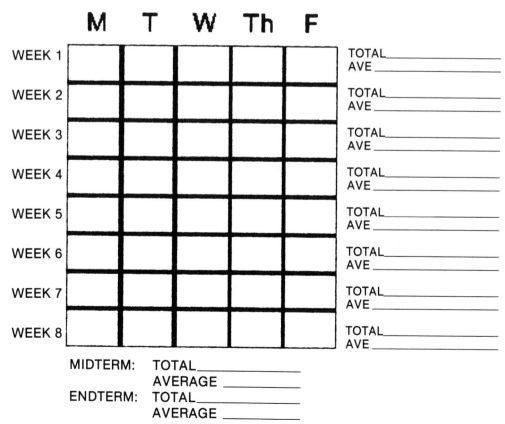

Fig. 8.13.

◇ *Personal Evaluation Criteria*

Each student should have ready access to these criteria when filling out the personal evaluation calendar.

1. Leadership behavior, amount of effort made in carrying out directions, willingness to assume personal responsibility for making corrections and improvements

2. Application of music skills, *growth* in the ability to read and analyze the musical score

3. Posture for best singing

4. Breath energy for producing quality tone

5. Vowel shape and space to affect the quality of tone and blend

6. Diction

Fig. 8.14.

Figure 8.15 is based on the learning objectives established by the teacher for a particular day of rehearsal. The values earned and recorded on these sheets can be used to provide data for filling in record sheets. Of course, the learning objectives must be clearly presented to the students. Either a brief list on the blackboard or repeated verbal statements of the objectives will do. If students are given the chance to sit out and observe the rehearsal from time to time, they will have the opportunity to evaluate the group, often reinforcing the director's instructions.

◇ *Performance Log*

1. List the objectives for class today.

2. Which of the above objectives did you effectively meet?

3. What will help you with the objective(s) you have not met yet? (Hint: Consider the criteria for personal evaluation or the music skills you are learning.)

Fig. 8.15.

The knowledge areas of the music performance include vocabulary, notation, elements, genres, styles, and historical periods. Generally both the skills and knowledge aspects of the group performance course target the growth of the individual. The elements of music in particular provide grounds for experimentation and discovery in a class where the material of the final product is predetermined.

Flexibility in the use of time and space exists only as it serves the group process. Time and space variations of the typical group rehearsal could include sectional rehearsals in separate parts of the classroom or in separate practice rooms, time for individual skills activities, time for knowledge activities, or time for evaluative activities. Such a division of time and space utilization does serve the group process by providing variety, building skills and knowledge, and giving students an opportunity to examine what has or has not been achieved by the group so far. Ideally, all student activities (group or individual) will somehow relate to the music being rehearsed. So, as the music serves as context for most of the learning, the skills, knowledge, and evaluative activities serve to illuminate the musical score.

— 9 —
Fancy Footwork
Interdisciplinary Units

INTERDISCIPLINARY STUDY

It is often suggested that interdisciplinary study helps students see relationships between different subject areas, provides opportunities for students to explore subject matter from less traditional, but possibly more personally compatible, points of view, and broadens student exposure to concepts and subject matter. In experimenting with interdisciplinary study within the Rewrite model, we noticed several other benefits as well. We found that our students often achieved a deeper understanding of the material as they saw how it related to areas of knowledge and practice other than those traditionally included in our courses. We noticed that they seemed to be able to analogize more freely across traditional subject area divisions and that they would often find solutions to problems in one field by applying knowledge from other fields. Some students, who had deep and abiding antipathies for language arts, found our classes more palatable and even (heaven forbid!) more interesting when they could combine our subject matter with subjects of personal interest to them. Consequently they learned more about language than they ordinarily would have because they were more actively involved in our classes.

As teachers, we found that we benefited from these interdisciplinary studies in several ways, too. We enlarged our knowledge and understanding of the subject matter by collaborating with colleagues from other areas and gained a collection of new ideas for teaching and activities by seeing how other subjects were taught. We were able to create opportunities for learning far beyond any we could have created working alone and built collegial bonds with other faculty members that were supportive both personally and professionally long after our interdisciplinary work had ended.

Although interdisciplinary study is often encouraged in the educational world, it is rare to find appropriate materials that are useful or even truly interdisciplinary. For example, there was recently a big push to include writing across the curriculum, but the types of materials and suggestions offered to in-service teachers consisted of having math students write out their answers in verbal form or having social studies students keep a learning log. Few materials actually taught writing as it applied to different subject areas.

Because interdisciplinary materials are so hard to find, it usually falls to classroom teachers to create them. The problems inherent in constructing these materials affect planning of unit content and schedules, blending diverse subject matters into unit tasks and other activities, and choosing evaluation criteria that draw from all involved subject areas. These problems are not insurmountable, however, and the benefits of interdisciplinary study can be enjoyed by teachers and students within the context of the Rewrite model.

There are basically two types of interdisciplinary study in secondary school situations. The first involves the teaching of two or more subjects within one course. This often happens when a curriculum committee somewhere decides that newly mandated material can easily be incorporated in an existing set of courses. An example of this would be the recent push to teach computer courses in public schools. This often resulted in math departments' being told to teach students about computers as part of their regular offerings as though the regular course content was not enough to fill up the entire term. The second type of interdisciplinary endeavor involves teaching one theme or set of subject matter in two or more different courses at once. Elementary school teachers do this regularly with great success, but because of scheduling and space constraints in secondary schools, it is usually difficult to accomplish this type of interdisciplinary study. Examples of this type of study include the simultaneous study of the history and literature of a given period. For example, a study of nutrition in health class coinciding with a unit in menu planning in home economics, and technical report writing taught in English class while students are working on science project reports in science class.

In this chapter, an example of each type of interdisciplinary study is included. The first, an example of two subjects in one class, is a plan for teaching mathematics and computer programming in an elementary algebra class. The second example, which involves one subject taught in two classes, is a plan for teaching composition in an English class and a general music class.

TWO IN ONE: COMPUTER PROGRAMMING IN MATH CLASS

Anyone who has ever taken a computer programming course is well aware that there is more than enough subject matter to fill up an entire course and turn one's eyes into watery square things that resemble miniature display monitors. So, when it is suggested to math teachers that computers should fit nicely into math class, the response is often a skeptical "Really? And when would you like me to teach math?" Similar incidents have been reported by home economics teachers asked to teach health and nutrition as part of a cooking class, English teachers asked to teach word processing as part of their writing classes, and history teachers asked to teach library research around the edges of their already full curricula. It is difficult to incorporate a second subject area into an established course without making some compromises, but the use of Rewrite programming can often reduce their magnitude, mainly by loosening up available resources of time, space, and information, streamlining management procedures to make more time for learning, and providing a coherent way to plan for multiple subjects in one unit.

Planning

Planning an interdisciplinary unit is not really very different from planning a monodisciplinary one. The same procedures used in chapters 3 and 5 can be applied here, but with a few additional caveats. First, additional time or units may need to be scheduled simply because there is more material to be covered. Second, be prepared to flex curriculum calendars and sequences a bit now and then. It may happen that a particular unit will deal almost exclusively with one of the subject areas in order to set up the necessary knowledge base for later work, thus delaying instruction in the other area. It may also happen that the new subject matter works better with a concept or curriculum area in the established subject area usually reserved for a different time of year. Third, as much as possible, apply the following guidelines to curriculum and unit planning procedures:

1. List the goals for each subject and try to correlate them according to (a) the need to know, (b) common concepts, and (c) complementary concepts.

2. Whenever possible, create unit tasks that draw from both areas.

3. Be sure to include evaluative criteria from each subject area in the rubrics.

List goals and correlate. Correlation of goals and objectives based on the need to know entails a certain streamlining and possibly some amount of rearrangement. What does the student need to know to master the support areas and successfully complete the unit task? If there is no real need to cover a particular aspect in a given unit, it should be relegated to another unit that does require it. Even though certain sets of concepts usually go together in a regular unit. they might not do so in an interdisciplinary one because it is so untraditional and different types of relationships are being emphasized. Whenever possible, common concepts should be presented simultaneously. This way, students' perceptions and understanding of interdisciplinary relationships can be reinforced. Complementary concepts are not shared by the disciplines under study, but are often necessary intermediate steps in instruction if a true interdisciplinary understanding is to be achieved. Because common concepts are taught together, complementary concepts should be scheduled simultaneously when there are no common concepts to cover.

Create unit tasks that draw from both areas. If the goals of a unit are truly interdisciplinary, then the unit task should reflect that. One of the purposes of interdisciplinary study is to enable students to investigate relationships across traditional barriers. If those barriers are rebuilt in the unit task, the interdisciplinary character of the unit evaporates.

Evaluative criteria. When writing the rubric, the teacher should be careful to use criteria from both areas. This reinforces the students' perception of the interdisciplinary character of the unit and gives them practice in applying higher order thinking to both areas.

A Sample Course

In the math/computer programming course spotlighted in this section, the course is divided up into five categories:

1. Unit tasks
2. Math and programming skills
3. Knowledge and vocabulary
4. Term project
5. Programmer's library

Unit tasks. Category 1 consists of programming assignments that function as tests of the students' understanding of math concepts and skills. They provide a medium for evaluation of students' abilities to synthesize the material learned in their mathematics instruction. By requiring that certain functions and relationships be demonstrated in the programs, teachers can substitute the programs for formal tests while showing students real applications of the subject matter.

Math and programming skills. This category includes both math and programming skills. They are graded on a mastery basis and are used for drill and practice. Depending upon the needs of the unit, these modules teach either math or computer skills or both when applicable. Whenever possible, these categories of skills can be separated, but in the interests of time and scheduling it may sometimes be necessary to create dual modules which teach skills from both areas in the same assignment.

Knowledge and vocabulary. Category 3 might not be enough to require a separate category in a regular math class, but in this combined class, the math vocabulary and facts can be augmented with the vocabulary and rules of Pascal programming language.

Term projects. Term projects in this course are programming projects the students set up for themselves and work on in their free time and on project days. (If computer equipment is limited, the teacher may want to establish a rotating schedule for computer time during the week for those students wishing to work on their projects.) Because programming is often a time-consuming activity, especially for beginners, large programming projects such as these are better relegated to quarter-long work periods than squeezed into unit tasks.

Programmer's library. This category is set up both as an opportunity for students to learn about problem solving and a way to cut back on the time needed for programming work. Over the course of the year, each student compiles all of his or her programs, both major and minor, in a notebook that serves as a personal library of programs. As students collect their programs in their library notebooks, they should be encouraged to use them to solve new problems. During the course of the year, the teacher can have students pull up programs from their libraries to use as germs for new, more elaborate programs which demonstrate mastery of more advanced skills. This gives students the opportunity to see interrelationships between different types of problems and, because students are not starting from scratch, the amount of time required to write a new program can be reduced and more time can be spent on the target math concepts.

A Sample Unit in Ratio, Proportion, and Decision Control

This unit spends rather more time on decision control in Pascal programming than it does on the relatively simple concepts of ratio and proportion. Consequently, the time normally spent on this area is drawn out. However, the basic patterns and subroutines written in this program will be applicable again and again and in the long run will allow more time for math in later units. Even so, it is prudent to use the Pascal goals and objectives to provide real-life contexts for the math concepts. The goals and objectives of the unit are as follows:

Goals

1. Students will learn to express analogies through statements of proportional relationships.

2. Students will learn how to think analogically.

3. Students will learn about Boolean data types and operations.

4. Students will learn what decision control is and how to use it in writing programs and in making life decisions.

Objectives

1. Students will write a computer program that will allow the user to convert amounts from one measurement system to another.

2. Students will be able to correctly identify the components of a proportion.

3. Students will be able to express proportional relationships correctly through the use of ratios and variables.

4.   Students will be able to solve for variables in proportional relationships.

5.   Students will be able to write a flow chart expressing at least two options for the user.

6.   Students will be able to correctly use Boolean data types in a Pascal program.

7.   Students will be able to correctly use IF-THEN and IF-THEN-ELSE statements in decision control.

8.   Students will be able to write compound instructions within an IF-THEN or IF-THEN-ELSE loop.

9.   Students will be able to correctly use ASCII codes and values along with Boolean data types and operations for user interface.

10. Students will be able to nest instructions within an IF-THEN-ELSE loop.

11. Students will program a working menu and any other interfaces needed to facilitate use input.

12. Students will add to their programmers' library notebooks programs for a user's menu and nested compound instructions used in response to user input.

Content

Unit Task

Write a Pascal program using Boolean data types, IF-THEN and/or IF-THEN-ELSE statements of compound instructions that convert a number value from one measurement system to another.

Skills

1.   (Math) Ratios and proportions; analogies
2.   (Programming) Boolean data types and operations; IF-THEN and IF-THEN-ELSE

Knowledge and Vocabulary

1.   (Math) Ratio, proportion, comparison, analogy, equivalence, conversion, extremes, and means
2.   (Programming) IF-THEN, IF-THEN-ELSE, Boolean data types, compound instructions, decision control, Boolean operations: AND, OR, NOT, TRUE, FALSE

Programmer's Library

Menu screen program

Nested decision control program (two choices)

Conversion program

Scheduling

The unit calendar (see figure 9.1 and the accompanying activities plan in figure 9.2, page 180) is rather different from most of the earlier calendars presented in this book. Notice that the support modules are all given during the first week and the unit task occupies all of the second week. This is because the support skills and knowledge must be mastered if the unit task instructions are to be in any way intelligible. It also ensures that the support concepts receive more consistent reinforcement and review than if they were allowed to drift along with little or no attention for five days. See figures 9.3, 9.4, and 9.5, pages 181-84, for the checklist, rubric, and programming work sheet that accompany this unit.

(Text continues on page 185.)

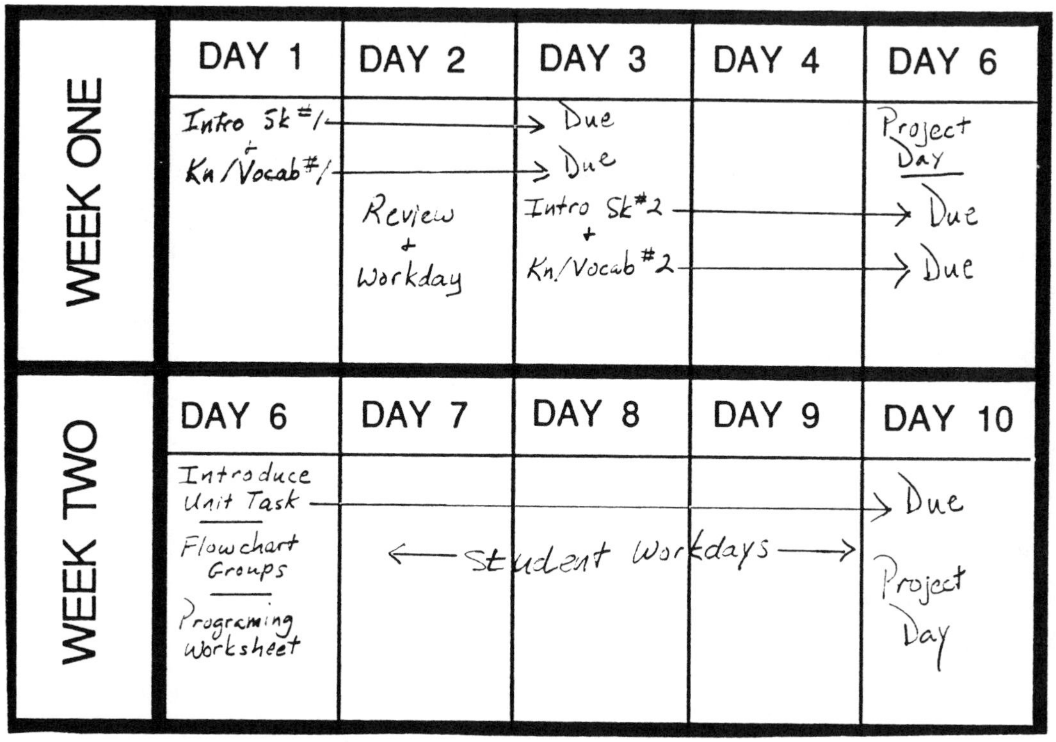

	DAY 1	DAY 2	DAY 3	DAY 4	DAY 6
WEEK ONE	Intro Sk #1 + Kn/Vocab #1	Review + Workday	→ Due, → Due, Intro Sk #2 + Kn/Vocab #2		Project Day → Due → Due

	DAY 6	DAY 7	DAY 8	DAY 9	DAY 10
WEEK TWO	Introduce Unit Task, Flowchart Groups, Programming worksheet	← Student Workdays →			→ Due, Project Day

Fig. 9.1. Math/programming unit calendar.

◇ *Math/Programming Unit Activities*

Day One

Introduce skill 1 and knowledge and vocabulary 1.

Day Two

Review and work day.

Day Three

Skill 1 and knowledge and vocabulary 1 due.

Introduce skill 2 and knowledge and vocabulary 2.

Day Four

Review and work day.

Day Five

Term project day.

Skill 2 and knowledge and vocabulary 2 due.

Day Six

Introduce unit task and work in flowchart groups.

Choose program foci and complete programming work sheet.

Days Seven, Eight, and Nine

Work days.

Day Ten

Term project day.

Unit tasks due.

Fig. 9.2.

◇ *Math and Programming*
Proportions and Decision Control 1
Unit Checklist

In this unit, you will learn how to tell the computer to make simple decisions based on user inputs. Your program should help the user to convert a measurement value from one unit of measurement to another. In order to do this, you will have to understand how to set up proportional statements using ratios. Complete all of the following items to be eligible for an A.

_____ 1. Attend or get the notes for the class presentation on IF-THEN statements, decision control, and compound instructions.

_____ 2. With one or two partners, write a flowchart using IF-THEN statements and compound instructions for one of the following people:

    a. A new babysitter who has to get two preschoolers to bed on time

    b. A short-order cook in a hamburger joint

    c. A new student in the lunchroom

    d. A bus driver on a new route with construction at different points in the route

_____ 3. Share your group's flowchart with the rest of the class. As a class, decide what attributes a good program should have. Make a chart with the attributes and rate the group flowcharts. Decide which flowcharts are the best and why.

_____ 4. Choose a type of measurement from the list below or suggest one of your own to the teacher as the kernel of your program. Then choose *two* equivalent measurement systems to work with (i.e., Fahrenheit and Celsius, francs and dollars, yards and meters, etc.):

    a. Temperature—Fahrenheit, centigrade, Kelvin, Celsius

    b. Currency units—American dollars and foreign currencies

    c. American units of measurement and metric

    d. American and European recipes

    e. Ancient systems of measurement and modern ones

_____ 5. Write a proportion that reflects the relationship between the two systems.

_____ 6. Make a flowchart for a program that does all of the following things:

    a. Converts from one measurement system to another and back

    b. allows the user to choose which way the conversion should go (i.e., francs to dollars or dollars to francs)

Fig. 9.3.

(Figure 9.3 continues on page 182.)

Fig. 9.3.—*Continued*

       _____ 6. c. Uses Boolean data types in IF-THEN statements

                         d. Uses compound instructions in the IF-THEN loops

                         e. Requires the user to input data for direction of conversion and amount to be converted

                         f. Gives the user clear instructions

       _____ 7. Write a rough draft for the program and debug it as well as you can by proofreading it and using the computer.

       _____ 8. Demonstrate your program for an editing group and get their suggestions and help for further debugging and refining.

       _____ 9. Revise and improve your program until it runs.

       _____ 10. Take the second version of your program to an editing group and demonstrate for them.

       _____ 11. Prepare your final draft of your program, draw your flowchart, and copy your program onto the unit disk for grading on or before the posted due date.

◇ ***Math and Programming***
Proportions and Decision Control 1
Rubric

An A program has all or most of the following:

1. A flowchart, two rough drafts, and a final draft of the program, and a copy of the program on the unit disk

2. Conversion from one unit of measurement to another and allows the user to choose which way the conversion should go

3. Clear instructions for the user and makes good use of the screen for communicating with the user

4. No bugs

5. Use of Boolean data types, IF-THEN statements, and compound decision control instructions within the IF-THEN loops

6. Correctly programmed proportional relationships

7. Few or no errors in flowcharting and Pascal language and format

Fig. 9.4.

Fig. 9.4.—*Continued*

A B program has all or most of the following:

1. A flowchart, one rough draft, final draft, and copy on disk

2. Conversion from one unit of measurement to another and allows the user to choose which way the conversion should go

3. Clear instructions for the user and makes fair use of the screen for communicating with the user

4. No serious bugs

5. Use of Boolean data types, IF-THEN statements, and compound instructions within the IF-THEN loops

6. Correctly programmed proportional relationships

7. Several minor errors in flowcharting and/or Pascal language and format

A C program has all or most of the following:

1. A flowchart or rough draft with final draft and disk copy

2. Conversion from one unit of measurement to another

3. Instructions for user that are easy to understand but makes poor use of the screen

4. Minor bugs that interfere with the running of the program

5. Use of Boolean data types and IF-THEN statements, but no compound instructions in loops

6. Errors in proportional relationships

7. Many errors in flowcharting and/or Pascal language and format

A D program has all or most of the following:

1. Only a final draft and disk copy

2. No conversion from one unit of measurement to another

3. Instructions that are difficult to understand

4. Serious bugs, doesn't run

5. Improper use of Boolean data types or IF-THEN statements

6. Serious errors in flowcharting and Pascal language and format

An F program has all or most of the following:

1. Only a final draft or disk copy

2. No measurement conversion

3. No understandable user instructions

4. Serious bugs, doesn't run

5. No use of Boolean data types or IF-THEN statements

6. Serious errors in Pascal language and format

Math and Programming
Proportions and Decision Control 1
Programming Work Sheet

1. What two measurements will be the focus of your program?

   a.

   b.

2. Write out the proportional relationship between these two measurements and then test your expression by filling in sample values.

   Proportion:

   Sample problem 1:

   Sample problem 2:

   Sample problem 3:

3. What will be the major steps in your program plan?

4. What information will you need from your user?

5. How will you ask the user for that information?

6. How will you display the answers for your user?

7. What will your IF-THEN loops do when they are selected by the user?

8. Draw a rough draft of your flowchart on the back of this sheet.

Fig. 9.5.

TWO COURSES—ONE SUBJECT: COMPOSITION IN MUSIC AND POETRY*

Special Concerns with Interdisciplinary Curriculum

Working together on interdisciplinary units can be exciting and enlightening for teachers and students. Teachers need to carefully examine the advantages and potential problems that will arise from collaboration. Determining the similarities and differences between the subject areas helps focus on these advantages or problems.

First, course activity categories are often different. Lining up the unit tasks, skills, and knowledge activities to coincide with another class takes much time and thought in the planning stages. Where an English class might have writing tasks, grammar and spelling modules, editing processes, and a creative writing project, the music class might have unit tasks, various skills assignments relating to the unit task, listening, performing (through singing, playing recorders, or playing in the class skiffling band), note-taking, and review tests. In coordinating curricular materials, the major question to answer is how to best reinforce one another's material. It may be quite simple to discover relationships between end products and structural tools used to build those products. But often the actual processes using the tools are quite different. For example, drawing parallels between music and poetry composition is not too difficult when looking at the end products or the structural tools. However, finding relationships between compositional processes from one medium to another is less clear-cut. Because music and poetry are, in fact, different media, there may not always be a direct relationship between what happens in the music class and what happens in the English class. As long as the activities are used within the contexts of the processes, it is not necessary to try to find analogous relationships between music and poetry in every phase of the curriculum.

Timing can also be a problem. If it is imperative that both classes stay on schedule so that corresponding learning activities are timed and sequenced to the greatest advantage for the students, a time margin for unforeseeable difficulties should be included within the schedule. It may happen that staying on schedule is not as critical for one class as for the other, especially if one class will be incorporating material from the other. The class providing the material to be incorporated in the other will be under greater pressure to stay on schedule than the class incorporating the material. For example, in our first experience using the music/poetry program, the music class got behind schedule in the first melody-writing task. Notating melodies and using composer techniques proved to be a greater leap from rhythm than had been anticipated. However, the delay in the music curriculum actually gave the English classes time to produce more poetry from which to choose for the final music composition which was to be set to one of the student's own poems.

Often one of the classes might face challenges unique to its subject area. Sometimes more groundwork will need to be laid in a previous term or unit to prepare the students for the interdisciplinary curriculum, or the nature of one class might be quite different from the other. Therefore, the class incorporating materials from another must allow time and means for adjustment of the final product to accommodate those materials.

My experience in teaching the music composition segment of a music/poetry collaboration provides examples of the challenges just mentioned. Where the English language was a ready tool for the students in the poetry class, the students of music composition were far less proficient with the language of music. Much preliminary groundwork was laid in the previous term to familiarize the students with the tools of music. Also, where the English class had a highly individualized curriculum, many of the learning classes in the music class involved team efforts such as singing as a class

---

*This unit was developed and written by Jean Simons and this author.

chorus, playing an instrument in the class skiffling band, and playing recorders in a class ensemble. Team efforts producing group products required the building of individual involvement and ownership in ways different from an individualized curriculum. Fitting music to words became another issue the English class did not have to cope with since students had already composed several poems from which to choose for their final music composition.

Interdisciplinary curricula can greatly enhance learning in all subjects involved by providing an opportunity for students to transfer principles and knowledge to new situations and subject areas. However, as with any collaborative effort, problems can arise from inherent differences in subject areas. But differences do not always pose problems. Some differences provide solutions; others are irrelevant. The key to success lies in determining whether the differences matter and then deciding whether the differences are problems requiring solutions or solutions to problems. Having thus examined the similarities and differences between subject areas, we become more perceptive of the advantages and more fully armed to meet the potential problems of interdisciplinary curricula.

Compare and Contrast

Music and poetry make a good combination for an interdisciplinary curriculum plan because they share many common concepts strategies, and processes. These similarities make it relatively easy to coordinate our materials so that they are mutually reinforcing. The parallel quarter plans shown in figure 9.6 illustrate how this is done.

 Parallel Quarter Plans

Music	**Poetry**
• Mapping of Nursery Rhymes	
• Rhythm composition: notation, repetition, contrast, variation, meters	• Five original poems: three invention techniques, basic rhythm patterns
• Melodic composition: composer techniques, repetition, sequence, fragment, retrograde	• Three original poems: invention techniques, onomatopoeia, rhyme, alliteration, tongue twisters
• Form: ABA, Theme and Variations	• Rigid poetic forms: haiku, tanka, cinquain, clerihew, limerick, metaphor, simile
• Final composition and performance	• Arts fair

Fig. 9.6.

Notice that, although the two curricula are not exactly matched, there is a general agreement in the progression of concepts and skills. The music curriculum begins first because students are not usually as familiar with the protocols of music as they are with their own language, but then the units march together until the English curriculum once again diverges. The first set of parallel units have to do with rhythms, although the English unit has an added emphasis on invention techniques. Next, the emphasis is sound—melodies in music and speech sounds in English. Finally, form is addressed in both classes. Then the English class goes on to learn about publishing, advertising, and coordinating activities through communication as they plan a school-wide arts fair to exhibit what they and other students have produced in different media throughout the year. At the same time, the music students polish their compositions and prepare them for performance at the fair.

The ideas of coordinating concepts and processes and facilitating transfer of them between the subject areas are similar to those ideas presented in the first part of this chapter. However, there are some important differences to be taken into account when working with more than one course. These differences have to do with the creation and evaluation of unit tasks.

In the two-in-one interdisciplinary unit, one unit task incorporates material from two subject areas. In the cross-curricular one-in-two situation, two unit tasks involve similar material used in different ways. Instead of the two subject area teachers creating one giant unit task to be used in both courses, they each put together separate unit tasks that run simultaneously (see figure 9.7). This allows students to work on the same idea from two different points of view. It also keeps those students who are not signed up for both classes from being penalized for missing a part of the work. This is an especially important provision to make in secondary schools where students do not stay with the same group of classmates for each subject.

 Unit Tasks

Rhythm Composition

Complete all of the following tasks to be eligible for an A:

_____ 1. On the attached sheet, write five motives (rhythm only), two measures each in 2/4, 3/4, or 4/4.

_____ 2. Perform your motives for a precomposition group. Your group should be able to answer the following questions:

   a. Can the composer perform it?

   b. Does it have a time signature with proper counts per measure?

   c. Is it interesting enough to repeat and/or vary?

_____ 3. Choose one of your motives to repeat, contrast, and vary in your own rhythm composition.

_____ 4. Using the motive you have chosen, list ways you can repeat, contrast, or vary the motive.

_____ 5. Now it is time to be a composer! Hook your motive and its repetitions, contrasts, and variation into an eight to twelve measure rhythm composition. You may not use all the ideas you came up with from item 4, but your composition should demonstrate examples of repetition, contrast, and variation of your motive.

Fig. 9.7.

(Figure 9.7 continues on page 188.)

Fig. 9.7. — *Continued*

_____ 6. Take your composition to an editing group, perform it, and have two class-mates edit using the following checklist.

Does the composition have:

_____ _____ A time signature?

_____ _____ Bar lines with the correct number of counts per measure?

_____ _____ One to two measure motive repeated, contrasted, and varied?

_____ _____ Eight to twelve measures of length?

_____ _____ Double bar line at the end?

_____ _____ Accurate performance by the composer?

Editor 1 _____ Editor 2 _____

_____ 7. Do a final draft in ink on a clean piece of paper with all corrections and additions to the rough draft. Turn in precomposition sheets, rough draft, and final draft.

Original Poems

You have learned three basic techniques for composing poems. You have learned that poems do not have to rhyme or have a steady rhythm like a nursery rhyme although you *have* learned that there are different kinds of rhythms in poetry. You may have also learned that you are a poet with a lot of good ideas to turn into poetry.

_____ 1. You will be writing five original poems for this unit task. To begin, use each of the three invention strategies you have learned to get ideas for five differ-ent poems. Be sure to use each strategy for at least one of the poems: para-poems, listing, and mind maps.

_____ 2. Take the rough drafts of five or more poems to an editing group. Use the rubric to guide you in your editing. If you have more than five poems, choose the five most promising ones to continue work on.

_____ 3. Revise your five poems and take them to another editing group.

_____ 4. Prepare your five poems for final publication.

_____ 5. Turn in all of your prewriting, rough drafts, and final draft on or before the due date.

Likewise, evaluation criteria are different for each course (see figure 9.8). In the music/poetry curriculum, musical values were stressed in music class and linguistic ones in English class. The fact that both courses were working with similar material provided enough continuity for a natural parallelism in what was being evaluated and how it was being evaluated.

 Rubrics

Rhythm

An A composition has all or most of the following:

1. A distinct motive that is *mostly repeated*, *sometimes varied*, and/or *contrasted*

2. A time signature, bar lines, and correct number of counts per measure

3. Eight to twelve measures long with double bar line at the end

4. Precomposition sheet, rough draft, and final draft in ink with at least two editors

A B composition has all or most of the following:

1. A distinct motive that may get repeated, varied or contrasted equally

2. A time signature, bar lines, and correct number of counts in most measures

3. Eight to twelve measures long and has double bar line at the end

4. A precomposition sheet, rough draft, and final draft in ink with at least one editor

A C composition has all or most of the following:

1. A motive that is difficult to recognize because it seldom gets repeated; is mostly contrasted

2. A time signature, bar lines with correct counts in some measures

3. Eight or fewer measures long, may or may not have double bar line at the end

4. A precomposition sheet and rough or final draft which may or may not have been edited

A D composition has all or most of the following:

1. A motive that is difficult to recognize because it does not get repeated, but only contrasted

2. A time signature and bar lines that may be misplaced and measures with incorrect number of counts

3. Eight or fewer measures long with no double bar line at end

4. Final draft only without editor comments

Fig. 9.8.

(Figure 9.8 continues on page 190.)

Fig. 9.8.—*Continued*

Poetry

An A task has all or most of the following:

1. Prewriting, two rough drafts, and final draft
2. Five original poems
3. All three invention techniques are used at least once
4. One main idea or theme per poem
5. A strong rhythm pattern
6. Correct class format with few or no mechanical errors

A B task has all or most of the following:

1. Prewriting, one rough draft, and final draft
2. Five original poems
3. All three invention techniques are used at least once
4. Confused main idea or theme in one or two poems
5. Average rhythm pattern
6. Minor errors in format and mechanics

A C task has all or most of the following:

1. Prewriting or rough draft with final draft
2. Four or five original poems
3. Two invention techniques
4. Foggy main idea or theme in three or four poems
5. Weak rhythm pattern
6. Several errors in format and mechanics

A D task has all or most of the following:

1. Only a final draft
2. Two or three original poems
3. One invention technique
4. No discernible main idea or theme per poem
5. No rhythm pattern
6. Many serious errors in format and mechanics

BREAKDOWNS

As teachers and planners we often become so involved in our curriculum preparation that the purposes and elements of what we are doing seem so obvious as to be hardly worth mentioning. But they are often not so obvious to our students, particularly when we break down traditional barriers that students take for granted. It is important to point out what barriers are being breached and why. This helps students understand the context of what they are being asked to do and helps them to see what new types of thinking they are expected to do. It also clearly shows them the possibilities inherent in interdisciplinary studies. All of these things are important for one other thing as well: avoiding breakdowns.

Breakdowns in communication have always seemed to me to be part of the territory in classroom teaching. I never took them too seriously because communication is an ongoing process, and I always try to train my students to ask questions about what they don't understand. But one day, about a week into our interdisciplinary music/poetry curriculum, another kind of breakdown occurred that was directly attributable to a communication breakdown. Cliff, one of my eighth-graders, broke down.

Cliff was generally a pretty stable fellow. (The only other time he'd lost his cool was when I had gotten a bad case of the giggles during his project presentation on Uranus.) He had been patiently working on the skills and vocabulary exercises on rhythms, doggedly learning to express rhythms using parsing marks as well as musical notations. Cliff always got A's. Cliff always worked hard. Cliff was a rock. That was why I was so shocked when he came in, sat down, looked at the musical notes on the board, and began to gasp and growl.

"Mrs. E!" he groused. "What's going on around here? This is English class, right?"

"Right."

"And Miss Simons' is music class, right?"

"Right."

"So what's going on? How come we're doing music in here and poetry in there? This isn't how it should be! Why are you doing this to us? When is it going to stop? When are the two of you going to figure out what you're teaching?"

It occurred to me that perhaps I should have been more explicit in introducing the interdisciplinary materials. The hostile looks I was getting from the rest of the class made it obvious that everyone else felt as Cliff did. I sat down and tried to explain. Most of the students were mollified, but a few were having problems with the redrawing of traditional educational boundaries. I decided to take time to explain interdisciplinary study to my other classes and to advise Jean to do the same.

Moral: If you want the kids to play your game, you've got to tell them the rules!

— 10 —
Final Exams

WHY? BECAUSE....

Testing is a subject that has only been mentioned in passing in this book. Attitudes on testing are quite often as highly charged as those on politics and religion and it is not the author's intention to resolve all differences in this chapter or even in this lifetime. Each teacher must decide what place testing has in the classroom and how tests will be used in a specific teaching situation. In this final chapter, the emphasis will be on reconciling the Rewrite program with the testing needs of traditional schools. Tests are a fact of life in our educational system, and whether we like it or not, our students will have to be able to pass them successfully to progress within that system. Gifted students in particular will likely need to take many more tests and more difficult tests than students who do not choose to attempt to pursue advanced studies.

Secondary schools often require teachers to administer final exams at the end of a course. Sometimes these tests are prescribed, as in achievement or matriculation tests, but usually the content and manner of the test are left to the discretion of classroom teachers. When the tests are prescribed, teachers have to prepare their students in both content and processes of test-taking. When the tests are composed by the classroom teacher, they can be constructed to test those elements that were emphasized by the teacher. Whichever situation exists in a given school, final exam time can provide positive opportunities for review, closure, and demonstration of progress to both students and teachers.

TEACHING *FOR* A TEST

The first time I was handed a copy of an SAT test and told to prepare my students for it was also the last time. I simply refused to coach my students to take it. I was never approached about it again once I had made my ethical position clear. If the test was to find out how well the students were doing, then that was what I wanted it to do. Coaching them for a particular test or test form would only show me how well they had learned the material for that particular test. It would reduce the standardized test from a measurement of general achievement to a glorified quiz, and my students would only learn how to take that particular test. Furthermore, they may have gotten a hidden message that cheating is okay.

Teaching *to* the test is a practice often criticized in teacher education classes—and rightly so. The test should not dictate what students learn; it should sample their knowledge to see what they have learned. The school curriculum should reflect the expectations of the society as expressed in the test foci. For example, students who have only studied biology should not be given a test section on chemistry, nor should those who have only studied elementary algebra and geometry receive a section on calculus. Finding out the questions and answers for a particular test and then feeding them to a class for drill and practice is teaching to the test at its worst. The test is no longer a test at that point; it is the curriculum.

Teaching *for* a test is an entirely different matter, however. Students should be taught how to take tests. Tests are a fact of life in our society and if we do not prepare our students to take them, they will be denied many opportunities for learning and accomplishment. The better students understand what tests are, what they are for, and what they require of test takers, the better they will be able to respond to tests and the more accurately will tests reflect the true competence of the students. Teaching for a test prepares students to approach tests confidently and competently. Managed well, teaching for a test can be instructive without compromising the purposes of a particular test.

Teaching for a test involves two parts: preparing students in the actual subject matter of the course and teaching them about tests and test-taking. If a course has been well-planned and executed throughout the term of study, then it only remains to prepare them for test-taking. This can be done in several ways, but most fall into two basic categories. The first category involves ongoing, periodic instruction and practice in test-taking strategies and skills throughout the course. Teachers can include different types of quizzes and tests in their unit activities and use them to both gauge student progress and to instruct students in the metacognitive skills and strategies of test-taking. The second category involves teaching one or two units exclusively on test-taking, using the standardized test administration as the culmination of the unit in the unit task. In these units, students would learn about the types of tests administered in the subject area, the types of questions typically used on those tests, and the types of listening, reading, thinking, and writing skills necessary to answer the questions well. They might also learn about managing stress, attention, and fatigue as well as strategies for preparation.

Even if one's school does not require prescribed tests for the students, it is still useful to teach for testing to some extent. If students are never exposed to this type of testing, they may not feel comfortable enough to perform at their best when presented with a standardized test later. Preparing them for test-taking prepares them for one more aspect of real life and grants them one more measure of independence.

TESTING WHAT WAS TAUGHT

The great purpose of a teacher's life is to become unnecessary. When students have learned, through the teacher's guidance, how to function competently on their own without that guidance, then the teacher has been truly successful. In the Rewrite model, both academic and personal competence are stressed and students are taught to use them in the synthesis and evaluation of original products. In order to test what was taught in such an environment, both academic and personal competence should be tested.

Testing of academic competence should give students the chance to show how well they are able to function in the subject area. How well have they mastered the strategies and processes of the methodologies? How well are they able to apply their skills in carrying out those methodologies? How well have they mastered the knowledge base of the subject area? Are the students really able to operate on their own in the subject area or do they still need constant supervision, direction, and advice?

Testing of personal competence should give students the opportunity to show how well they are able to manage their time and behavior in accomplishment of a set of goals. Are they able to identify a goal and choose a course of action for achieving it? Are they able to follow that course of action, modifying it as necessary? Are they able to plan out their time and use it wisely and productively? In short, are they able to take responsibility for themselves and their work or do they still need to be told what, how, and when to do something?

Final exams that test both of these areas require a different structure from the one- to three-hour sit-down exam so typical of finals. Instead, they need to be structured to allow students to examine the problem(s) at hand, to decide on a solution or solutions, and to work independently over a stretch of time to attain the final solution(s). This involves a change in the time element and in the manner and content of testing.

Despite the testimonies of generations of students who have left final exams feeling as if they have fallen down Alice's rabbit hole, the "sit-down-and-take-it-now" type of final exam doesn't really test the full array of student abilities. How can it when the testing situation bears so little resemblance to the actual circumstances of study and work within a given subject area? In a Rewrite classroom, students learn not only about background knowledge and skills, but about how those elements are used in methodological contexts in the synthesis of original products over a period of time. Unless the time frame of the final exam is considerably expanded, it is impossible to gauge how well students are able to do what they were taught to do. How much is "considerably"? It is enough to be comparable to the time frames of units. It might be a week long or even two, so that students have a chance to really show how well they have internalized the academic and Rewrite hidden curricula. Sitting in a chair for three hours filling up papers gives the teacher little or no feedback on how well these larger goals were accomplished during the course. Working actively and independently on a complex project or problem for a week or two does.

How is such an exam constructed? It is done in much the same way as a unit, with three important differences. First, there is no direct instruction in new knowledge or techniques; second, no new material is introduced, and third, no support modules are given. Instead, the exam is drawn up as a complex, authentic task that requires one to two weeks of constant class time work to complete. It requires the application of subject area knowledge, skills, and methodologies in the creation of a new product. Evaluation criteria, as always, are specified at the beginning of the task and peer tutoring and review are encouraged and required. Students are encouraged to find out what they need to know to complete the task and any necessary resources are made available to them. The only thing they may not do is pump the teacher for information unless their questions are purely procedural. After all, the final exam is the teacher's chance to see how unnecessary he or she has become.

By way of an example, the following scenario describes a Rewrite final exam in a language arts class. The actual exam task is a short story. The students have been given two weeks to do all of their prewriting, drafting, and postwriting. By the end of that two weeks, they must turn in all of their prewriting materials and rough drafts along with a final draft and a completed questionnaire on their story. The final draft is slated for publication in a class literary anthology to be handed out the last day of school. This provides the added incentive of a real audience of peers, teachers, and family, and makes the task a real one. There is no length requirement for the final draft, but there are specific procedural and content requirements. Figure 10.1, "Final Exam Assignment," describes these requirements. It is passed out at the beginning of the two-week period with a tape of the "Mission: Impossible" theme playing in the background. A final exam checklist, editing checklist, and overview work sheet are also provided (see figures 10.2 through 10.4, pages 196-98).

(Text continues on page 199.)

◇ *Final Exam Assignment*

It's almost over! Our year-long exploration of language and literature is drawing to a close, and now it's time for you to dazzle everyone with what you have learned! This will be your final assignment of the year and your final exam. The rules for this exam are as follows:

1. You will have two weeks to complete your exam.

2. Until you complete this exam, *all* of your class time will be devoted to it except for term project days.

3. You must complete *all* of the activities on the checklist.

4. You must find whatever information you need on your own *without* the teacher's help.

5. You may ask the teacher *only* about exam procedures and editing groups.

6. You may *not* disrupt anyone else's work. If you do, you *will* be penalized!

Your assignment is to write a short story using what you have learned about the writing process and literary forms and techniques. Your story will be published in a class literary anthology and distributed at the end of school. You may choose the subject and format of your story. There is no length requirement for the story, but keep in mind that your time is limited and you must include all of the following elements:

1. At least two well-rounded characters

2. A conflict

3. Direct and indirect characterizations

4. A believable setting

5. A developed plot to include exposition, rising action, climax, falling action, and resolution

6. At least two techniques for building and/or maintaining suspense

See the attached checklist, editing group evaluation form, and overview work sheet for further details.

Fig. 10.1.

◇ *Final Exam Checklist*

Complete each of the activities below to be eligible for an A. If you have *any* questions about the exam or its activities, be sure to ask the teacher for help and explanation. Remember that this is your final exam. Make sure you are clear on what is required. The teacher is here to help.

_____ 1. Select and use at least two prewriting techniques to find a subject for your story.

_____ 2. Sketch out a rough plot for your story.

_____ 3. Construct your round characters by assembling personal histories and character profiles for each of them.

_____ 4. Research your setting and write or draw a detailed description of it.

_____ 5. Write a rough draft of your story.

_____ 6. Take your rough draft to a peer editing group. Use the evaluation form to go over one another's work.

_____ 7. Revise your story and get it edited again.

_____ 8. Prepare your final draft. It must be typewritten or neatly handwritten in ink on 8-½" × 11" paper so that it will fit the format of the class anthology.

_____ 9. Answer the questions on the overview work sheet.

_____ 10. Hand in all of the following items on or before _____.

   a. Prewriting work

   b. Plot diagram

   c. Character backgrounds

   d. Setting research and description/drawings

   e. Two rough drafts

   f. Completed evaluation form

   g. Overview work sheet

   h. Final draft ready for publication

Fig. 10.2.

◇ *Editing Checklist*

Listed below are the higher and lower order concerns you will need to look for while editing one another's papers for the final exam. Put a check next to each concern that still needs work before the writer can turn in a high-quality exam paper. Write any comment you have in the large squares at the bottom of the page or on the back. Be sure to sign your comments or the writer will not get credit for an editing group.

Concerns	Editing Group 1	Editing Group 2
Round characters		
Clear conflict		
Direct characterization		
Indirect characterization		
Setting		
Exposition		
Rising action		
Climax		
Falling action		
Resolution		
Suspense techniques		
Grammar		
Voice tone		
Usage		
Format		
Spelling		
Group 1 Comments		Group 2 Comments

Fig. 10.3.

◇ *Overview Work Sheet*

1. Identify your round characters and tell how you made them "round" instead of "flat."

2. Describe the basic conflict in your story and identify one to three sentences in your story that highlight it.

3. Give two examples of direct characterization used in your story.

4. Give two examples of indirect characterization used in your story.

5. Draw a plot map on the back of this sheet and identify transition points between expo/rising, rising/climax, climax/falling, and falling/resolution by writing the sentence(s) from your story where each point occurs.

6. Identify the suspense techniques you used and tell how you used them.

7. Add any other explanations or observation about your work here.

Fig. 10.4.

THE ANSWER LADY REVISITED

It takes a lot of creativity and persistence to get through a Rewrite final exam, particularly if you're the teacher. The students have plenty to do for two weeks, but you've been excluded from the activities. What's a teacher to do for such an eternity? Plenty, you say. There are plenty of things to catch up on and two weeks won't begin to make a dent in it all.

That's what the answer lady thought, too, until she found herself held prisoner in a classroom for seven hours a day for two weeks while her students labored away without her. The answer lady does not carry that appellation for nothing, however, and so she has compiled a set of suggested activities for those teachers who may find themselves at a loss after the novelty of free time wears off.

The activities fall into four basic categories:

1. Organizational and clerical work (figure 10.5, page 200)

2. Professional educator's work (figure 10.6, page 201)

3. Quality control work (figure 10.7, page 202)

4. Harmless amusements (figure 10.8, page 203)

For each of these categories, the answer lady has developed a checklist to help you make it through the exam period. Use the checklists as guides and feel free to modify items or to add any ideas of your own to the checklists. The answer lady is not sensitive about such things. She only wishes to help you become more autonomous and competent — extremely worthy goals.

◇ *Organizational and Clerical Work*

_____ 1. Update gradebook entries.

_____ 2. Fill out any forms the office has been asking for.

_____ 3. Fill out any forms the office hasn't been asking for.

_____ 4. Fill out any surveys, questionnaires, or order blanks that were lost among the forms from the office.

_____ 5. Take care of any other correspondence.

_____ 6. Look through the brochures on workshops and seminars that were hidden under the above-mentioned items and see if there are any left to attend.

_____ 7. Do your textbook inventory and list students who owe money or books.

_____ 8. Make up little forms to notify students of fines.

_____ 9. Fill out the little forms and deliver them.

_____ 10. Look through your desk drawers to see if you've forgotten anything.

_____ 11. Sort books and journals into two piles: toss and read.

_____ 12. Sort your files into three categories: leave well enough alone, toss, and read.

_____ 13. Go through the classroom library records and make out overdue and fine notices. Deliver them.

_____ 14. Clean out your desk drawers.

_____ 15. Write anonymous suggestions for improving the school and slip them secretly into the principal's box.

Fig. 10.5.

◇ *Professional Educator's Work*

_____ 1. Grade any work left in the in boxes.

_____ 2. Help students who have failed revisions.

_____ 3. Keep your nose out of the final exam work.

_____ 4. Think up four cute ways to answer silly questions.

_____ 5. Go through textbook samples received by the department and try to find one you like enough to try to order in May.

_____ 6. Read the books and journals in the "read" pile.

_____ 7. Read through the files in the "read" pile.

_____ 8. Look through a poster catalog and choose some for next year.

_____ 9. See how many teachers will go in on the order with you.

_____ 10. Go through the year's curriculum plans and note needed improvements.

_____ 11. Work on making improvements for next year.

_____ 12. Work on curriculum plans for any new classes next year.

_____ 13. Try to find a useful activity for the kids to do the last four days of school.

_____ 14. Copy recipes from clippings you've collected this year.

_____ 15. Formalize your teaching philosophy and see if you can use it in a class for in-service credit.

Fig. 10.6.

◇ *Quality Control Work*

_____ 1. Throw out any dead plants in the room.

_____ 2. Throw out any papers with footprints on them.

_____ 3. Check all your pens and markers to see if they work.

_____ 4. Throw out any dried-up pens and markers.

_____ 5. Check all the pencil erasers to see if they erase.

_____ 6. Make out repair requests for broken equipment.

_____ 7. Take down the winter bulletin board.

_____ 8. Put up the end-of-the-year bulletin board.

_____ 9. Switch your broken stapler for somebody's good one.

_____ 10. Fix the tape on sagging posters.

_____ 11. Take down any lunch menus older than two months.

_____ 12. Take down any announcements older than two months.

_____ 13. Give good advice to people.

_____ 14. Clean the blackboards and try to make the eraser lines symmetrical.

_____ 15. Dust the room.

_____ 16. Make sure all calendars show the correct month.

_____ 17. Look for any stale or spoiled food left in hiding places.

Fig. 10.7.

◇ *Amusements*

(Warning! These activities are only to be undertaken in times of extreme boredom and must be done in such a way as to appear to be legitimate faculty duties!)

_____ 1. Read the books you were saving for summer vacation.

_____ 2. Start a journal.

_____ 3. Plan a vacation you can't afford.

_____ 4. Plan a new wardrobe.

_____ 5. Figure out which car you *really* need.

_____ 6. Learn to make pig noises without using your lips.

_____ 7. Stare at students.

_____ 8. Check the hallway.

_____ 9. Ask kids whether they have passes.

_____ 10. Watch the teachers in the other rooms.

_____ 11. Make up your own chain letter.

_____ 12. Look out the window.

_____ 13. Count planes, cars, trucks, and cycles.

_____ 14. Give unwanted advice.

_____ 15. Take the final exam yourself.

Fig. 10.8.

Index

About the Author

Pamela Everly earned her B.A. in Teaching of Russian from the University of Illinois at Urbana-Champaign and an M.A. in gifted education at the University of Colorado at Colorado Springs. For fifteen years she has taught English, Russian, German, and reading in both regular and gifted classrooms. She is a Teacher/Consultant of the Utah Writing Project and has conducted numerous workshops on the teaching of writing. She is currently working as a freelance curriculum writer and educational consultant and teaches gifted enrichment classes as well as teacher workshops on the Rewrite model.